956.7
IRA   37009000039766

THE HISTORY OF NATIONS

Iraq

The History of Nations

Iraq

Other books in the History of Nations series:

Canada
China
England
France
Germany
India
Indonesia
Italy
Japan
Mexico
North Korea
Pakistan
Russia
Spain

The History of Nations

Iraq

David Schaffer, *Book Editor*

NORTH DELTA SECONDARY SCHOOL LIBRARY

Daniel Leone, *President*
Bonnie Szumski, *Publisher*
Scott Barbour, *Managing Editor*

GREENHAVEN PRESS®

San Diego • Detroit • New York • San Francisco • Cleveland
New Haven, Conn. • Waterville, Maine • London • Munich

© 2004 by Greenhaven Press. Greenhaven Press is an imprint of The Gale Group, Inc., a division of Thomson Learning, Inc.

Greenhaven® and Thomson Learning™ are trademarks used herein under license.

For more information, contact
Greenhaven Press
27500 Drake Rd.
Farmington Hills, MI 48331-3535
Or you can visit our Internet site at http://www.gale.com

ALL RIGHTS RESERVED.
No part of this work covered by the copyright hereon may be reproduced or used in any form or by any means—graphic, electronic, or mechanical, including photocopying, recording, taping, Web distribution or information storage retrieval systems—without the written permission of the publisher.

Every effort has been made to trace the owners of copyrighted material.

Cover credit: © David Lees/CORBIS

LIBRARY OF CONGRESS CATALOGING-IN-PUBLICATION DATA

Iraq / David Schaffer, book editor.
  p. cm. — (History of nations)
  Includes bibliographical references and index.
  ISBN 0-7377-1661-4 (pbk. : alk. paper) — ISBN 0-7377-1660-6 (lib. : alk. paper)
  1. Iraq—History. I. Schaffer, David. II. History of nations (Greenhaven Press)
DS70.9.I718 2004
956.7—dc21   2003049019

Printed in the United States of America

Contents

Foreword — 13

Introduction: Iraq's History: Of Dynasties and Decimation — 15

Chapter 1: Mesopotamia: Civilization's Breeding Ground

1. The Roots of Civilized Societies
by Geoff Simons — 37
The earliest known human civilizations existed in what is now Iraq, in a region between the Tigris and Euphrates Rivers known as the Fertile Crescent. From these pioneering societies came the first known written documents and historical records, inventions such as the wheel and canal irrigation for crops, the earliest instruments of warfare and conquest, and the first great kingdoms and empires of human history.

2. The Early Culture of Mesopotamia
by Seton Lloyd — 45
The early civilization of Sumeria was the first known to have produced written language. Much of these written pieces are pictograms on works of pottery and sculpture, but there is also a major historical chronological record known as the king-list that describes the sequential rulers of Sumeria.

3. The Ishtar Gate: An Example of Babylonian Magnificence
by Robert Koldewey — 54
The Ishtar Gate of Babylon was considered one of the greatest man-made wonders of the ancient world. German archaeologist Robert Koldewey, one of the earliest to research ancient Mesopotamia, describes the Ishtar Gate's beauty and how its structural complexity reflected the advancement of Babylonian civilization.

4. Infusions of Foreign Powers
by Georges Roux   59
After being surrounded by newly emerging rival kingdoms and empires, the civilizations of Mesopotamia began to be conquered and dominated by outside powers, beginning with the conquest by the Persian ruler Cyrus the Great in the fifth century B.C.

Chapter 2: The Baghdad Caliphate: A Global Power Center

1. The Rise of Islam and Arab Conquests
by Walter M. Weiss   68
The Islamic religion and Arab nationalist expansion began in the Arabian Peninsula, but Iraq became swept up in both movements and was strongly impacted by them. Arabism and Islam came to be the dominant cultural forces in Iraq during the Middle Ages.

2. Hustling, Bustling Baghdad
by Gaston Wiet   72
Arab and Islamic power came to rule over an area well beyond Iraq in the eighth century, but at that time the major city of the Arab Islamic empire was Baghdad, the historically famous city in central Iraq. In addition to being a political and religious power center, Baghdad also became one of the leading cultural, literary, scientific, and artistic cities of the world. Islamic historian Gaston Wiet describes Baghdad's achievements, energy, and intellectual stature during its heyday.

3. A New Era of Foreign Domination
by Rom Landau   76
After suffering gradual decline for many centuries, Baghdad and Iraq once again became susceptible to conquest and domination by foreign forces. Certain groups of central Asians in particular—Persians, Turks, and Mongols—came to play especially important roles in the fate of Iraq beginning in the eleventh century.

4. The Aftermath of Recurrent Conquests
by Marco Polo   82
The legendary Italian explorer traveled through what is now Iraq and described his experiences. The accuracy of his accounts are suspect on some important points, but Polo does convey a sense of social and cultural confusion that pervaded Iraq after a series of conquests and infiltrations by foreign powers.

Chapter 3: Provinces and Protectorate: Iraq Under the Ottomans and British

1. The Ottoman Takeover
by Geoff Simons   87
After a series of frequent incursions by invading forces, Iraq began a long period of sustained rule under the Ottoman Turkish Empire.

2. The Political and Social Roots of Modern Iraq
by Charles Tripp   92
The geopolitical foundations of modern Iraq took shape under the Ottomans. Three provinces, with capitals in the northern city of Mosul, the central city of Baghdad, and the southern city of Basra, together came to essentially comprise the area that would constitute the territory of the modern nation of Iraq.

3. Turbulence in the Early Twentieth Century
by Phebe Marr   102
Sentiment favoring independence in the early twentieth century led to a revolt against a new Turkish government and a subsequent revolt against the British, who triumphed over the Ottomans in World War I.

Chapter 4: The Emergence of Modern Independent Iraq

1. National Transition to Independence Under King Faisal
by Majid Khadduri   110
Iraq first emerged as a British protectorate after World War I, a transitionary status it would maintain until 1932 when it would become a fully indepen-

dent nation. During this time Iraq was ruled by King
Faisal, a monarch appointed by Britain, who played a
major role in the birth of the contemporary nation
Iraq.

2. Internal Opposition and Factionalism in Postindependent Iraq
by Stephen Hemsley Longrigg and Frank Stoakes   118
After becoming fully independent, Iraq was long
beset by internal division and violent political factionalism. Many coups and counter-coups, internal government power struggles, and another period of
British occupation during World War II all contributed to the chaos and turmoil that afflicted Iraq
during the mid–twentieth century.

3. Pan-Arabism: A Decisive Force in Iraq's Destiny
by Michel Aflaq   127
The ideology known as Pan-Arabism, which emerged
during the twentieth century, proved to be greatly
appealing to the long-oppressed Arab peoples, including those in Iraq.

4. From Monarchy to Anarchy
by Sandra Mackey   133
Sentiments for Arab independence and against foreign influences in Arab land culminated in Iraq in a
revolution against the British-installed monarchy in
1958. This proved to be a critical turning point in the
political fate of the Iraqi nation.

Chapter 5: The Reign of Saddam Hussein

1. The Making of Hussein's Persona and Character
by Efraim Karsh and Inari Rautsi   143
Saddam Hussein, the ruler that would come to loom
so large in Iraq, was affected by his early life experiences and influences. These led Hussein to adapt
adamant pro-Arab, antiforeign positions and adopt a

militancy that would enable him to survive and flourish in a brutally violent and treacherous environment.

2. Ruthless Rule Yields Social Progress
by Samir al-Khalil   157
Although they continued to employ the same ruthless governing methods as previous governments, Saddam Hussein's Ba'ath Party stabilized the country and even fostered support for their rule by improving social and economic conditions.

3. The Iran-Iraq War
by Sandra Mackey   165
In 1980, one year after he took full control of Iraq, Hussein went to war against its historic rival Iran. Lasting eight years, the Iran-Iraq War was the longest conventional war fought directly between two nations during the twentieth century and one of the costliest and bloodiest ever fought in history.

4. The War over Kuwait
by George H.W. Bush   178
Iraq invaded and conquered Kuwait in August 1990. The war that ensued proved to be greatly detrimental to Iraq militarily and politically.

5. Hussein's Quest for Nuclear Weapons
by Khidhir Hamza with Jeff Stein   183
Since Iraq used chemical weapons in its war with Iran, much suspicion and scrutiny has centered on whether it has weapons of mass destruction. Former Iraqi nuclear scientist Khidhir Hamza left Iraq in 1994 and revealed extensive secrets about Iraq's nuclear weapons program following his escape.

Chapter 6: The U.S. War on Iraq and Its Aftermath

1. Iraq Poses a Threat to World Peace
by George W. Bush   195
The nation of Iraq and the regime of Saddam Hussein became targets of U.S. president George W. Bush in his war against terrorism. An October 2002 speech

by Bush was specifically dedicated to spelling out his policy on Iraq and providing a rationale for taking military action against that regime.

2. Opposing Military Intervention
by Brent Scowcroft   202
An opponent of military action against Iraq argues that such a war would detract from other U.S. policy priorities and would have detrimental long-term consequences.

3. Iraq Stands Firm Against World Opinion
by Saddam Hussein, interviewed by Tony Benn   206
In February 2003 Saddam Hussein came forward to respond to the threats and verbal attacks being made against Iraq. Hussein claimed the United States and other Western powers had ulterior, self-serving motives for threatening to attack Iraq.

4. Achieving Lasting Stability in Iraq
by Niall Ferguson   212
In order to ensure Iraq's long-term stability, the United States must mollify local leaders by promising to leave the country while remaining in firm control of the political and economic systems for the foreseeable future.

Chronology	218
For Further Research	224
Index	227

Foreword

In 1841, the journalist Charles MacKay remarked, "In reading the history of nations, we find that, like individuals, they have their whims and peculiarities, their seasons of excitement and recklessness." At the time of MacKay's observation, many of the nations explored in the Greenhaven Press History of Nations series did not yet exist in their current form. Nonetheless, whether it is old or young, every nation is similar to an individual, with its own distinct characteristics and unique story.

The History of Nations series is dedicated to exploring these stories. Each anthology traces the development of one of the world's nations from its earliest days, when it was perhaps no more than a promise on a piece of paper or an idea in the mind of some revolutionary, through to its status in the world today. Topics discussed include the pivotal political events and power struggles that shaped the country as well as important social and cultural movements. Often, certain dramatic themes and events recur, such as the rise and fall of empires, the flowering and decay of cultures, or the heroism and treachery of leaders. As well, in the history of most countries war, oppression, revolution, and deep social change feature prominently. Nonetheless, the details of such events vary greatly, as does their impact on the nation concerned. For example, England's "Glorious Revolution" of 1688 was a peaceful transfer of power that set the stage for the emergence of democratic institutions in that nation. On the other hand, in China, the overthrow of dynastic rule in 1912 led to years of chaos, civil war, and the eventual emergence of a Communist regime that used violence as a tool to root out opposition and quell popular protest. Readers of the Greenhaven Press History of Nations series will learn about the common challenges nations face and the different paths they take in response to such crises. However a nation's story may have developed, the series strives to present a clear and unbiased view of the country at hand.

The structure of each volume in the series is designed to help students deepen their understanding of the events, movements, and persons that define nations. First, a thematic introduction provides critical background material and helps orient the reader. The chapters themselves are designed to provide an accessible and engaging approach to the study of the history of that nation involved and are arranged either thematically or chronologically, as appropriate. The selections include both primary documents, which convey something of the flavor of the time and place concerned, and secondary material, which includes the wisdom of hindsight and scholarship. Finally, each book closes with a detailed chronology, a comprehensive bibliography of suggestions for further research, and a thorough index.

The countries explored within the series are as old as China and as young as Canada, as distinct in character as Spain and India, as large as Russia, and as compact as Japan. Some are based on ethnic nationalism, the belief in an ethnic group as a distinct people sharing a common destiny, whereas others emphasize civic nationalism, in which what defines citizenship is not ethnicity but commitment to a shared constitution and its values. As human societies become increasingly globalized, knowledge of other nations and of the diversity of their cultures, characteristics, and histories becomes ever more important. This series responds to the challenge by furnishing students with a solid and engaging introduction to the history of the world's nations.

Introduction

Iraq's History: Of Dynasties and Decimation

The nation of Iraq, as it currently exists, originated only after World War I and has enjoyed official independence as a nation since only 1932. However, the area that makes up Iraq has as rich a history of human civilization and culture as any place in the world. The area once known as Mesopotamia, which composes a large portion of Iraq, was the location of the first-known human civilizations and the earliest examples of human writing, crop raising and agriculture, astronomical observation, and nation-state governments headed by a king. It is where major developments such as irrigation and canal construction and the invention of the wheel first took place. The splendorous ancient city of Babylon lay in Mesopotamia, as did the important ancient city of Ur, the birthplace of the biblical figure Abraham. Centuries later the Iraqi city of Baghdad would rank as one of the wealthiest and most advanced cities in the world, and a massive empire united by devotion to the Islamic religion would be ruled from central Iraq. In more recent times Iraq has again propelled itself to global prominence, due largely to its strategic location in the critical Middle East region and along the Persian Gulf, through which an enormous portion of the world's oil supplies pass. Iraq's own rich oil reserves, large army, and military arsenal have also contributed to making Iraq a force to be reckoned with in world affairs during the late twentieth and early twenty-first centuries.

However, there have also been prolonged periods during Iraq's history in which it has been subject to heavy influence and outright domination by foreign powers. Iraq's location near the Middle Eastern crossroads of Europe, Africa, and Asia has subjected it to many migrations, aggressions, and conquests by peoples from various locations. During these times of foreign involvement and control, Iraq has often suffered marginalization, decay, reversion to primitive conditions, and even brutal destruction. This alternation between periods of great glory and world prominence and subjugation to secondary status recurred throughout the history of Iraq.

Civilized Origins

The city of Sumer, located between the Tigris and Euphrates Rivers in Iraq, is recognized as the precursor to all subsequent civilized nation-states throughout history. Archaeologists and historians have established that Sumer existed as long ago as 6000 B.C. Tablets written in a symbolic language known as cuneiform provide the earliest known recorded historic documents of any civilization. These tablets, along with other artifacts, came to light as a result of extensive excavation and archaeological exploration beginning in the eighteenth century. The realization of how important Sumer was in the development of human history is described in *Sumer: Cities of Eden,* written and produced by the editors of Time-Life Books:

> As more became known about them . . . the Sumerians finally received their due as one of the great creator civilizations, employing the potter's wheel and plow, mastering such techniques as riveting, soldering, engraving, and inlaying, and constructing large edifices with the aid of arches, vaults, and domes. Most important of all, the Sumerians inaugurated the era of recorded history by developing its prerequisite, the art of writing. Their cuneiform . . . script was humankind's first medium for expressing language in signs.[1]

Wandering and foraging groups of people likely began to settle in the fertile plains between the Tigris and Euphrates Rivers as early as the seventh millennium B.C. But it was around 5000 B.C. that the development of sophisticated irrigation systems enabled an advanced, civilized society to evolve. The editors of *Sumer: Cities of Eden* explain how this came about:

In Sumer during the fifth century B.C., people were, for the first time in human history, spared the demands of catching or growing food for their own sustenance. A farmer could produce more than he or his family needed and could barter the surplus to neighbors who were free to devote themselves to other occupations; to crafts such as pottery and metalworking, to administrative jobs in the world's first bureaucracies, to the service of the gods. So civilization—with all its mixed blessings—was born.[2]

Naturally, as the place where organized, civilized states originated, Sumer was the center of civilization at the beginning of recorded history. Rural and nomadic dwellers were attracted to the cities and towns, and new city-states in the surrounding areas also rose up. Eventually, the advanced form of society the Sumerians created would be adapted by people who would use these advancements against them.

The First Interstate Warfare

With population increases and cities developing in closer proximity, another activity common throughout human history, military warfare, soon emerged in Sumer. Axes and spears are among the artifacts found from that time. The original Sumerians found themselves overwhelmed by a unified tribal people known as the Akkadians, who resided to the north of Sumer in Mesopotamia, around 2300 B.C. The Akkadian conquest of Sumer was led by Sargon I, who, according to *Sumer: Cities of Eden,* "commanded what may have been the world's first standing army: '5,400 warriors ate bread before him,' boasted one inscription. Certainly, he controlled a military force far more potent than anything Sumer—or possibly the world—had seen."[3] The Akkadians combined many aspects of Sumerian culture with their own, including Sumerian arts and sciences. This merging of the two cultures led to the emergence of Babylon, a thriving and prosperous city-state revered far and wide as a wonder of the world.

Babylonian greatness came to its zenith under the leadership of Hammurabi, a king who ruled from 1792 through 1750 B.C. Hammurabi conquered additional territories for Babylon and was widely renowned for his warrior prowess, but he also made notable contributions in other fields. Probably his single most noteworthy achievement was the establishment of the Code of Hammurabi, a legal code that was precedent-setting in terms of its progressiveness and humanitarianism. The significance of the Code of Hammurabi is indicated in *Iraq: A Country Study*, a publication from the Federal Research Division of the Library of Congress edited by Helen Chapin Metz, who has edited several country studies for the U.S. federal government:

> The Code of Hammurabi, not the earliest to appear in the Middle East but certainly the most complete, dealt with land tenure, rent, the position of women, marriage, divorce, inheritance, contracts, control of public order, administration of justice, wages, and labor conditions.
>
> In Hammurabi's legal code, the civilizing trend begun at Sumer had evolved to a new level of complexity. The sophisticated legal principles contained in the code reflect a highly advanced civilization in which social interaction extended far beyond the confines of kinship. The large number of laws pertaining to commerce reflect a diversified economic base and an extensive trading network. In politics, Hammurabi's code is evidence of a more pronounced separation between religious and secular authority than had existed in ancient Sumer.[4]

Babylon's status as a seat of high civilization and human achievement lasted for about two thousand years, but during that time it was not always peaceful. Local ethnic factions fought each other, and various groups held power during different periods of time, but Babylonian customs and culture survived, adapted by each new group of interlopers to take control of the city. Among those coming to power during this time were the Assyrians, who were descendants of colonists from Babylon who resettled to the north. The Assyrians ruled over Babylon as part of an extensive empire that reached as far west as the Mediterranean and included the sacred Hebrew city of Jerusalem. The Assyrians alternated in power over Mesopotamia with other ethnic factions for a period of about five hundred years during the first millennium B.C., but these competing factions were all based in Mesopotamia. In the sixth century B.C., Mesopotamia would begin to be impacted and dominated by foreign powers, setting the trend that would recur in Iraqi history from that time on.

Two "Greats" Come to Babylon

The models for civilized society that had emanated from Mesopotamia had, by the last millennium B.C., spread throughout the known world. Nation-states and empires larger than any ever based in Mesopotamia were appearing. One such empire was that of the Persians, which rose up during the sixth century B.C. and conquered Babylon in 539 B.C. Persia was led by Cyrus the Great, one of the most renowned emperors in world history. So large is Cyrus on the stage of world history that Michael Hart, a historical author who wrote a biographical compilation entitled *The One Hundred: A Ranking of the Most Influential Persons in History*, includes Cyrus on the list at number eighty-six. One particular aspect of Cyrus's influence is of great relevance to Iraqi history:

> For over twenty-five centuries, the Sumerians and the various Semitic peoples who succeeded them . . . had been at the very center of civilization. For all that time, Mesopotamia had been the richest and most culturally advanced region of the world (with the exception of Egypt, which was [by Cyrus's time] roughly on the same level). But Cyrus's career . . . brought that chapter of world history to an end. From then on, neither Mesopotamia nor Egypt was the center of the civilized world. . . .
>
> Furthermore the Semitic peoples [of Mesopotamia] were not to regain their independence for many centuries to come.[5]

After two hundred years of Persian rule, another major empire, Macedonia, to Mesopotamia's west, would defeat the Persians under the leadership of Alexander the Great, another hugely important historic figure. Both Cyrus and Alexander had great respect and admiration for Babylon's civilization and culture, but not all of their successors shared their feelings. Although Alexander made grand plans for Babylon, saying he would make it an eastern capital for his empire, he died shortly after taking up residence there in 323 B.C. and never could carry out his plans. Alexander's successors were not able to maintain control over Babylon, and during the next five centuries the Mesopotamian territories underwent recurrent conquests by various Iranian peoples and the Romans, until one group of Persians, the Sasanians,

came to power in A.D. 227 and remained in control of Persia and Mesopotamia for more than four centuries. However, the Sasanians showed no concern for maintaining or preserving the civilizations or achievements of the Mesopotamian peoples. According to *Iraq: A Country Study,* by the end of the Sasanians' reign, "Mesopotamia was in ruins, and Sumero-Akkadian civilization was entirely extinguished."[6]

The area of Mesopotamia would undergo a renewal and once again emerge as a centrally important place in the world, but with a new ethnic and religious composition among its people. The rise of the religion of Islam among Arabs, which spread through much of the world through military campaigns, was enormously important in shaping the history of Iraq. Arab armies started moving into Iraq and battling the Sasanian Persians around 630. The Sasanians had more armed men and superior military apparatus and techniques, but their readiness and combat worthiness had been greatly reduced through constant warring with the Byzantine Empire, based in Constantinople, Turkey. In a series of battles, culminating with the Battle of Kadisiya in 636, the Arabs defeated the Sasanians and came to control Iraq and Persia as well as other territory in southwest Asia. Iraq underwent a massive influx of Arab people and an infusion of Islamic influence, creating social conditions that have remained prevalent in Iraq ever since.

A seat of Islamic power that would reign over Muslims throughout the world was established in the city of Damascus, Syria. A clan known as the Umayyads came to rule there, and the Umayyad caliphate, or supreme religious leadership, came to dominate the power structure of a new Islamic empire. Under Umayyad rule Arabs came to rank among the most civilized and advanced people of the world, but the Umayyad lineage did not survive long; in 749 a rebellious sect based in Iran known as the Abbasids staged a successful revolt against the Umayyads, who had come to be seen as abusive of power, decadent, and insensitive to their followers.

After the Abbasids took power they moved their capital from Syria to Iraq, forming a new city that would come to be known as Baghdad. That city would prove to be of immense importance not just to the history of Iraq but also to the entire world. Bernard Lewis, an international studies professor and author of dozens of books on Islam and the Middle East, describes Baghdad as the place where "the caliphs of the House of ['Abbas] reigned as heads of most of the Islamic world for five centuries."[7] In fact, Baghdad's importance would go beyond being a major cultural and urban center for Arabism and Islam; under the Abbasids, Baghdad would become arguably the most advanced and culturally enriched city anywhere in the world.

A World-Class City

Baghdad reached the heights of power and cultural advancement that it did because of its position as the center of Islamic and Arab civilization. During the last few centuries of the first millennium, Islamic-Arab society was among the most sophisticated, artistic, and affluent cultures in the world. Some of the heights of grandeur Baghdad enjoyed during this time are described in *Iraq: A Country Study*:

> Baghdad became a center of power where Arab and Iranian cultures mingled to produce a blaze of philosophical, scientific, and literary glory. . . . It was the second Abbasid caliph, Al Mansur (754–55), who decided

to build a new capital.... Within fifty years the population outgrew the city walls as people thronged to the capital to become part of the Abbasids' enormous bureaucracy or to engage in trade. Baghdad became a vast emporium of trade linking Asia and the Mediterranean. By the reign of Mansur's grandson, Harun ar Rashid (786–806), Baghdad was second in size only to Constantinople.[8]

As Arab power and Islamic adherence spread across great distances, new power centers arose in places like Egypt, Spain, and Iran, and the importance of the caliph as a leader of the Islamic world became more symbolic than actual. Local leaders acknowledged the caliph's spiritual supremacy but ruled their own areas independent from Baghdad's authority; consequently, the Abbasids became, in the words of Bernard Lewis, "nominal suzerains."[9] During the ninth century the caliphs also began to lose real authority within Baghdad itself, as military commanders and political governors they appointed gained enough clout to overshadow the caliphs and even control who was designated to hold the position. In *The Middle East*, Lewis explains how this loss of power for the caliphs came about:

> A spendthrift court and a bloated bureaucracy created recurring financial crises, aggravated by the loss of provincial revenues and, subsequently, by the exhaustion or loss to invaders of gold and silver mines. The caliphs found a remedy for their cash-flow problems in the farming-out of state revenues, eventually with the local governors as tax-farmers. These farmer-governors soon became the real rulers of the Empire, the more so when tax-farms and governorships were held by army commanders, who alone had the force to impose obedience. From the time of al-Muʻtasim (833–842) and al-Wāthiq (842–847), the caliphs became the puppets of their own generals, who were often able to appoint them and depose them at will.[10]

The figurative role of the Abbasid caliphs did contribute greatly to the establishment of a large and strong Islamic alliance in the world, but their weakened position left Iraq open to new conquests and domination by foreign forces.

Renewed Foreign Forays

Many of those who gained power under the caliphate's state revenue assignment system were of Turkish origin, as large numbers of Turks from Central Asia, to the north of Iraq, migrated to the new, flourishing society that had emerged. By the mid-tenth century these Turks had established themselves strongly in Iraq. Indeed, they were among those who could pick and choose the caliphs. These Turks were the earliest of the steppes people in Iraq—ethnic racial groups who originated in the higher elevations in central Asia in the layered, flat-lying, low mountain areas generally referred to as steppes. These peoples would come to influence Iraq just as significantly as the Arabs, Persians, and Greeks had before them.

In 945, however, foreign intervention took the severe form of actual military occupation by an Iranian military clan known as the Buwayhids. The conquest of the Baghdad caliphate by the Buwayhids was central to two major, long-lasting historical conflicts. One was the nationalistic rivalry between Arabs and Persians. The other was between two separate branches of Islam, known as the Shia and Sunni. These two groups had come into conflict following the death of Muhammad. The Shias believed that only a direct descendant of Muhammad could qualify as a supreme Islamic leader, but the Sunnis believed any highly educated and moral Muslim was worthy of the highest levels of leadership within the faith. Over the years tensions between the two branches had at times been severe, even violent. The Buwayhids were Persian Shias. *Iraq: A Country Study* incisively claims, "The humiliation of the caliphate at being manipulated by Shias, and Iranian ones at that, was immense."[11] In fact, when a particularly powerful Turkish dynasty called the Seljuks undertook conquests in the mid-eleventh century, the Sunnis of Baghdad urged the Seljuks, who were also Sunni, to overpower the Shia Buwayhids holding Baghdad. After successful conquests in Iran, the Seljuks were welcomed as invaders of Baghdad.

The Fall of Baghdad

Under both the Iranian Buwayhids and the Seljuk Turks, the caliphate was preserved; and as Muslims, both groups had reason to exploit the status of the caliphate to bolster their own claims to leadership. The caliphs may have been powerless, but to some extent the Islamic-Arab culture and civil society that had flourished under the early Abbasids had also been maintained along with the institution of the caliphate. Indeed, under the Seljuks Islamic-Arab culture experienced one of its most productive periods. However, another group from the steppes would soon gain power in Iraq who had no use for the Islamic faith.

That group was the Mongols, originally headed by the historical figure Ghengis Khan. In 1258 an army led by Hulagu, a descendant of Khan, attacked Baghdad and won the surrender of the last Abbasid caliphate, al-Musta'sim, who was slaughtered by the Mongol conquerors along with his family and many thousands of others within the massive city. City treasures were plundered and sacred sites desecrated by the Mongols, who wreaked havoc over Baghdad and throughout Iraq. After surviving infiltrations and incursions by a variety of ethnic and tribal factions who all shared the Islamic faith, the Abbasid caliphate of Baghdad was finally terminated by the Mongol horde, which became renowned for widespread conquest and extreme destruction.

As if to offer further testament to the lasting strength of Islam, the Mongols themselves, at least those in southwest Asia, became mostly Muslim by the end of the thirteenth century. However, that was of no benefit to Baghdad or to Iraq. Southwest Asia became a battleground for competing Mongol factions as the larger empire fell into disunity. The area was particularly badly ravaged by the descendant Mongol ruler known as Timur the Lame, or Tamerlane, at the turn of the fourteenth and fifteenth centuries. Russian historical author Michael Prawdin wrote a comprehensive history of the reign of the Mongols called *The Mongol Empire: Its Rise and Legacy*, in which he excerpts a passage from a historical chronicler of the time. The chronicler was from Georgia, a country north of Iraq along the southern Russian border, but the description he gave of the aftermath of Tamerlane's onslaught applied to a large portion of southwest Asia, including Iraq:

> The Tartars [descendants of the Mongol conquerors] tormented the populace in every possible way, by hunger, by the sword, by imprisonment, by intolerable martyrdoms, and most cruel treatment. They carried off masses of spoils and made numerous prisoners, in a way that none can venture to report, nor to describe the misery and gloom.... It is estimated that the num-

ber of those killed exceeded the number of those who were left alive.[12]

Among the ruin Tamerlane wrought on Iraq was another massacre of Baghdad, where once again as many as hundreds of thousands of people were killed, and all but a few of the city's buildings were destroyed. From heights of splendor and worldwide leadership Baghdad and Iraq had suffered a huge decline into subjugation and social decimation. These conditions would persist in Iraq for a great many years.

Tamerlane's empire would disintegrate following his death, allowing for a new Persian dynasty, the Safavids, to briefly conquer northern Iraq. Like their Persian predecessors the Buwayids, the Safavids imposed Shia Islam upon the mostly Sunni adherents of the area. However, another emerging empire, headed by another group of Turks called the Ottomans, was gaining power in Asia, Africa, and Europe. The Ottomans wrested control of Iraq from the Safavids only a few decades after the Safavids first came to power there. The Ottoman Empire that emerged during the sixteenth century was ultimately one of the largest and longest-lasting in world history, but Iraq would be of little significance to the empire for most of its existence. Conflict with the Persians over Iraqi territory persisted well into the nineteenth century, and as *Iraq: A Country Study* says, "the frequent conflicts with the Safavids ... sapped the strength of the Ottoman Empire and ... weakened control over its provinces."[13] This led to a major revival of factional tribal authority and rivalry within Iraq and an ongoing decline in social conditions in the urban and settled areas of the country. For hundreds of years under the Ottomans, Iraq remained a marginal territory, beset by social and cultural regression. Iraq would once again emerge as an important nation at the center of world affairs and attention, but it would not be for another four centuries.

Breathing New Life into Iraq

Under the Ottomans Iraq was administered as three separate provinces or *vilayets*: one centered in the northern city of Mosul, another in Baghdad, and another in the southern city of Basra. Not only did Ottoman disregard for these areas keep them on the periphery of the empire, but great ethnic and religious divisions among the three districts also contributed to social and cultural disunity in Iraq. These divisions—between Arabs in the south and central regions and another ethnic group known as Kurds in the north, as well as divisions between Sunni Muslims, based largely in central Iraq, and Shias concentrated in the south—made Iraq an unlikely place for a solidified nation-state to develop, and these differences continue to afflict Iraq's national unity.

Then again, some things did work in Iraq's favor. Thanks largely to increased commercial interest on the part of the British, who saw great potential in Iraq's natural resources, some progress toward modernization was made in Iraq during the late nineteenth century. After the introduction of steamboats on the major rivers and the introduction of telegraph communications, Iraq benefited greatly from an Ottoman political appointment. That appointment was of a man named Midhat to the position of pasha, or governor, of Baghdad. Midhat implemented major reforms in Iraq that he had been promoting for all the provinces of the empire. These included strengthening central government agencies and creating new governing bodies, establishing legal codes, and improving the strength and efficiency of the army. Midhat's achievements marked a definite move away from tribal concentrations of power in Iraq and toward the urban classes and official government. So important were Midhat's contributions that Stanford J. Shaw and Ezel Kural Shaw, both historians at the University of California in Los Angeles, called him "the founder of modern Iraq"[14] in their book *History of the Ottoman Empire and Modern Turkey.*

With measures toward modernization came improved education and an increasing realization among the people of Iraq that they were denied national independence. Along with other Arabs subject to Ottoman dominance, a growing number of Iraqis began to want to rule themselves, free of the subjugation of their distant and disengaged Turkish rulers. When in the early twentieth century revolutionaries in Turkey, known as Young Turks, seized power and appeared to offer the promise of greater local autonomy in government, independence-minded Iraqis were quick to support the Young Turks. However, when these new Turkish rulers showed that they were determined to reassert Turkish rule over the empire and integrate those areas culturally with Turkey, Iraqi independence supporters became alienated from them. A description of the impact of the Young Turk movement upon Iraq is given in *Iraq: A Country Study:* "The

Young Turks aggressively pursued a 'Turkification' policy that alienated . . . Iraqi intelligentsia and set in motion a fledgling Arab nationalist movement. Encouraged by the Young Turks' Revolution of 1908, nationalists in Iraq stepped up their activity."[15]

Britain Becomes the Major Power in Iraq

Growing Arab nationalism and hope for independence played well into the hands of the British, who increasingly became the foreign power of greatest consequence to Iraq in the later years of the Ottoman reign. The British had always been concerned about instability in Iraq under Ottoman rule, as they had large colonial holdings in Asia, and sought to ensure safe and reliable transportation and communication links with those areas. When the Ottomans sided with Germany in World War I against the British and other European countries, the British held out the promise of independence for the Ottoman-controlled Arab areas in return for the Arabs' alliance in the war. It was World War I that finally ended the existence of the Ottoman Empire, with the British defeating them in Iraq, among other places. However, the Arabs' hopes for their own nation or nations were not so easily realized.

Following World War I the League of Nations, an international organization usually considered the precursor to today's United Nations, authorized Britain to set up nation-states in much of the formerly Ottoman-controlled Arab territory, including Iraq. The government Britain devised for Iraq was regarded with disappointment by many of the Arabs who had supported the British in the war. It consisted of a monarchy modeled after those of many Western countries. Britain would continue to keep military personnel and equipment stationed in Iraq and have a say in policy decisions affecting British interests. The British-appointed Iraqi monarch, King Faisal I, had been an active proponent of Arab independence before and during World War I, and he was disappointed at the low level of independence granted to Iraq. Nevertheless, he accepted the appointment and tried to cooperate with and accommodate the British.

Yet there were a great many Iraqis who were not so willing to accept the British role in Iraq. Dilip Hiro, a journalist and author recognized as a leading authority on Iraq and the Middle East, claims in his book *Iraq in the Eye of the Storm* that after the League of Nations mandated that Britain oversee the new Iraqi state, the

British became "targets of the Mesopotamian hostility that had so far been directed against the Ottoman Turks."[16] Even though Iraq was officially an independent nation, the fact that it was categorized as a British protectorate and that the British had so much discretion regarding the government's formation and policies led to frustration among those who had long sought true Arab independence. When the plan for British oversight of Iraq was announced, a major nationalist rebellion ensued.

The Kurds and Shia Muslims were especially opposed to the British-appointed government and put up strong resistance, setting a long-lasting precedent for opposition to the central government among those groups, but there was opposition among Iraq's mainstream Sunni Muslims as well. Although the rebellion was quickly put down by the British, it helped to unify Iraq's various factions and set the stage for the possible creation of a cohesive state in the future. As explained in *Iraq: A Country Study*,

> The Great Iraqi Revolution (as the 1920 rebellion is called) was a watershed event in contemporary Iraqi history. For the first time, Sunnis and Shias, tribes and cities, were brought together in a common effort. In the opinion of Hanna Batatu, author of a seminal work on Iraq, the building of a nation state in Iraq depended upon two major factors: the integration of Shias and Sunnis into the new body politic and the successful resolution of the age-old conflicts between the tribes and the riverine cities and among the tribes themselves.... The 1920 rebellion brought these groups together, if only briefly; this constituted an important first step in the long and arduous process of forging a nation-state out of Iraq's conflict-ridden social structure.[17]

Iraq Becomes a Nation

Following the rebellion, the British agreed to grant Iraq full independence in 1932, earlier than was originally planned. The monarchy remained, but a nationalist civil government with real authority was also formed. However, Britain maintained a strong military presence in the country as well as the right to intervene when its security interests were threatened. The person who was most prominent in Iraq politics for the next twenty-five years, holding various high-ranking government positions, was Nuri as-Said, who was strongly pro-British in his policies. Many Iraqis with strong sentiments for independence and Arab nationalism remained dissatisfied.

The conflict between independence advocates and pro-Western forces was just one factor contributing to severe factionalism within Iraq that persisted for nearly four decades after the nation gained full independence. Along with the Kurdish-Arab conflict and the ongoing split between Sunni and Shia Muslims, contentiousness between nationalist and pro-Western forces made it very difficult for the new Iraqi government to stabilize itself and assert authority over the nation. The military staged a coup against the civil government in 1936, and the military would involve itself in ruling Iraq from that time on. The only exception was during World War II, when the British reoccupied the country and took over its governance when it appeared that Iraq was going to side with the Axis powers of Germany, Japan, and Italy in the war. Following the British withdrawal after the war, Iraq was just as divided among strongly opposing factions as it had been before the war; civil unrest and militant opposition to the government only grew worse.

These deteriorating conditions were foreseen by King Faisal at the time of Iraq's official independence. Andrew and Patrick Cockburn, brothers who are both international journalists with strong experience in covering the Middle East, include this passage from a memo written by Faisal in 1933 in their book *Out of the Ashes: The Resurrection of Saddam Hussein*:

> There is still—and I say this with a heart full of sorrow—no Iraqi people, but unimaginable masses of human beings devoid of any patriotic ideas, imbued with religious traditions and absurdities, connected by no common tie, giving ear to evil, prone to anarchy, and perpetually ready to rise against any government whatsoever.[18]

The Emergence of the Ba'ath Party

One ideology that gained widespread support in Iraq during the turbulent years following independence was Pan-Arabism, which advocated Arab independence and opposed foreign intervention in Arab lands, supported Socialist economic policies, and sought to unite all Arab peoples into a single nation. In Iraq Pan-Arab ideals were espoused by the Ba'ath Socialist Party, one of the most revolutionary and violent groups active in Iraq's civil unrest following World War II.

Like most strong advocates of Arab independence, the Ba'ath favored eliminating the monarchy in Iraq. However, it was another group of monarch opponents, military leaders known as the Free Officers, who in fact successfully eliminated the Iraqi monarchy in July 1958, killing the king and the crown prince, usurping all powers of the central government, and establishing Abdul Karim Kassem as the new leader. On the morning of the coup the government radio station opened its broadcast with the announcement, "Citizens of Baghdad, the Monarchy is dead! The Republic is here!"[19] It soon became clear though that the unrest and internal conflict that had long plagued Iraq had not been ended by the change in government.

The next ten years were just as violent as those that had gone before. Just a year after the 1958 coup Iraq's new leader, Kassem, was subjected to an assassination attempt. Playing a critical role in the attempt was a young Ba'ath Party member named Saddam Hussein. Both he and the Ba'ath would soon be playing an important role in Iraqi history, but immediately following the assassination attempt, which failed, Hussein was forced to flee Iraq altogether. He spent the next few years in Syria and Egypt before returning home.

During the 1960s the Ba'ath Party was involved in two more successful coups. After the first one, in 1963, the party was purged from the new government by Abdul as Salaam Arif, a military officer who had taken part in the 1958 coup supporting Kassem but had subsequently been active in the attempt to depose Kassem. Five years later, the Ba'ath Party again cooperated with military officers to stage another coup. This time the party acted first, purging its military coup partners from the new government before it could be kicked out itself. Following this coup Iraq finally had the opportunity to exist with a long period of continuity in government.

Saddam Hussein Becomes Iraq's Supreme Leader

The official head of the new Ba'ath government was Ahmad Hasn Bakr. However, even from the earliest days of the regime, Bakr's cousin and kinsman from the city of Tikrit, Saddam Hussein, played a critical role in the Ba'ath government. As chairman of the Revolutionary Command Council, Hussein led efforts to purge all government bureaus and agencies of anyone even suspect of disloyalty to the Ba'ath. He installed people throughout the government and in other important leadership positions within Iraqi society whom he could count on being supportive of the Ba'ath. And he was responsible for the formation of a militia under the control of the Ba'ath Party that could counterbalance the power of the state military. All these measures, along with efforts to increase public spending and improve living conditions that were geared toward encouraging support for the national government among the masses, enabled the Ba'ath to succeed where so many others had failed: They maintained central power in Iraq.

In 1979 Hussein officially replaced Bakr as the head of Iraq. He immediately embarked on a campaign to purge any potential foes from the government, going so far as trying and executing people on television. The great significance of Hussein's attainment of absolute power in Iraq is explained by Andrew and Patrick Cockburn in *Out of the Ashes:*

> For the sixty years after Britain created Iraq, it was paralyzed by its own divisions. Despite growing oil wealth, it remained a third-rate power, unable to mobilize its resources. The purge of the Ba'ath Party leadership in 1979 gave Saddam total control. He eliminated competitors for power within the party. He had already disposed of those outside....
>
> Internal feuding in the 1960s and 1970s made Iraq a marginal power in the Middle East and a very small player in world affairs. Saddam now started on a sustained effort to win control of the Persian Gulf and leadership in the Arab world.[20]

Indeed, Hussein would catapult Iraq back into being at the center of world affairs, but it would take engagements in extremely costly wars to achieve this goal.

Leading His Nation to War

A little more than a year after taking full control of Iraq, Hussein led his nation into war with Iran, its neighbor to the east. Iran had just undergone a revolution, replacing a pro-Western monarchy with a fundamentalist Islamic government that was openly eager to spread its revolution. The new government in Iran had specified Iraq as a place where it would like to see another Islamic revolution, and Iran helped Shia dissidents in Iraq with arms, supplies, and training. Hussein began the war in the fall of 1980. Lasting eight years, it would be the longest war fought directly between two national governments during the twentieth century.

The Iran-Iraq War was enormously costly for both sides: Total deaths reached at least six hundred thousand and there were more than 1 million casualties. Some of the most modern and destructive weapons in existence were employed, and the total cost of war damages reached at least $400 billion. At least publicly, Hussein stated that the war was being waged over disputed territory, but when the war finally ended, both sides agreed to a peace plan that restored the original border.

Still, Iraq emerged from the war stronger than it was before. This was due largely to the extensive international support Iraq received during the conflict. With Iran threatening to spread Islamic fundamental authoritarianism throughout the Middle East, a wide variety of nations, some of whom were often at odds with each other over other international matters, provided Iraq with various forms of assistance and support during the war.

The Cockburns elaborate on the improvement in Iraq's status stemming from its war with Iran:

> The war with Iran made Iraq a regional power and the strongest of the seven countries that border the Gulf. It started the war [with] ten divisions and ended it with fifty-five divisions. By the end of the war it had a tank force of four thousand and rockets that could reach Tehran and Tel Aviv.... Iraq won support from both superpowers, the Europeans, and much of the Arab world.[21]

Iraq clearly did not at this time reach the levels of preeminence in the world that it enjoyed during the Mesopotamian or Abbasid caliphate eras, but being the most powerful military power in regions as strategically critical as the Middle East and Persian Gulf while establishing numerous partnerships with powerful nations did give Iraq a much more elevated status in the world than it had experienced for a long time.

This improvement would prove to be short-lived. In 1990, just two years after the long and costly war with Iran ended, Iraq attacked another neighbor, this time Kuwait to the south. Kuwait and Iraq had had a long-standing border dispute, and tensions had been compounded when Kuwait had pressed Iraq for quick repayment on loans Kuwait had extended during the Iran-Iraq War. Attempts at negotiation had proven futile, and Iraq had been publicly angered by Kuwait's unwillingness to make accommodation considering the great burden Iraq had borne in the war with Iran, a country that was seen as a threat to many of the Arab national governments, including Kuwait's. When relations between the two nations collapsed, Iraq invaded Kuwait, deposed the government, and declared it to be a province of Iraq. Although this conquest was quickly and easily undertaken by Iraq, it proved to be a disastrous blunder in the long run.

Iraqi History Repeats Itself

In response to Iraq's invasion of Kuwait, nearly the same international coalition that came together to assist Hussein in the first Gulf war now turned against him, combining forces to drive him out of Kuwait. Once again Iraq paid heavily in terms of casualties and damage, but this time much of the military power it had built up by the end of the 1980s was destroyed. Hussein was forced to accept peace terms that subjected him to international economic sanctions and allowed international inspectors to have access to critical information and government and military locations within Iraq. It was a long way to come down so quickly; the Cockburns describe the country as having been "reduced to semicolonial servitude."[22]

The resolution of this war was followed by a period in which major world nations such as the United States and Britain maintained consistent policies against Iraq. Although these policies did weaken Iraq militarily, economically, and socially, they did not ultimately achieve the objectives of removing Hussein from power or forcing the Iraqi government to verifiably disarm. Following the terrorist attacks against the United States in September 2001, the U.S. and British governments intensified their efforts to remove or disarm Hussein's regime, claiming that Iraq not only had illegal weapons but also shared those weapons and cooperated with international terrorists such as those who carried out the September 11 attacks. Eventually another international military coalition, this one consisting almost entirely of U.S. and British forces, again attacked Iraq, this time invading the country and forcibly removing Hussein's Ba'ath regime.

This military campaign was impressive in its swiftness and effectiveness, with coalition forces launching their attack in mid-March 2003 and achieving conquest of the nation in less than a month. In a gesture of dramatic triumph, U.S. president George W. Bush spoke to U.S. military troops aboard the aircraft carrier *Abraham Lincoln*. Bush claimed that the success in Iraq was "one victory in a war on terror that . . . still goes on."[23] Although Bush was optimistic in his assessment of the war's achievement, there were soon signs that the social factionalism and instability that had plagued Iraq before the reign of the Ba'ath regime might be reemerging.

A particularly severe problem for the coalition forces was a breakdown of social order and rampant lawlessness that ensued following the collapse of the extremely authoritarian Iraqi government. Looting and violent gang activity challenged the coalition, and its inability to stop such activity soon led to resentment of the occupying forces among the Iraqi people. A *New York Times* article claimed that "in the space of a few weeks, awe at American power in war has been transformed into anger at American impotence in peace."[24] Although the United States and Britain possessed vast resources and had the determination to bring stability to Iraq, the nation's history of domestic turbulence and resistance to foreign domination indicated that the latest attempt by foreign powers to control Iraq would also be frought with difficulty.

Notes

1. Editors of Time-Life Books, *Sumer: Cities of Eden*. Alexandria, VA: Time-Life Books, 1993, pp. 11–12.
2. Editors of Time-Life Books, *Sumer,* pp. 12–13.
3. Editors of Time-Life Books, *Sumer,* pp. 122–23.
4. Helen Chapin Metz, ed., *Iraq: A Country Study*. Washington, DC: U.S. Government Printing Office, 1990, p. 10.
5. Michael Hart, *The One Hundred: A Ranking of the Most Influential Persons in History.* New York: Galahad Books, 1978, pp. 455–56.
6. Metz, *Iraq*, p. 14.
7. Bernard Lewis, *The Middle East: A Brief History of the Last Two Thousand Years.* New York: Scribner, 1995, p. 77.

8. Metz, *Iraq*, p. 21.
9. Lewis, *The Middle East,* p. 77.
10. Lewis, *The Middle East,* p. 80.
11. Metz, *Iraq*, p. 23.
12. Quoted in Michael Prawdin, *The Mongol Empire: Its Rise and Legacy.* Trans. Eden and Cedar Paul. New York: Free Press, 1967, p. 469.
13. Metz, *Iraq*, p. 26.
14. Stanford J. Shaw and Ezel Kural Shaw, *History of the Ottoman Empire and Modern Turkey.* Vol. 2. Cambridge, UK: Cambridge University Press, 1977, p. 68.
15. Metz, *Iraq*, p. 29.
16. Dilip Hiro, *Iraq in the Eye of the Storm.* New York: Thunder's Mouth/Nation Books, 2002, p. 22.
17. Metz, *Iraq*, p. 35.
18. Quoted in Andrew Cockburn and Patrick Cockburn, *Out of the Ashes: The Resurrection of Saddam Hussein.* New York: HarperCollins, 1999, p. 66.
19. Quoted in *Time,* July 28, 1958, p. 25.
20. Cockburn and Cockburn, *Out of the Ashes,* pp. 78–79.
21. Cockburn and Cockburn, *Out of the Ashes,* p. 82.
22. Cockburn and Cockburn, *Out of the Ashes,* p. 85.
23. Quoted in David E. Sanger, "Bush Declares 'One Victory in a War on Terror,'" *New York Times*, May 2, 2003, p. 1.
24. Edmund L. Andrews and Susan Sachs, "Iraq's Slide into Lawlessness Squanders Good Will for U.S.," *New York Times*, May 18, 2003, p. A1.

The History of Nations
Chapter 1

Mesopotamia: Civilization's Breeding Ground

The Roots of Civilized Societies

By Geoff Simons

Most of present-day Iraq is located on the site of the world's first civilization: Mesopotamia. The earliest civilizations of Mesopotamia made enormous contributions to history and humanity. The first known written historic documents, dating from the fourth millennium B.C., originated in this area. Innovations such as the wheel, the plow, and canal irrigation of agricultural lands also originated among Mesopotamia's first societies.

International author Geoff Simons has written more than forty books, including a history of Iraq titled Iraq: From Sumer to Saddam. *In the following excerpt from that book, Simons provides a chronological summary of the major civilizations and cultures that arose in Mesopotamia during the earliest days of known history.*

The region of the world that the ancient Greeks called Mesopotamia (land 'between the rivers') and that we know today as Iraq was a fount of civilisation—a veritable crucible, cockpit, cradle, womb of cultural progress (the metaphors run through the books). Here it was that restless tribes and peoples jostled for land and power, contending with their neighbours, being shaped by defeats, successful conquests, and the collisions of different cultures. Here it was that the first cities were born, writing began, and the first codified legal systems were established. Here it was—through such ancient lands as Sumer, Akkad, Babylonia and Assyria—that the vital cultural brew was stirred, the quite remarkable concoction from which Western civilisation would emerge. . . . We may reflect also that a modern Iraqi is entitled to contemplate with awe and pride the fructifying richness of the cultures that first emerged in his land more than five thousand years ago. . . .

Geoff Simons, *Iraq: From Sumer to Saddam*. New York: St. Martin's Press, 1994. Copyright © 1994 by Geoff Simons. Reproduced by permission of Palgrave Macmillan.

Sumer

The descendants of the early Stone Age farmers struggling to subsist on the edges of the marshes became known as the Sumerians, the inhabitants of Sumer. At that time most of the world's population were nomads, moving from one area to another in search of the necessary resources. They followed the wild herds through the seasonal migrations, clothing themselves in animal skins and seeking shelter in caves and crude lean-to structures. The settled communities were at first rare and insecure, though some evolved into larger stable communities. Some relied on a single prized commodity, such as salt (at Tell es-Sultan) and obsidian (at Catal Huyuk), used in the manufacture of mirrors, jewellery and knives. If communities were to be more durable they needed to develop more flexible economies; they needed to become more self-reliant. In fact the people of the Middle East were among the first to domesticate sheep and goats and to cultivate crops of wheat and barley. No longer were such people threatened by the whims of passing traders or the exhaustion of a local commodity.

The Sumerians, building on the achievements of their ancestors, worked to irrigate a difficult terrain and so to bring vast areas of alluvial desert into cultivation. The resulting surplus of grain gave the Sumerians time and resources for ambitions beyond mere subsistence. They became traders and merchants, artisans and engineers, and in due course scribes, the complex order of social classes sustained by the many developments in farming production. Sumerian scribes became the first people known to have written down epic poems, a type of recorded history, and to have speculated on the meaning of life.

The farmers began by simply carrying water to where it was needed, a laborious task that necessarily limited the area that could be irrigated. Next they diverted water from the rivers by means of small mud dams that directed the flow into well-placed ditches. From here the *shaduf* (a counter-weighted bailing bucket) was employed to convey the water into irrigation channels. The Sumerians also invented the plough, at first nothing more than a tree branch pulled by one person and pushed by another, but later, during the 4th millennium BC, they invented a copper plough that could be pulled by oxen. By 3000 BC ploughs made of bronze, an alloy of copper and tin, helped the Sumerian farmers to work large plots of land. And the successes in agriculture yielded many further developments. Planners and engineers were needed to lay out the patterns of dams and dykes, just as mathematicians were required to calculate rates of water flow, distances and the angles of slopes. Instruments were developed to aid such computations, which in turn led to observations of the sun and moon to develop a reliable calendar, whereupon farmers could be advised when to plant and harvest their crops.

The invention of the wheel is often attributed to the Sumerians, its first form probably being used in pottery making. Then they thought of throwing the potter's wheel on its side and using it for locomotion. This again extended the scope of Sumerian agriculture by enabling farmers to work land far from their villages: an ox or donkey hitched to a wheeled cart could move a much heavier load than could be carried on its back or dragged on a sledge. The invention of the wheel, we may surmise, also assisted in the construction of the stepped ziggurats, the ever larger temples built on the Sumerian plain. The interiors of the ziggurats were adorned by frescos and sculptures, a further indication of the importance of the temples in Sumerian culture. A priestly class farmed extensive tracts of land connected to the ziggurats and used the produce to support themselves and other citizens deemed to be in special need. The temple staffs expanded over the years and the ziggurats themselves came to function as centres of urban life. Administrators, accountants and priests all came to enjoy a well-rewarded existence and there were, in addition, a vast army of singers, musicians, cooks, weavers, cleaners and others, all drafted to serve the expanding religious culture. Agricultural activity was increasingly consigned to slaves, who toiled with evident success. It is recorded that soon after 3000 BC the temple in the city of Lagash was producing a daily bread and beer ration for around 1200 people, a significant achievement for the times.

The successes of the Sumerian economies gave a great stimulus to the greatest innovation of all, the invention of writing. To keep track of the expanding flow of products it was necessary to develop some means of keeping a permanent record. Thus the earliest written works were no more than inventory lists, charting the fluctuating contents of storehouses, but once a flexible system of writing had been invented it went far beyond the needs of straightforward economic administration: for the first time it was possible to use a symbolic system to record legends, poetry and historical detail. The earliest scripts were pictographic symbols used for individual words and concepts but such cumbersome systems eventually gave way to systems of symbols used for sounds. The Sumerians evolved one of the most successful systems, where clay tablets carried wedge-shaped impressions made by a stylus. This 'cuneiform' system (Latin *cuneus* = wedge) was later adopted by the Akkadians, the Babylonians, the Assyrians, the early Canaanites, the Hittites and the Hurrians; and so served Semitic, non-Semitic and Indo-European languages....

Great tribes, sometimes as federated unions comprising entire nations, moved with restless energy through the ancient Middle East. Expelled from their homes by invaders or seeking expansionist conquests of their own, they inevitably came into collision with the settled urban communities, of which the Sumerian developments were the most successful examples. They had created a rich agricultural economy and an unprecedented urban civilisation: suddenly they were to encounter the onrush of warlike hordes hunting for loot and land. It was one such confrontation around 2500 BC that came to threaten the existence of the Sumerian urban system. The Sumerians called the invaders the Amurru, who were probably the same Semitic tribes that the Hebrews referred to as the Amorites or Canaanites. In any event, they swarmed across the open Mesopotamian plains, capturing the ancient cities, killing the local kings, and then settling down to enjoy the fruits of their conquest. It was the collision of the Sumerian civilisation with the culture of the conquering tribes that was to generate the civilisation of Babylonia....

Babylonia

Babylonia emerged historically and ethnically from the union of the Sumerians and the Akkadians, a merging in which the Semitic Akkadian strain proved dominant. The military success of the Akkadians against the Sumerians led to the establishment of Babylon as the capital of lower Mesopotamia. Babylon was to flourish for almost two thousand years from about 2225 BC to its conquest by Alexander the Great in 331 BC. The biblical scribes of the Old Testament reckoned that the Euphrates, on which Babylon was sited, ran through the Garden of Eden. The Greeks declared that Babylon contained two of the Seven Wonders of the World, and the Romans saw it as 'the greatest city the sun ever beheld'....

At the start of the history of Babylon stands the great figure of Hammurabi 1792–1750 BC, a conqueror and law-giver through a reign of some forty-three years. He was depicted on seals and inscriptions as a youth full of fire and skill, a great warrior who crushes all his enemies, who marches over mountains and never loses a battle. Under Hammurabi the tumultuous states of the lower valley were forced into unity and disciplined by the famous Code. The diorite cylinder carrying the engraved Code of Hammurabi, conveyed from Babylon to Elam around 1100 BC, was unearthed at Susa in 1902 (it is now in the Louvre [museum in Paris]).

There is full acknowledgement of the role of the gods but the Code is essentially a body of secular legislation. Enlightened laws accompany barbarous punishments, and the primitive *lex talionis* and trial by ordeal are set against complex judicial procedures that have a modern ring. In all there are 285 laws arrayed systematically under the headings of Personal Property, Real Estate, Trade and Business, the Family, Injuries, and Labour. The Code, from which the Mosaic Code borrows or with which it shares a common source, is more enlightened than many judicial systems that were to follow in the centuries ahead.

Hammurabi retained the principle of the *lex talionis* ('an eye for an eye') but he sought to reduce its impact. Misdemeanours that formerly attracted mutilation or even death were now punished by fines, an advance that has been interpreted as a great civilising influence. The Sumerians long before had discovered the advantages of paying a wronged person compensation instead of waiting for the aggrieved party to exact revenge, and Hammurabi developed this idea into a penal sanction. It has been suggested that this development encouraged the emergence of the entire fabric of law, with all the associated apparatus of lawyers, solicitors, juries and the complex fabric of jurisprudence in civilised societies.

The idea that justice should be tempered with mercy was a Babylonian innovation, a vital contribution to the morality of law. But the idea was expected to apply only in domestic situations: there was no thought that one's enemies should be treated with compassion. This attitude accords well with how Middle Eastern rulers were in general expected to slaughter their opponents, even innocent non-combatants. . . . However, in urging a just approach to family morality Hammurabi laid the basis for a moral general social compassion, a position that is well represented (though often impotent) in the modern world. Here Hammurabi followed a much earlier Sumerian code, the earliest known legal canon, that attributed to Ur-Nammu who founded the Third Dynasty of Ur (2113–2096 BC), and who included the stipulation that 'the orphan is not to be given over to the rich, nor the widow to the powerful, nor the man of one shekel over to him of one mina'. It is clear that there were compassionate law-givers long before Hammurabi.

The Code bears importantly on aspects of marriage and women's rights (innovations here are sometimes contrasted with much repressive legislation in later Christendom). The 136th clause, for example, declares that if a man abandons his wife, leaving her without proper support, she is then free to remarry without being involved in the complexities of the courts. In the same spirit the 124th clause of the Code states: 'if a woman hates her husband and refuses him his conjugal rights, her case shall be examined in the district court. If she can prove she has kept herself chaste and has no fault while her husband has been unfaithful and so has demeaned her, she shall not be punished but may take her dowry and return to her father's house'. (Though this still smacks of sexism it should be set against a grossly anti-feminist Christianity happy for almost two millennia to tolerate marital rape.)

Hammurabi concludes his Code with the words:

> In my bosom I carried the people of the land of Sumer and Akkad ... in my wisdom I restrained them, that the strong might not oppress the weak, and that they should give justice to the orphan and the widow. ... Let any oppressed man, who has a cause, come before my image as king of righteousness! ... In the days that are yet to come, for all future time, may the king who is in the land observe the words of righteousness which I have written upon my monument!

... Hammurabi had aimed to lay the basis of a state that would endure 'for all future time', but the glory of the empire scarcely survived his death. His son, Samsu-iluna (1749–1712 BC), faced fresh revolts in southern Macedonia and new invasions from the north. The state of Babylonia survived until 1595 BC when the capital was sacked by the Hittites, a nomadic horse-breeding tribe of Indo-Europeans. Their warrior-chieftains ('kings') thought in basic military terms wherever the tribe settled: they were quick to organise massive fortifications linked by subterranean tunnels. It was inevitable also that they would absorb much of the culture of the Babylonians, adopting, for example, their systems of writing and the fabric of their law. When King Mursilis I led his Hittite warriors to end the Hammurabi dynasty it may have been expected that a new line of rulers would be established. However, Mursilis was forced to withdraw his army, and soon afterwards he was assassinated. Other tribes rushed to fill the Mesopotamian vacuum, among them the Hurrians and the Kassites.

These tribes swarmed down from the eastern heights, skilled charioteers eager to exploit a Babylonia mortally wounded by the brief Hittite conquest. For four centuries after the collapse of Babylon the region was ruled by a Kassite dynasty. The new conquerors adopted the Akkadian language, with the use of Sumerian reserved for religion, law and learning. The temples and palaces built by the Kassites at the new capital of Dur-Kurizalgu were designed and constructed in traditional Babylonian style. . . .

The Assyrians ('children of Ashur') were a Semitic race, at first colonists from Babylonia and its subjects. Later, around 1300 BC, they rose up and conquered Babylon. The state of Assyria grew around four cities watered by the Tigris and its tributaries: Ashur (later Kala'at-Sherghat), Arbela (Arbil), Kalakh (Nimrud), and Nineveh (Kuyunjik, near to Mosul). Archaeologists have found obsidian knives at Ashur, along with black pottery with geometric patterns that suggest links to central Asia. A town has been unearthed at Tepe Gawra, near the ancient site of Nineveh, for a long time the capital of the Assyrian empire. The town—with its many temples and tombs, its combs and jewellery, and the oldest dice known to history—dates to around 3700 BC. The Assyrian kings were first based in Ashur, but then built Nineveh (named after the god Nina, the equivalent of the Babylonia Ishtar), as a more secure retreat from the invading Babylonians. Here at the height of Ashurbanipal's power 300,000 people lived and Assyria's 'Universal King' was recognised by all the western Orient. . . .

[Babylonian king] Nabopolassar [(625–604 BC)] ended the Assyrian control of Babylonia and created the Chaldaean empire. When he died he bequeathed the liberated empire to his son Nebuchadnezzar II, the villain of the Old Testament Book of Daniel. In his inaugural address to the god Marduk he praised the deity for his sublime appearance and then declared: 'At thy command, O merciful Marduk, may the house that I have built endure forever, may I be satiated with its splendour, attain old age therein, with abundant offspring, and receive therein tribute of the kings of all regions, from all mankind.' He did much to realise his great ambitions; as warrior, statesman and builder he has been rated among Babylonian kings as second only to Hammurabi. He crushed an Egyptian force that was conspiring with the Assyrians against him, and brought Palestine (after the siege of Jerusalem in 586 BC) and Syria under his control. Enjoying the protection of Nebuchadnezzar, Babylonian merchants were again in charge of all the trade in the region.

He took tribute and raised taxes to spend on civic projects, as Hammurabi had done. He built new temples and palaces, embellishing all new buildings with frescos and sculptures; like Hammurabi, he remembered to keep the priests well fed. Again Babylon had become the grandest metropolis in the ancient world. The building bricks often carried brilliantly coloured enamel tiles of blue, yellow or white, embellished with glazed relief shapes of animals and human beings. Most of the bricks recovered from the site of Babylon bear the words: 'I am Nebuchadnezzar, King of Babylon'.... But the glories of Nebuchadnezzar were not to last: even before he died there were signs of dissolution and decay, even the suggestion that he became insane....

Soon after the death of Nebuchadnezzar the Babylonian army was falling into disorder; the traders were interested only in profiteering; and the parasitical priestly class did no more than accumulate treasure, a beckoning finger to envious peoples beyond the gates. When Cyrus, at the head of a disciplined Persian army, stood outside Babylon in 538 BC, the gates were opened to him; and for two centuries Babylonia was ruled as part of the Persian empire. Then Alexander the Great came to Mesopotamia, conquered Babylon in 331 BC, and soon afterwards died following a banquet in the palace of Nebuchadnezzar—killed, some commentators have decided, by alcoholism. Babylon survived the death of Alexander, though it had sunk into a period of irreversible decline. In 50 BC the great Sicilian historian Diodorus commented of Babylon: 'only a small part of the city is now inhabited and most of the area within its walls is given over to agriculture'; and in the same vein St Jerome (AD 345–420) wrote: 'The whole area within the walls is a wilderness inhabited by all manner of wild animals.' Perhaps ancient Babylon ended its days as nothing more than an abandoned desolation.

The Early Culture of Mesopotamia

BY SETON LLOYD

There has been extensive archaeological study and activity in Iraq for over a hundred years, much of it focused on the civilizations of Mesopotamia. English archaeologist Seton Lloyd has studied and written about many ancient civilizations. In his 1978 book The Archaeology of Mesopotamia, *Lloyd includes a section on the development of written historical records and pictorial depictions on works of art in Sumer that portray that civilization's beliefs and way of life. Lloyd discusses one document in particular, the king-list, which is recognized as the first written historical government record known to the world.*

In sculpture surviving from the Protoliterate [ca. 3000 B.C.] period, the scenes depicted are predominantly religious. At this point, therefore, a digression may not be out of place regarding the character and composition of the Sumerian pantheon.

From the earliest written formulations of religious belief, the names of three male gods, Anu, Enlil and Enki emerge as dominating figures. Anu, the sky-god, whose temple we have noticed at Uruk, was originally recognized as the highest power in the universe and sovereign of all the gods. Later in Sumerian history, he seems to have been replaced in this capacity, first by Enlil, patron god of Nippur and secondly by Marduk, tutelary deity of Babylon. Enki of Eridu was in a class by himself as god of wisdom and learning. Generally speaking, though the whole country worshipped a common pantheon, each individual city retained its own patron god and its own set of legends. For the rest, in the words of [French historical author] George Roux,

> The heavens were populated with hundreds of supremely powerful, manlike beings, and each of these

Seton Lloyd, *The Archaeology of Mesopotamia: From the Old Stone Age to the Persian Conquest*. London: Thames and Hudson Ltd., 1978. Copyright © 1978 by Thames and Hudson Ltd. Reproduced by permission.

gods was assigned to a particular task or a particular sphere of activity. One god for instance might have charge of the sky, another of the air, a third of the sweet waters, and so forth, down to humbler deities responsible for the plough, the brick, the flint or the pickaxe.

These gods had the physical appearance as well as all the qualities and defects of human beings. 'In brief', as Roux concludes, 'they represented the best and the worst of human nature on a superhuman scale'.

Examples of those associated with particular cities, who became also the object of a general cult, include the moon-god, Nanna (Sin) of Ur and his son, Utu (Shamash) of Sippar and Larsa; Ninurta, the warrior-god; Nin-khursag (Nintu), mother and wife of Enlil; Inanna (Ishtar), goddess of love and her husband Dumuzi (Tammuz). Inanna is of course the Great Mother, worshipped throughout the land, to whom the Eanna precinct at Uruk was dedicated: a female principle of creativity, expressing godhead through fecundity. As for Dumuzi, Roux points out that, though undoubtedly associated in the Sumerian mind with productivity in the vegetable and animal world, so that his union with Inanna must symbolize fertility, the theory which long associated him with the 'dying and resurrected' god of [Sir James] Frazer's *The Golden Bough* [book on the origins of magic and religion] has more recently been rejected. Other minor gods and goddesses are too numerous to mention.

Examples of Ancient Sculpture

A well-known stone vase from Warka, 90 cm high, has three registers of figures very finely carved in relief. Above, the goddess Inanna appears in front of two reed bundles terminating in loops and streamers, which are her perpetual symbol, and a ritually naked priest offers her a basket of fruit. Behind this the relief is damaged, but a small fragment remains of a figure which may well be that of a 'king' or leader, and an attendant supports the tasselled girdle which he is perhaps about to present. Inanna is supported by minor deities, mounted on model temples and appropriate beasts, with other symbols including a pair of vases like that on which they are carved. In the second register, naked priests bring further offerings and in the third, beasts and plants represent her two 'kingdoms'. Another sacred symbol present here is the stylized rosette with eight petals. Again, on the sculptured sides of a stone trough in the British Museum, sheep and rams from the 'sacred herd' return to her temple, here represented as a marsh-dweller's reed building, and from it their lambs emerge

SUMERIAN SAYINGS

The texts of Sumerian cuneiform tablets have been shown to include everything from business and financial records to legendary tales similar to those found in the Bible. Among the most interesting writings of the Sumerians are short amusing sayings and proverbs. The following are some of these sayings (reprinted in Sumer: Cities of Eden, *by the editors of Time-Life books).*

Do not return evil to your adversary; maintain justice for your enemy, do good things, be kind all your days. What you say in haste you may regret later.

Making loans is as [easy] as making love, but repaying them is as hard as bearing a child.

Go up to the ancient ruin heaps and walk around; look at the skulls of the lowly and the great. Which belongs to someone who did evil and which to someone who did good?

Who has not supported a wife or child, his nose has not borne a leash.

Commit no crime, and fear [of your god] will not consume you.

Bride, [as] you treat your mother-in-law, so will women [later] treat you.

The gods alone live forever under the divine sun; but as for mankind, their days are numbered, all their activities will be nothing but wind.

Sumer: *Cities of Eden.* Alexandria, VA: Time-Life Books, 1993, pp. 132–33.

to meet them. This also is a scene perpetually repeated, for example on the faces of a stone bowl from Khafaje, where cattle replace sheep, and much later in an architectural relief from the Early Dynastic temple at Al'Ubaid.

Secular subjects are less common. There is the fragmentary stela of black granite from Warka, carved with difficulty, to show two scenes in which the same 'king' figure hunts lions; and there is the extraordinary life-size head in limestone.... It is only a component part of a composite figure, the remainder of which could have been made from other materials such as wood and bitumen. The eye and eyebrow inlays are missing, as is the metal-foil covering of the hair. With these restored, the head looks a little outlandish; but the bare stone mask, as found, is strikingly beautiful. Animals carved in the round—a couchant ram from Warka and a wild boar from Ur—seem to have been ornaments attached by metal to larger contrivances, while stone vases also are sometimes decorated with animals—lions or bulls—carved partly in the round and partly in relief. Dating from the Jemdet Nasr period [early third millennium B.C.] at Warka, there are crudely carved 'king' figures, foreshadowing the *ex-voto* 'personal' statues of Early Dynastic times. Nearer still to these is a single votive statue of a woman from Khafaje. Of the same period are jars of animal form with an opening on top, usually of dark-coloured stone. These are often decorated with coloured inlays in geometrical patterns.

Cylinder-Seals

Another innovation which runs parallel to the pictographic writing of Protoliterate times is the cylinder-seal, a device used for establishing ownership or recording an agreement. These small objects of stone or shell, pierced through the centre for suspension, were delicately carved on their curved sides with a variety of devices or designs, to create a tiny frieze of ornament when rolled over soft clay. They have been found in great numbers and their impressions on tablets or clay jar-stoppers are even more plentiful.

The cylinder-seal is a device which makes its first appearance ... at Uruk. In the examples dating from this period, therefore, we should expect to see the Sumerian craftsman's first, and perhaps awkward, experiments in an extremely difficult form of carving. On the contrary, though it is clear that he had not yet completely mastered the intricacies of repetitive design, the variety of his subjects and the ingenuity of their decorative treatment testify to an achievement seldom rivalled during the centuries that followed. Already his work has the quality of relief carving, rather than mere linear drawing, as is shown by the vigorous modelling and articulation of the individual figures.

The pictorial themes and mythical symbols contributing to the composition of these designs have been the subject of much study and are today partly understood. Most evident in the religious scenes is the invocation of two deities never personally depicted, but symbolized by ideograms implying their attributes. There is a god who ... personifies the generative force in nature, graphically represented by certain animals and plants. Other symbols of the god include an eagle, sometimes lion-headed, and a snake. Equally prominent is Inanna, whose curiously shaped emblem (identified by some as the 'gatepost' of a reed-built temple), afterwards became her name-sign in pictographic writing. A decorative combination of these symbols alone can provide the subject of a seal design. Alternatively, when the performance of some religious ritual—sacrifice or oblation—is portrayed, human figures appear. . . . Flocks and herds make frequent appearances and are defended against lions by such figures as the 'bull-man' and 'lion-headed eagle', familiar features of Sumerian imagery in later times. Game animals also appear: boars, stags, ibex and moufflon, and from their shapes heraldic patterns are composed to supplement the seal-cutters repertory of designs. Occasionally there are secular subjects, including the 'king' figure, either hunting or at war. . . .

First Historical Documents

The Protoliterate period must be regarded, not as a prelude to Sumerian civilization, but as a first formative phase in its development, during which major contributions were made to the establishment of its identity. All that we know about it has been learnt from the results of excavations; but once it is ended, we find ourselves on the threshold of written history, and from now onwards must check our archaeological conclusions against the testimony of contemporary documents. The phase with which we shall next be dealing is generally referred to as the 'Early Dynastic' period: a title which is explained by the contents of a single, primarily important written document. This is the so-called 'king-list', in which the political anatomy of the Sumerian commonwealth and the succession of its rulers were at some time committed in writing to the memory of Mesopotamian posterity. Several slightly varying versions of this text have survived, and among them is one which can be dated (partly by the point which it stops) to the beginning of the 18th century BC. The earlier part of the same list even reappears in Greek, among the writings of Berossus, an obscure historian of the Hellenistic age.

Before speaking further about this document, in which the concept of 'kingship' is at least implicit, it may be well to enlarge a little upon the titles variously attributed to the rulers of Sumerian city-states during successive phases of their political evolution. In the early inscriptions, a number of different terms are used to imply forms of state leadership which are not precisely defined. Among these are *ensi* ('lord'), *en* (perhaps 'overlord'), *lu-*

GILGAMESH: A LEGENDARY FORERUNNER

Among the written works of the Sumerian cuneiform tablets was The Epic of Gilgamesh, *a part-realistic, part-supernatural tale that has come to be recognized as an early precursor of many legendary tales of different historic civilizations. The main character, Gilgamesh, was an actual king, but the epic includes many fantastic elements, including the attainment of immortality by a man named Uta-napishti, who recounts to Gilgamesh how he was able to attain eternal life by surviving a great deluge. The tale imparted by Uta-napishti bears striking resemblances to the biblical story of the flood and Noah's Ark, as these excerpts indicate.*

'[Everything I owned] I loaded aboard:
   all the silver I owned I loaded aboard,
all the gold I owned I loaded aboard,
   all the living creatures I had I loaded aboard.
I sent on board all my kith and kin,
   the beasts of the field, the creatures of the wild, and
      members of every skill and craft....

'The weather to look at was full of foreboding,

gal ('great man' or 'king'), and the distinction between them has been the subject of much thought and some controversy. The fluctuating conclusions of authorities on the subject are usefully summarized by [H.W.F.] Saggs and [Cyril John] Gadd, both writing in 1962. Saggs recollects the interesting proposal presented by [Thorkild] Jacobsen in 1943. He reached the conclusion that 'Sumerian kingship was not primitive but evolutionary and that its action was, at least sometimes, controlled by an assembly of elders and community heads or even by the mass of free men'. This theory was based on a study of early literary sources: '. . . the myths, the tales of the behaviour and exploits of the gods, which are generally thought to reflect the sociology of the times at which Sumerian society crystallized in the city-state . . .', probably very early in the 3rd millennium BC. According to

---

I went into the boat and sealed my hatch.
To the one who sealed the boat, Puzur-Enlil the shipwright,
   I gave my palace with all its goods. . . .

'The stillness of the Storm God passed over the sky,
   and all that was bright then turned into darkness.
[He] charged the land like a *bull* [*on the rampage,*]
   he smashed [it] in pieces [*like a vessel of clay.*]

'For a day the gale [winds *flattened the country,*]
   quickly they blew, and [*then came*] the [*Deluge.*]
Like a battle [the cataclysm] passed over the people.
   One man could not discern another,
nor could people be recognized amid the destruction. . . .

'For six days and [seven] nights,
   there blew the wind, the downpour,
the gale, the Deluge, it flattened the land.

'But the seventh day when it came,
   the gale relented, the Deluge *ended.*
The ocean grew calm, that had thrashed like a woman in labour,
   the tempest grew still, the Deluge ended.'

The Epic of Gilgamesh. Trans. and with an introduction by Andrew George. London: Penguin Books, 1999, pp. 89–94.

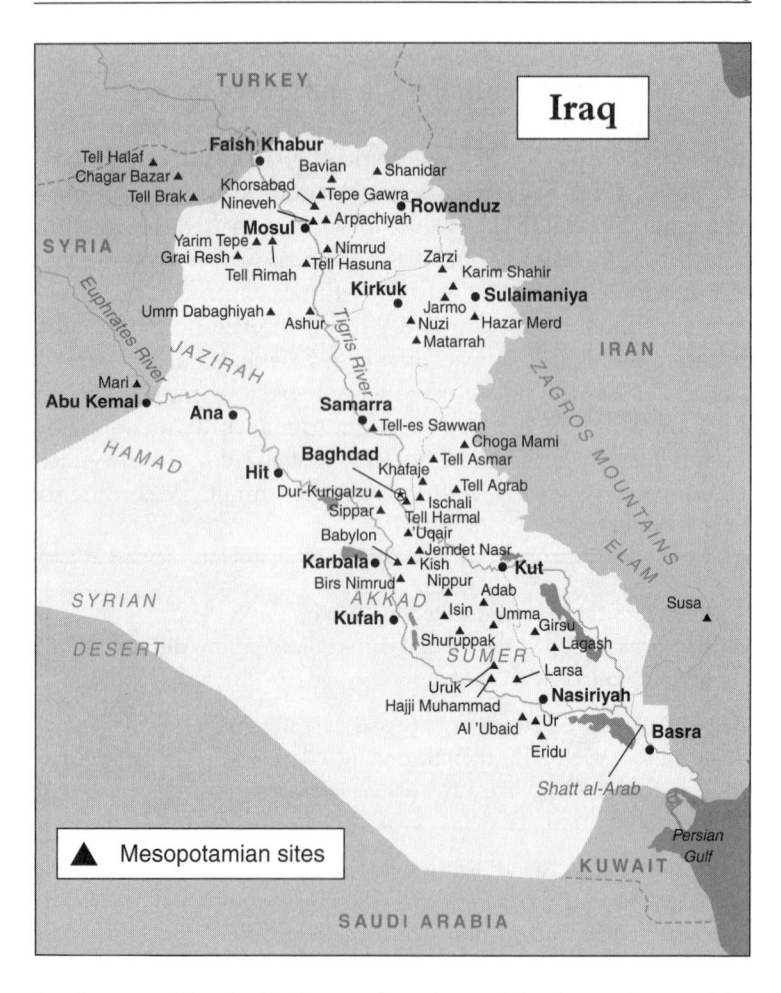

[Map: Iraq — Mesopotamian sites]

Jacobsen writing in 1943, one function of the 'general assembly' was to choose an official called *En*, who was 'primarily a cult-functionary, being the consort of the city's patron deity, and playing a vital role in the Sacred Marriage upon which the fertility of the city state depended'. His secondary administrative functions, in connection with the temple lands, gave him great political importance, and at one stage he became virtually the ruler. Very early, there came about some division between the priestly and secular functions of the *En*, who no longer lived in the temple but in a pretentious palace of his own. Later, during the historical period, the actual ruler

> was no longer the *En*, but an official originally con-

cerned in the agricultural operations, who bore the title *Ensi*. Cultic duties were delegated to a special priest or priestess.... In the event of an attack from the outside, the assembly had to choose a war-leader or king (*Lugal*).... The office of neither *En* nor *Lugal* was originally hereditary or permanent, that of the *Lugal* at least being granted only for the duration of the emergency.

The *En* or *Lugal* might attempt to perpetuate his position of authority and the two functions might then be vested in the same man. He could not be an absolute ruler, and could act only as authorized by the assembly.

Jacobsen's view of Sumerian society and its political structure, which aroused much interest when originally presented, is today less generally accepted, owing to a lack of further confirmation by new historical texts. The bare facts of what we are justified in concluding about the status of Sumerian rulers are that *lugal* remained the general designation of a 'king' and that an *ensi*, though a governor in his own right, might be subordinate to a *lugal* in another city.

Here are some features of the king-list as we know it today. It presents us first with the names of eight semi-legendary rulers 'before the Flood', and of the cities with which they are believed to have been associated. 'After the Flood', we are told, 'Kingship was sent down from on high'. A more factual chronicle then follows, introducing us to a federation of city-states, only one of which at any given time held supremacy over all the others. A succession of dynasties is accordingly listed, each based upon an individual city, whose hereditary rulers on such occasions became 'Kings' of 'the Land' and accepted responsibility for its welfare. Occasionally genealogical information is given, or mention is made of some happening which explains the transfer of hegemony from one state to another. This secondary list, as has often been pointed out, 'was not composed for the benefit of modern scholars', and from their point of view has manifest defects. The stated lengths of individual reigns are, for instance, fanciful and it has long been realized that certain dynasties in fact ruled concurrently in their own cities. Yet it does serve to emphasize the Sumerians' overall conception of the Land as an entity. Also it embodies for the first time a catalogue of the principal Sumerian cities—Sippar, Shuruppak, Kish, Ur, Adab, Mari, Akshak, Lagash, Isin, Larsa and others about which less is known.

The Ishtar Gate: An Example of Babylonian Magnificence

By Robert Koldewey

One of the earliest archaeologists to dig at ancient Mesopotamian sites was German Robert Koldewey. In 1914 an English translation of his findings appeared in a book titled The Excavations at Babylon. *In this excerpt from that book, Koldewey describes the elaborate beauty and craftwork of the Ishtar Gate, one of the most impressive and prominent structures of ancient Babylon.*

The magnificent approach by way of the Procession Street corresponds entirely with the importance, the size, and the splendour of the Ishtar Gate. With its walls which still stand 12 metres high, covered with brick reliefs, it is the largest and most striking ruin of Babylon and—with the exception of the tower of Borsippa which, though now shapeless, is higher—of all Mesopotamia.

It was a double gateway. Two doorways close together, one behind the other, formed into one block by short connecting walls, lead through the walls of crude brick, which are equally closely placed. At a later period the latter formed a transept which stood out square across the acropolis and afforded special protection to the inner part, the Southern Citadel. Apparently these walls were originally connected directly with the inner town wall still extant at Homera, for inscriptions found there prove conclusively that to it belonged the name Nimitti-Bel, while the Ishtar Gate

Robert Koldewey, *The Excavations at Babylon*, translated by Agnes S. Johns. London: Macmillan and Company, Ltd., 1914.

is itself frequently spoken of in other inscriptions as belonging to both Imgur-Bel and Nimitti-Bel. Imgur-Bel and Nimitti-Bel are the two oft-mentioned celebrated fortress walls of Babylon, of which we shall presently speak.

Of each of the two gateways two widely projecting towers close to the entrance are still standing, and behind them a space closed by a second door. This space, which is generally called the gateway court, although it was probably roofed in, shows clear signs that its primary object was to protect the leaves of the double door which opened back into it from the weather, and also that it strengthened the possibilities of the defences. In the case of smaller gates which do not possess these interior chambers, the leaves of the doors were inserted in the thickness of the wall, which afforded a protection; an embrasure which is absent in the gateways. On the northern gate the gateway chamber lies transversely, on the southern it extends along the central axis. Here also it is enclosed with walls of such colossal thickness that it may be supposed to have supported a central tower of great height, but nothing remains in proof of this.... Here, as in all the other buildings, we have little to guide us as to the superstructure. Among the ornaments in a grave in the Southern Citadel was a rectangular gold plate which on the face represents a great gateway. On it, near the arched door, we see the two towers overtopping the walls, while on their projecting upper part triangular battlements and small circular loopholes can be seen. Of the latter we found thick wedge-shaped stones under the blue enamelled bricks, and also part of the stepped battlements in blue enamel which, on the whole, may have had an appearance of triangles.

Detailed Design and Construction

The gateway itself was not placed immediately in the mud wall, but between four wing-like additions of burnt brick, in each of which was a doorway. Thus the Ishtar Gate had three entrances, the central one with fourfold doors, and one to right and left, each with double doors. The foundations of the main building are so deep that, owing to the present high water-level, we could not get to the foot of them. The gateway wings are not carried down so far, and the walls that stretch northward still less. It is conceivable that those parts of the wall where the foundations are specially deep do not sink so much in the course of time as those of shallower foundations, and settlement is unavoidable even with these, standing as they do upon earth and mud. Thus where the foundations are dissimilar there must be cleavages in the walls, which would seriously endanger the stability of the building. The Babylonians foresaw this and guarded against it. They devised the expansion joint, which we also make use of under similar circumstances. By this means walls that adjoin each other but which are on foundations of different depths are not built in one piece. A narrow vertical space is left from top to bottom of the wall, leaving the two parts standing independent of each other. In order to prevent any possibility of their leaning either backwards or forwards, in Babylon a vertical fillet was frequently built on to the less deeply rooted wall, which slid in a groove in the main wall. The two blocks run in a guide, as an engineer would call it. In the case of small isolated foundations, the actual foundation of burnt brick rests in a substructure of crude brick shaped like a well, filled up with earth, in which it can shift about at the base without leaning over, which gives it play like the joints of a telescope. In this way the small postament near the eastern tower of our gate is constructed, and also the round one which stands to the westward of it on the open space in front of the gate. On these postaments and on similar ones in the northern gateway court and in the intermediate court must "the mighty bronze colossi of bulls and the potent serpent figures" have stood which Nebuchadnezzar placed in the entries of the Ishtar Gate.

Where the southern door adjoined its western buttress there were some remarkable and rather considerable ancient cavities in the wall, for which I cannot discover any certain explanation. They were filled with earth, and had not been meddled with in modern times. Later than these, but also of ancient times, there is a well hewn out in the northern wing. A narrow staircase led down to it, and could only be reached by a passage 50 centimetres wide cut through the wall, which opened on to the space in front of the gate. The exit was hidden away in a corner, and almost entirely concealed.

The Wall Decorations of Bulls and Dragons

The decoration of the walls of the Ishtar Gate consisted of alternated figures of bulls and dragons (*sirrush*). They are placed in horizontal rows on the parts of the walls that are open to observation by those entering or passing, and also on the front of both the northern wings, but not where they would be wholly or partially invisible to the casual observer. The rows are repeated one above another; dragons and bulls are never mixed in the same horizontal row, but a line of bulls is followed by one of sirrush. Each single representation of an animal occupies a height of 13 brick courses, and between them are 11 plain courses, so that the distance from the foot of one to the foot of the next is 24 courses. These 24 courses together measure almost exactly 2 metres, or 4 Babylonian ells, in height. As these bricks change their standard when in use as binders or stretchers at the corners, the reliefs on one side of a corner are invariably either one course higher or lower than on the wall on the adjoining side.

From top to bottom of the wall there are 9 rows of these animals visible in relief. The two lowest rows are frequently under the water-level, which has risen so considerably in recent years. In 1910, however, it was possible to penetrate as low as some of these reliefs. Above there was a row of bulls in flat enamels, a good portion of which was found *in situ* on the south-east pier of the north gate. Above this must have been at least one row of sirrush and one of bulls in flat enamels, and a row of sirrush in enamel reliefs; the whole ruin was bestrewn with an extraordinary number of fragments from these upper rows. Those fragments have recently been brought to Europe, and it now remains to determine from them the actual numbers of the figures, so far as they can be counted. When this is done, we shall be able to decide whether or not there were more of these rows. The succession of the rows in the meantime may be schematized thus:

Row 13. Sirrush in enamelled relief.
" 12. Bulls in enamelled relief.
" 11. Sirrush in flat enamel.
      Upper level of pavement of shadu an turminabana stone.
" 10. Bulls in flat enamel, the top row of those found still *in situ*.
" 9. Bulls in brick relief, carefully worked.
      Older road pavement of burnt brick.
" 8. Sirrush in brick relief.
" 7. Bulls in brick relief.
      Traces of an older pavement (?).
" 6. Sirrush in brick relief.
" 5. Bulls in brick relief.

"   4. Sirrush in brick relief.
"   3. Bulls in brick relief.
"   2. Sirrush in brick relief, in 1910 only above water-level.
"   1. Bulls in brick relief, in 1910 only above water-level.

Each of the 8 lower rows containe at least 40 animals, and the upper 5 rows 51 animals. For in the latter there were certainly 5 more on the south-eastern angle of the northern gateway court and 6 more on the front of the northern wings. This gives a minimum number of 575 animals. After the excavations 152 pieces were to be seen still in position, and about as many more may yet be discovered in the part not yet uncovered.

The whole of this collection of creatures was certainly at no period visible at the same time and from the same point of view. The level on which the Ishtar Gate stood was repeatedly raised by artificial means. The traces of the two last heightenings can be seen between the 10th and 11th and the 8th and 9th rows. The traces of a pavement between the 6th and 7th rows are not clear. It is possible that when the gate was first built the roadway lay at the same level as the surrounding plain, but there is no proof of this. It may also be surmised that, for some time at least, the lower part of the gate was used as such, but in any case with the successive heightenings of the road the lower part of the building gradually disappeared below the surface. The filling-up shows the existence of great foresight, and of most scrupulous care expended on the work. The reliefs were carefully smeared over with mud, and those of the 8th row were actually covered with a fine clean white stucco.

Infusions of Foreign Powers

BY GEORGES ROUX

The power and glory of Mesopotamia's early civilizations ended in the sixth century B.C. Beginning with the conquest by legendary Persian emperor Cyrus, the area came under the domination of outside forces, a situation that would last for more than a thousand years. Georges Roux is a French national who has spent many years living and studying in the Middle East. The following excerpt from his book Ancient Iraq *describes this period of Iraqi history, during which time the territory was alternately conquered and controlled by various Persian factions, the Greeks under Alexander the Great, and, for a brief time, the Romans.*

The last king of an independent Babylon, Nabû-na'id or—as we call him after the Greeks—Nabonidus (556–539 B.C.) is one of the most enigmatic and fascinating figures in the long series of Mesopotamian monarchs. He was the son of a certain Nabû-balatsu-iqbi, 'wise prince and governor', and of a votaress of the god Sin in the city of Harran, both probably of royal blood. A man in his sixties when he ascended the throne, he had held important administrative functions under [previous Babylonian ruler] Nebuchadrezzar.... Extremely fond of his mother—she died in 547 B.C. at the age of one hundred and four, and was buried with royal honours—he had inherited from her a keen interest in religious affairs and a special, almost exclusive devotion for the god she had served all her life. After the death of Nabû-na'id the pro-Persians of Babylon, anxious to please their new sovereign, did everything in their power to sully his memory. In a libel known as 'the Verse Account of Nabonidus', they accused him of being a madman, a liar boasting of victories he had never won and, above all, a heretic who blasphemed [Babylonian god] Marduk and worshipped, under the name of Sin, 'a

Georges Roux, *Ancient Iraq*. Cleveland, OH: The World Publishing Company, 1964.

deity which nobody had ever seen in the country'. These vicious accusations met with a success that their authors themselves could hardly have expected. Through a confusion of names they gave birth to the story of Nebuchadrezzar's madness as told in the Book of Daniel, and found an echo in a fragment of the famous Dead Sea Scrolls. Even the most cautious of modern historians are obliged to admit that they contain a spark of truth. Some at least of Nabonidus' inscriptions suggest that Sin ranked higher in his esteem than the national god Marduk, and the sanctuaries of the moon-god throughout the country were the objects of his special attention: not only did he splendidly restore the ziqqurat and several temples of Ur, but the rebuilding of E.hul.hul, the temple of Sin in Harran, which had been destroyed by the Medes [an ethnic group based near the Persians in Iran] during the war against Assyria, appears to have been the *idée fixe* of his reign. To say, however, that Nabû-na'id for political and sentimental reasons wanted to replace Marduk by Sin at the head of the Babylonian pantheon is perhaps going too far. Other temples in Mesopotamia—including the great temple of Marduk in Babylon—also benefited from his zeal, and the eagerness with which, before building anew, he sought the *temenu*, or foundation-deposit, which authenticated the sacred ground testifies to his attachment to the religious traditions of Sumer and Akkad. On account of his lengthy excavations in search of these written documents, Nabonidus has been nicknamed 'the royal archaeologist', though neither his aims nor his methods had anything to do with archaeology. Nevertheless, the king certainly shared with his subjects that passion for the study of the past which characterizes his epoch.... To quote an amusing example: when Sir Leonard Woolley was excavating at Ur the palace of Bêl-shalti-nannar—Nabonidus' daughter and high-priestess of Sin—he was puzzled to find in the same building, in the same occupation-level, objects of widely different period, such as a Kassite *kudurru*, a fragment of a statue of King Shulgi and a clay cone of one of the Kings of Larsa. Only later did he realize that he had been exploring Bél-shalti-nannar's private museum!

Cyrus the Great

In complete contrast with this devout and apparently weak monarch stands the formidable figure of Cyrus II, 'Great King, the Achaemenian, King of Parsumash and Anshan', who ascended the Persian throne in 559 B.C., three years before Nabonidus was crowned.

The Persians—an Indo-European speaking people—had entered Iran at the end of the second millennium.... Moving slowly along the folds of the Zagros [mountains in east Iraq], they had eventually reached and occupied the mountainous range still known as Fars, to the south of the Iranian plateau. At the close of the seventh century B.C. when their history becomes better known, they were divided into two kingdoms ruled by the descendents of Teispes, son of Achaemenes (*Hahamanish*). In Persia proper (*Parsa* or *Parsumash*), i.e. the region between Isfahan and Shiraz, reigned the family of Ariaramnes, elder son of Teispes, while further west, along the border of Elam, the country of Anshan, or Anzan was ruled by the family of Ariaramnes' brother, Cyrus I. Both kingdoms were vassals of the Medes. For one or two generations, the House of Ariaramnes held sway over the House of Cyrus, but Cyrus' son, Cambyses I (*circa* 600–559 B.C.) reversed the situation and added to his prestige by marrying the daughter of Astyages, his Median overlord. From this marriage was born Cyrus II. At the beginning of Nabonidus' reign, Cyrus (*Kurash*) from his palace at Pasargadae ruled over a large but isolated district of Iran, paying tribute to his grandfather. But the Persian prince lacked neither ambition nor intelligence. He had already started reducing to obedience the Iranian tribes of the neighbourhood and was slowly enlarging his kingdom, when the King of Babylon himself gave him an opportunity to acquire an empire.

We have seen that Nabonidus' most cherished dream was to rebuild the temple of Sin in Harran. Not only was this sanctuary dear to his heart, but the possession of the market-place and strategic city commanding the roads from northern Mesopotamia to Syria and Asia Minor was of extreme importance to the economy and security of the Babylonian kingdom. Unfortunately, Harran had been in the hands of the Medes since 610 B.C., and against the Medes Nabonidus alone was powerless. Seeing in the Persians the true successors of the Elamites upon whose assistance the Babylonians had so often relied in the past, he called upon Cyrus for help. Cyrus accepted. Astyages got wind of the plot, summoned his grandson to Ecbatana, but met with a refusal to obey. A bitter war ensued, ending with the victory of the Persians. Betrayed by his own general, Astyages was captured by

Cyrus who, in one day, found himself the master of both the Persian and the Median kingdoms (550 B.C.). This important event, long known to us from the works of classical authors, is also mentioned in contemporary cuneiform texts. In one of his inscriptions, Nabonidus tells us that Marduk appeared to him in a dream and ordered him to rebuild E.hul.hul in Harran.... Following his victory over the Medes, Cyrus embarked upon a series of brilliant military campaigns which, after ten years, gave him an empire considerably larger than anything the world had ever witnessed. His first objective was Lydia, where reigned the fabulously rich Croesus. Rather than cross the Armenian highlands, Cyrus led his troops along the road that ran parallel to the Taurus range, through the steppe of Jazirah. Crossing the Tigris below Nineveh and marching westward *via* Harran, he occupied Cilicia, then a vassal-state of Babylon, thereby breaking the alliance he had just formed with Nabonidus and throwing the Babylonians on the side of Lydia and her traditional allies, the Egyptians. But neither the Egyptians nor the Babylonians could send troops to the aid of Croesus, who met the Persians alone and was defeated at Pteryum (547 B.C.). Lydia absorbed, the Greek cities of Ionia fell one by one, and the whole of Asia Minor submitted to Persian rule. No sooner was the conquest achieved than Cyrus turned his weapon in the opposite direction. Successively, Parthia and Aria, kingdoms of eastern Iran, Sogdia and Bactria in Turkestan and Afghanistan, and part of India fell into his hands. The Persian empire now stretched from the Aegean to the Pamirs, a distance of almost three thousand miles. Confronted with such a giant, Babylon had no hope of survival....

The Persian Conquest

Cyrus attacked Babylonia in the autumn of 539 B.C. Nabonidus ... ordered Belshazzar [his son, a military commander] to deploy his troops along the Tigris in order to cover the capital city. But the Persians had overwhelming numerical superiority. Moreover, Gubaru (Gobryas), governor of Gutium (i.e. Assyria), who ought to have protected the left flank of Belshazzar's army, went over to the enemy....

Belshazzar was killed in the battle at Opis and Nabonidus, probably in Babylon, although, according to other sources, Cyrus appointed him governor of Carmania (Central Iran). Far from being destroyed ..., Babylon was treated with the utmost respect.

From the first day of Persian occupation (October 12, 539 B.C.), care was taken not to offend the Babylonians in any way, and every effort was made to resettle them in their homes, to enforce law and order throughout the country.... Cyrus made it known to all that he considered himself as the successor of the national rulers, that he worshipped Marduk and 'praised his great godhead joyously'. Indeed, we can believe the Persian conqueror when, in an inscription written in Akkadian on a clay cylinder, he declares that the Babylonians accepted his rule with enthusiasm:

> All the inhabitants of Babylon, as well as of the entire country of Sumer and Akkad, princes and governors, bowed to him (Cyrus) and kissed his feet, jubilant that he had received the kingship, and with shining faces happily greeted him as a master through whose help they had come to life from death and had all been spared damage and disaster, and they worshipped his name.

... The first Persian kings, conscious of their duties towards one of their richest and most civilized provinces, carried out some of the royal tasks traditional in Mesopotamia. We know, for instance, that Cyrus restored the precinct of the temple of Sin at Ur, that he and [Persian king] Darius repaired the E-Anna of Uruk. In Babylon, his winter residence, Darius built an arsenal, a palace for the crown prince and an *apadana* (i.e. a hall supported by columns, in the Persian style) for his own palace. But Xerxes and his successors, engaged in an endless and costly war against Greece, do not seem to have cared much for their Babylonian satrapy. The entire period between the accession of Xerxes (485 B.C.) and the conquest of Alexander (331 B.C.) is exceedingly poor in architectural remains and building inscriptions. In southern Iraq, business documents found *in situ* prove that Babylon, Barsippa, Kish, Nippur, Uruk and Ur—to mention only the main cities—were alive, some of them even fairly prosperous, but none of their monuments appears to have been rebuilt or repaired....

Adverse economic conditions perhaps contributed to the decline of the Mesopotamian civilization. The main artery of the Persian empire, the 'Royal Road' from Sardis to Susa, ran at the foot of the mountains and bypassed Babylon. Trade with India and the East in general was monopolized by the Persians, nearer to these countries. Syria had been detached from Mesopotamia by Darius or Xerxes. Babylonia and Assyria, forming together the ninth satrapy, were grossly overtaxed: they paid to the Crown an annual tribute of one thousand talents of silver and supplied the Persian court with food during four months of the year. In addition, they had to bear the full burden of a greedy local administration. If we are to believe [Greek historian] Herodotus, the satrap of Babylonia received daily the content of an *artaba* (about 100 pints) of silver and kept 800 stallions and 16,000 mares, while his Indian dogs were fed by four villages! . . .

Oppressed, impoverished and partly 'denationalized', such was Mesopotamia, it would appear, in the last decades of the fourth century B.C., when Alexander came to give her a new, though entirely different life.

The Hellenistic Period

The battle of Gaugamela (near Erbil), on October 1, 331 B.C. opened for Alexander the road to Babylonia and Persia, as the battle of Issus, two years before, had opened for him the road to Syria and Egypt. The Persian troops stationed in Babylon surrendered without fighting, and the Macedonian conqueror made a triumphal entry into the old Semitic metropolis. Realizing, like Cyrus, that he could never rule over 'a hundred different nations' unless he won their hearts, he made sacrifice to Marduk and ordered the rebuilding of the temples thought to have been destroyed by Xerxes—a gigantic task which was never to be completed. The Babylonians hailed him as their liberator and immediately acknowledged his kingship. After a month's stay in Babylon, he proceeded to Susa, and thereafter embarked upon the great armed expedition to the East which took him as far as the river Ganges. When he returned, nine years later, his mind was full of grandiose projects: Babylon and Alexandria in Egypt were to become the twin capital cities of his empire; they would be linked by sea around the Arabian peninsula, shortly to be conquered; the coasts of the Indian Ocean would be explored; the Euphrates would be rendered navigable up to the Persian Gulf; a great port would be built at Babylon and another at the mouth of the river. But most of these plans remained a dead letter: on June 13, 323 B.C., Alexander died in Babylon, probably of malaria, at the age of 32.

At that date, Alexander's only son, the future Alexander IV, was not yet born, and it was his brother, Philip Arrhideus, who was proclaimed king in Macedonia. But the authority of this young and mentally retarded prince remained purely nominal. The real power lay in the hands of Alexander's generals—the *Diadochi*—who, having divided the empire between themselves, struggled for forty-two years to prevent each other from reconstructing it. During this period—one of the most complex in the history of antiquity—Babylon changed hands several times. At first the seat of a military junta presided over by the regent Perdiccas, it was allotted to Seleucus, chief of the Macedonian cavalry, by his colleagues in 321 B.C., after they had murdered Perdiccas. In 316 B.C., Antigonus, the ambitious satrap of Phrygia, dislodged Seleucus from Babylon, forcing him to take refuge with Ptolemy in Egypt. But Seleucus came back in 312 B.C., recovered his satrapy, and for four years successfully protected it from repeated attacks launched by Antigonus and his son Demetrius. It was a fierce and bitter war which brought terrible suffering upon Babylon and its territory—'there was weeping and mourning in the land' repeats, as a leit-motif, a Babylonian chronicle describing these events. Finally, Antigonus was defeated and killed at Ipsus, in Phrygia (301 B.C.), and Seleucus added to Babylonia the satrapy of Syria and the eastern half of Asia Minor. The war, however, continued, this time in the West, between Seleucus, Ptolemy, Demetrius and the Macedonian ruler of Thrace, Lysimachus. In September 281 B.C., a few months after he had defeated Lysimachus at Korupedion (near Sardis), Seleucus was stabbed to death by a son of Ptolemy. He had taken the title of king in 305 B.C., but for the Babylonians, the 'years of *Silukku*', the Seleucid era, began on the first New Year's Day following his return from Egypt: April 3, 311 B.C. It was the first time that a continuous numerical dating system was used in Mesopotamia.

After Ipsus, Seleucus ruled directly or indirectly over a huge territory extending from the borders of India to those of Egypt, and from the Black Sea to the Persian Gulf. But this empire lacked cohesion and started disintegrating almost as soon as it was formed. By 200 B.C., the descendants of Seleucus had lost practically all their provinces and protectorates beyond the Taurus and the Zagros, and after Babylonia had been conquered by the Parthians (126 B.C.), all that remained was a small state in northern Syria, torn apart by dynastic crisis, which fell an easy prey to the Romans in 63 B.C. . . .

The Parthian Period

The Parthians—a branch of the Scythians [from what is now southeast Europe and southwest Asia]—appear for the first time in history *circa* 250 B.C., when Arsaces led his nomadic tribesmen out of the steppes of Turkestan to settle in the north-eastern corner of Iran. By 200 B.C., the 'Arsacids' were firmly established along the southern shore of the Caspian sea. Between 160 and 140 B.C., Mithridates I conquered the Iranian plateau in its entirety and, reaching the Tigris, pitched his camp at Ctesiphon, opposite Seleucia. The Seleucid Demetrius II succeeded in recovering Babylonia and Media for a short period, but in 126 B.C., Artabanus II reasserted his authority over these regions, and from then on the Tigris-Euphrates valley remained in Parthian hands—save for two brief periods of Roman occupation under Trajan and Septimus Severus—until it fell under Sassanian domination with the rest of the Parthian kingdom, in A.D. 227.

THE HISTORY OF NATIONS
Chapter 2

The Baghdad Caliphate: A Global Power Center

The Rise of Islam and Arab Conquests

BY WALTER M. WEISS

The emergence of Muhammad as a major religious and Arab nationalist leader in the seventh century, and the explosive spread of Islam and Arab power that followed, strongly affected Iraq. Arab armies defeated Persians in major battles at Kadisiya and Ctesiphon, both in what is now Iraq, bringing Islamic and Arab dominance to the area. The following excerpt from Walter M. Weiss's book Islam: An Illustrated Historical Overview *describes how Islam came to be the dominant religion and Arabism the prevalent culture in Iraq. Walter M. Weiss is a German author and professor of history, journalism, and political science who has traveled extensively in the Muslim world.*

The Prophet [Muhammad] had no sons, nor had he designated a successor. Upon his death, therefore, Muhammad's closest followers met according to ancient Arab tradition to elect the new head of the community. They decided in favor of Abû Bakr, Muhammad's disciple from the earliest days, and father of his second wife 'Â'ishah. Abû Bakr was the first of the so-called four legitimate caliphs (Arabic *khalîfah*, "successor," "representative"), whose lives and deeds are held by the Sunnites to be exemplary in every respect. Abû Bakr was in turn succeeded by the caliphs 'Umar, 'Uthmân and 'Alî.

During his reign of only two years, Abû Bakr's primary task was to stabilize the Muslim state, whose unity already threatened to disintegrate. A number of important Arab tribes had accepted Muhammad's leadership, but considered themselves to be released from the terms of treaties with Medina at the Prophet's death. At

Walter M. Weiss, *Islam: An Illustrated Historical Overview*. Happauge, NY: Barron's Educational Series, Inc., 2000. Copyright © 2000 by Barron's Educational Series, Inc. Reproduced by permission.

the same time numerous false prophets had cropped up, vying with each other for acceptance by the tribes and causing considerable disturbance. In the Wars of Apostasy (633), Abû Bakr put a temporary end to these schismatic trends.

The second "legitimate caliph" was 'Umar (634–644), who is remembered in Islamic history as a pioneering figure. About him Muhammad reportedly said, "If God had wanted another prophet to follow me, it would have been 'Umar." With enormous energy, he drove forward the victorious campaign which, within a few years, transformed the Bedouins of Arabia into the rulers of a new world empire.

Arab-Muslim Expansion

By 633, while still under the command of Abû Bakr, Muslim troops had conquered Palestine and Transjordan. A short time later they achieved an important victory over the Byzantines, and in rapid succession more cities and kingdoms succumbed to their power. Damascus fell in 635; the following year, the Battle of Yarmuk brought them the remainder of Syria, and the Battle of Qâdisiyyah allowed them to enter Ctesiphon, the Sassanid [rulers of Mesopotamia] capital situated on the Tigris River [in present-day Iraq]. In 638 they took Jerusalem, and in the following year, the commander 'Amr ibn al-'âs crossed the border into Egypt, leading to the surrender of Alexandria in 642. Thus, within just two decades after the death of the Prophet, the *dâr al-islâm* (Arabic "House of Islam"), or the living area of the Muslim tribal family, stretched from the North African Cyrenaica to the Caucasus, and in the east beyond Iran to the Oxus River (today Amu Darya) in present-day Afghanistan. Within a short period of time, Arabs had established numerous large fortified cities, namely Basra and Kûfah in southern Iraq, as well as Fustât in Egypt. Furthermore, the Arab language began to replace such ancient languages of the Near East as Aramaic and Coptic.

The reasons for this unique military success have been the subject of much speculation. One reason surely lies in the fact that decades of murderous conflict had weakened the two superpowers, Byzantium and the Sassanid realm, to such an extent that they mounted only enervated resistance to the Arabian onslaught. In addition, Oriental Christians greeted the Muslims as liberators from the Byzantine yoke. Certainly, the new self-consciousness of the nomads, which had already been awakened before

Muhammad, played an important role—as did their continuous desire for booty. Moreover, climatic changes resulting in a gradual drying of the Arabian peninsula furthered what was to become a kind of tribal migration into more fertile regions. The decisive element, however, was surely the complete and boundless devotion to a thoroughly new religious idea.

Dissent and Divisiveness

Naturally, discontent as well as social and religious tensions also accrued with the growth of conquered territories. Caliph 'Umar had already ensured that the state would continue to maintain sole control over new possessions by decreeing that land won through warfare would not be divided up among the soldiers, but pass into the hands of the state. The revenues from these lands would be used as pensions for the descendants of the Prophet's original companions and for those taking part in the campaigns, the amount to be recorded in the *dîwân*, a kind of military civil service list. But soon the Arabs who had been short-changed demanded equal rights, as did the newly converted Muslims among the conquered peoples, in particular, the former Iranian and Byzantine elite.

Protest against the alleged misuse and unjust distribution of revenues and offices was directed especially against the third caliph, 'Uthmân, who stemmed from the tribe of the Banû Umayyah. He is remembered for having authorized the first canonical compilation of the Koran, a version still valid today, but was murdered in 656. Immediately afterwards the first civil war broke out, lasting five years. Of the three parties involved, one was led by 'Alî, the Prophet's son-in-law, who after numerous unsuccessful attempts at power was finally chosen to be the fourth caliph. A second faction, led by Talhah and Zubayr, two early converts who were supported by 'A'ishah, the influential widow of the Prophet, marched against 'Alî from Basra. The third adversary was Mu'âwiyah, the powerful governor of Syria, who called for vengeance for the death of 'Uthmân in the name of legitimate succession of the Prophet.

'Alî defeated the two opponents from Basra in 656 at the Battle of the Camel in southern Mesopotamia, and he subsequently came to an agreement with Mu'âwiyah after the Battle of Siffîn in 657. The compromise, however, seemed suspect to many followers, and 'Alî was himself murdered in 661 by an outraged former adherent. The disintegration of the much-acclaimed unity of the Muslim community was thus ensured; its division into three large, irreconcilable groups, the Sunnites, Shî'ites and Khârijites, was no longer to be averted. Mu'âwiyah profited from the confusion. He forced 'Alî's son, Hasan, to abdicate the title of caliph, and after having assumed this highest honor for himself, moved his residence to Damascus, thereby establishing the rule of the Umayyad dynasty which was to last for almost a century.

Hustling, Bustling Baghdad

By Gaston Wiet

The Umayyad's were displaced by the Abbasids, a rival clan based in Persia, in the eighth century. The Abbasids built a new Islamic capital in Iraq, the historic city of Baghdad. The Abbasids further expanded the thriving Islamic empire, and Baghdad became the central place of power for the Islamic rulers. However, Baghdad was not only a religious and political power center during the reign of the Abbasids; it also became a thriving metropolis where commerce, science, art, and culture flourished. As honorary professor at the College of France in Paris, Gaston Wiet wrote extensively about Islamic history. In the following excerpt from his book Baghdad: Metropolis of the Abbasid Caliphate, *Wiet cites ancient accounts of the city in its heyday to depict ninth-century Baghdad's strength and vitality.*

The first [Abbasid] caliph, Saffah, went to Iraq to settle, and he chose as his capital Kufa, already a famous city founded in the early days of Islam. There was probably friction between the Khurasanian guard [army loyal to the Abbasids] and the local inhabitants, who had been ungovernable in the days of the caliph Ali [Prophet Muhammad is son-in-law fourth caliph]. This friction could also have been the reason for three other successive and rapid moves of the caliphate which terminated in the founding of Baghdad. It is not by mere chance that the city has a Persian name. It was originally a retrenched camp where the caliph lived in safety under the protection of his Khurasanians.

The description left by [Islamic geographer] Ya'qubi one and one-half centuries after the city's founding deserves to be reported in its entirety. Undoubtedly it is a piece of bravura, but it contains evident truths that are of some use.

Gaston Wiet, *Baghdad: Metropolis of the Abbasid Caliphate*, translated by Seymour Feiler. Norman: University of Oklahoma Press, 1971. Copyright © 1971 by the University of Oklahoma Press, Publishing Division of the University. Reproduced by permission.

"I mention Baghdad first of all because it is the heart of Iraq, and, with no equal on earth either in the Orient or the Occident, it is the most extensive city in area, in importance, in prosperity, in abundance of water, and in healthful climate. It is inhabited by the most diverse individuals, both city people and country folk; people emigrate to it from all countries, both near and far; and everywhere there are men who have preferred it to their own country. All the peoples of the world have their own neighborhoods there, their trade and commercial centers; that is why there is gathered together here what does not exist in any other city in the world. It stretches out on the two banks of those two large rivers, the Tigris and the Euphrates, and watches commercial products and staples flow to it on land and on water. For it is with great ease that each commercial object is transported endlessly from East and West, from Moslem and non-Moslem regions. Indeed, merchandise is brought from India, Sind, China, Tibet, the land of the Turks, the Khazars, and the Abyssinians—from everywhere in short—to such a degree that it is found in greater profusion in Baghdad than in its country of origin. It is procured so easily and surely that one would think that all the goods of the earth are sent there, all the treasures of the world gathered there, and all the blessings of the universes concentrated there.

"Besides, it is the capital of the Abbasids, the center of their empire, and the seat of their sovereignty, where no one has appeared before them, and where no other princes have lived.

The Center of the World

"Its name is famous and its reputation is universally known. Iraq is indeed the center of the world. For, according to the unanimous opinion of the astronomers exposed in the writing of the ancient sages, it is located in the fourth climate, the median climate, where the temperature equals itself by epochs and by seasons. It is extremely hot during summer days, the cold is intense during winter days, and a moderate temperature is enjoyed in autumn and in spring; the change from autumn to winter and from spring to summer takes place without violent contrasts. Thus the passing of the seasons brings repeated and regular variations of temperature. Not only is the climate regular but the terrain is excellent, the water is sweet, the trees flourish, the fruit is of perfect quality, the harvests are magnificent, good things abound, and the water supply is almost at ground level. As a result of this normal temperature, of the quality of the soil, of the freshness of the water, the inhabitants are of a happy disposition, their countenances are bright, and their intelligence is of an open nature. The people also excel through their knowledge, their understanding, their good education, their perspicacity, their distinction, their commercial, industrial, and business sense, their ingenuousness in all controversy, their competence in all trades, and their ability in all industry. No one is better educated than their scholars, better informed than their authorities in tradition, more solid in their syntax than their grammarians, more supple than their singers, more certain than their readers of the Koran, more expert than their physicians, more capable than their calligraphers, clearer than their logicians, more zealous than their ascetics, better jurists than their magistrates, more eloquent than their preachers, more artistic than their poets, or more voluptuous than their gay blades."

This is doubtless exaggerated appreciation, and some of the points should be taken with reservations. Legend even has the founder of the city, the caliph Mansur, make this wonderful prediction:

"This is indeed the city that I am to found, where I am to live, and where my descendants will reign afterward. Princes had lost all track of it, before and since Islam, so that the previsions and orders of God could be accomplished through my efforts; thus traditions are confirmed, signs and prognostics become clear. Assuredly, this *island*, bounded on the east by the Tigris and on the west by the Euphrates, will prove to be the crossroads of the universe. Ships on the Tigris, coming from Wasit, Obolla, Ahwaz, Fars, Oman, Yamama, Bahrein, and neighboring countries will land and drop anchor there. It is there that merchandise will arrive by way of the Tigris from Mosul, Azerbaijan, and Armenia; that too will be the destination of products transported by ship on the Euphrates from Raqqa, Syria, the borderlands of Asia Minor, Egypt, and the Maghreb. This city will also be on the route of the peoples of Jebel, Ispahan, and of the provinces of Khurasan. I shall erect this capital and live in it all my life. It will be the residence of my descendants; it will certainly be the most prosperous city in the world."

A Political and Economic Capital

It is appropriate to compare this enthusiasm with the judgment of a contemporary orientalist who is no less laudatory. Jean

Sauvaget writes: "The founding of Baghdad, and then of Samarra, completely transformed marketing conditions; conveniently well placed to maintain relations by sea with southern Asia, these large cities, exceptionally well populated for the time, sheltered the Abbasid court containing all the members of the caliph's family and gathered together in one spot thousands of people used to living in mad splendor."

These excerpts have the great advantage of showing that the site of the new city contained all the necessary conditions for the security and the development of a political and economic capital, since its location gave it control over strategic and commercial routes. Situated between two rivers, Baghdad believed that it was protected from invasion and thought that its name, Madinat-al-Salam, the City of Peace (or City of Safety), was justified. This was indeed the official name of the Abbasid capital as it appeared on coins as well as on the cloth manufactured in the weaving shops of the caliphate. The name was a deliberate reminder of an expression in the Koran (VI, 127), *Dar-el-Salam*, which refers to Paradise. The observation was made to Caliph Mansur himself: "Commander of the Faithful, you will live between two rivers so that your enemies will be able to reach you only by crossing a wooden or stone bridge; when the wooden bridge is cut or the stone bridge is demolished, your enemy will not be able to approach you."

Later events will show that such reasoning was a little naïve. The important fact is that the two rivers were to facilitate the transportation of men and goods. It should not be forgotten that Basra, a port for ships going to China and India, was near by.

Mas'udi's speech is no less lyrical: "It is the most excellent region on earth as far as essential needs and food are concerned. For the most precious possessions in the world, after safety, honor, and power, are pure water and air. Besides, the best rivers in the world are the Tigris and the Euphrates, and the best spot on earth has always been the confluence of the Tigris and the Euphrates."

A New Era of Foreign Domination

By Rom Landau

The gradual decline of Baghdad and the devolution of power from there to various distant parts of the Islamic empire led to a long period in which Iraq was dominated by outside forces. Rom Landau was a professor of Islamic and North African studies at the College of the Pacific in California when he wrote Islam and the Arabs *in 1958. In the following excerpt, Landau reviews how two groups, the Seljuk Turks and the Mongols, came to hold power in Iraq for a period lasting from the eleventh to the fifteenth century.*

About 970 a group of Oghuz Turks from central Asia made their way into the eastern fringes of Muslim territory. To keep them from moving into Persia the sultan of the area gave one of the tribes some land farther to the west. This attempt at applying the age-old formula of 'divide and conquer' met with complete failure; for the Seljuks, so named after their leader, turned on their erstwhile hosts and destroyed their power for ever.

Following this battle, the Seljuks elected one of their number, Tughril Beg, as leader. Through his brilliant leadership they soon controlled Iraq, Syria, Palestine and Anatolia and established Tughril in Baghdad with the title of al-Sultan, 'he with authority'. The new sultan received two crowns from the Abbasid caliph, showing that he was king both of Persia and Arabia and [as stated Ameer Ali] was 'Sultan of the East and the West'. Although the Seljuks were orthodox in their religious belief, they did not allow the caliph any real power but kept him merely to

Rom Landau, *Islam and the Arabs*. New York: The Macmillan Company, 1959.

give themselves an aura of legitimacy.

The Seljuk history that included the reign of Tughril, his nephew, Alp Arslan, and the latter's son, Malikshah, marked the zenith of this dynasty's rule. The armies of the Seljuks, led by Alp Arslan, drove the Byzantines out of most of their Asian holdings, but it is during the reign of Malikshah that the dynasty showed itself at its best. This sultan's era is probably best known because of his far more famous Prime Minister, Nizam al-Mulk, who reorganized the economy of the country from a purely monetary one to a modified feudal system. It was apparent to him that unless the undisciplined troops of the Seljuks had some personal interest in the country's prosperity, they would merely extract money from the inhabitants with no thought of responsibility. In exchange for their loyalty to the throne, Nizam al-Mulk gave the land itself to worthy officers. When the officers realized that their personal fortunes were tied up in the land, they began to take a serious interest in efficiently managing their holdings. Thus with a minimum of effort, the Prime Minister was able to establish a flourishing economy.

Even more far-reaching was Nizam's contribution to culture. In 1065 he provided for the establishment of the Nizamiyah, the first well-organized academy or university in Islam. He also brought about the reformation of the calendar assisted by the famous poet-mathematician Omar Khayyam. Nizam al-Mulk's noteworthy administration was brought to an untimely close by the activities of the infamous 'Assassins' who had entered Islamic history in the latter part of the eleventh century.

The Empire Splits

In 1090 the leader of the Assassins, Hasan-i-Sabbah, gained control over several virtually inaccessible mountain fortresses in northern Persia and Syria from which he directed his fanatical followers. It was their policy to eliminate by murder any person whose existence they felt was inimicable to their interests—the promulgation of radical Ismailism. This scourge in the heart of the Muslim world was not completely eliminated until the Mongols destroyed it in the thirteenth century.

After the death of Nizam al-Mulk at the hands of the Assassins, the Seljuk empire split up along the lines of the feudal holdings that he instituted. Without a strong man in Baghdad to control the grasping, petty nobles, constant feuds broke out among them; and small, independent provinces replaced the once unified nation. This period of weakness was one of the contributing causes for the initial, and at times recurrent, success enjoyed by the Crusaders. The westerners were able to defeat the indi-

THE BLUDGEONING OF BAGHDAD

Rival factions of Muslims respected Baghdad's status as a pinnacle of Islamic culture and power. The Mongols, however, had no such reverence for the city. The Mongols had no reservations about ravaging and destroying Baghdad when they gained control of it. In The Mongol Empire: Its Rise and Legacy, *Russian author Michael Prawdin describes how the caliphate was defeated by Mongol forces led by Hulagu, a grandson of the first Mongol conqueror, Ghengis Khan, and brother of the legendary Kublai Khan.*

The Mongol army crossed the Tigris, and Hulagu's envoys rode to the court of Caliph Mustassim.... For five hundred years the Abbasid Dynasty of the Caliphs of Bagdad had held spiritual sway over the Mohammedan world, though most of their temporal dominions had been lost. All the sultans and all the shahs had had to bow before their doctrinal decisions. But now Hulagu demanded that the fortifications of Bagdad should be destroyed, that the Caliph should pay homage and render tribute.

The Caliph answered: "Young man, misled by the days of good fortune, you have become in your own eyes the Lord of the Universe, and think that your commands are the decisions of fate. You ask what will never be given. Do you not know that from West to East all who hold the true faith are my servants? Did I wish to do so, I could make myself master of the whole of Iran, but I have no wish to conjure up war.".... Mustassim's envoys declared that anyone who laid hands upon the sacred person of the Caliph would infallibly perish; and Hulagu's astrologer, a pious Moslem, prophesied six terrible misfortunes should the Mongols attack the capital of Islam.

vidual Muslim principalities and, on occasion, even were able to play one Muslim leader against another.

Although the dynasty's control of a unified empire was at an end, some individual officers, notable among whom was Zangi,

> This prophecy cost the astrologer his life, and the next prophet hastened to foretell Hulagu's complete success. Within a week the Caliph's army had been routed, and a day later the Mongolian advance-guard was close to Bagdad, the religious capital of Islam. After three weeks' siege, the suburbs were stormed, and the Caliph surrendered unconditionally. For six days and six nights the town was pillaged, the mosques were burned, and the inhabitants massacred. Then Hulagu announced that the place had become his property, that the surviving inhabitants were his subjects, and that no further acts of violence must be performed. No harm had been done to the Christians, who had taken refuge in their churches, for it was the traditional policy of the Mongols to win over those sections of the population which were hostile to the rulers against whom they were fighting.
>
> The Caliph was forced to reveal where his treasures were hidden, and all the riches which the Abbasids had got together in the course of half a millennium were heaped up before the tent of Jenghiz [Genghis] Khan's grandson. To the Caliph, who, since being taken prisoner, had been given nothing to eat, Hulagu held out an ingot of gold, saying: "Eat that!"—"No one can eat gold," replied the Caliph. "If you knew that, why did you not send it to me?" rejoined the Mongol. "Had you done so, you would still have been eating and drinking peacefully, and without a care, in your palace." Then he had Mustassim trampled to death by the hoofs of his horses.
>
> Thereafter the Mongols ran riot over Mesopotamia and Syria. Only the towns that surrendered promptly were spared. Only princes who came at once to pay homage were allowed to retain their dignities and their possessions.
>
> Michael Prawdin, *The Mongol Empire: Its Rise and Legacy.* Trans. Eden and Cedar Paul. New York: Free Press, 1967, pp. 308–309.

were able to set up some semblance of a Seljuk state. However, following Salah al-Din's success in Egypt and Syria, his new dynasty, the Ayyubids, took over the petty Seljuk provinces in the east. The remaining Seljuks in Persia were swallowed up by a rising new menace from central Asia.

The Mongol Invasion

In the steppe country of Mongolia the savage tribes had been united under the control of Temujin (Ghengis Khan). He was able to subdue China by 1219 and to turn westward to the divided Islamic empire. Within a year Temujin had crossed the Oxus River and swept through Persia with the relentless pressure of a bursting dam. The petty kingdoms that had struggled from the wreckage of the Seljuk empire were thrust aside like so much dust, and the Mongol horde was on its way to Egypt. Pressed as they were on the east by the troops of the Khan and attacked on the west by the Crusaders, the situation looked hopeless for the Muslims. Then, in 1227, the death of Ghengis Khan gave Islam the respite it needed while the Mongols moved eastward to choose a new leader.

Less than twenty-five years later the Mongol pressure again began to make itself felt along the borders of Persia. This time the invasion of the Muslim countries proved to be a forerunner of the scorched earth policy so successfully followed by subsequent armies to the present day. Led by a grandson of Genghis, Hulagu, the Mongols captured the traditional seat of the Abbasid caliphs—Baghdad. Even though he was told that 'if the caliph is killed, the whole universe is disorganized, the sun hides its face, rain ceases and plants grow no more', Hulagu executed the last of the direct line of the Baghdad caliphs—men who had been the spiritual heads of Islam for the previous five hundred years.

Although the Mongols put a stop to intellectual and cultural life for nearly a century in the areas they devastated, they did make positive contribution to the Muslim world. The invaders from the steppes had no more toleration for the 'Old Man of the Mountains' and his Assassins than had the Muslim dynasties. In a series of surprisingly easy battles, the strongholds of this Ismaili sect were destroyed and the scourge of the previous two centuries was eliminated.

After the Mongols invaded Syria and were checked by the Mamluk, Baybars, they consolidated their gains in Persia and Iraq and settled down to rebuilding the land they had so ruthlessly devastated. This surprising change of policy was effected by the civilizing and stabilizing influence of Islam. After conquering the Muslim empire, the Mongols found themselves in the position of so many other victors—overcome by the religion and culture of their victims.

The Aftermath of Recurrent Conquests

BY MARCO POLO

The recurrent conquests of Iraq by foreign powers resulted in a diverse mix of peoples and cultures in the area. They also left the region without strong governing authority and afflicted by social disorder. The Venetian traveler Marco Polo, who became famous for his long voyage across Asia from Europe to visit with the Mongol ruler Kublai Khan in the thirteenth century, recorded some observations as he passed through Iraq that reflected these social conditions. Polo mistakenly identified Baghdad as being at the same location as Babylon, and some historical observers doubt that Polo was ever actually in Baghdad. Polo's writing also reveals prejudice and ignorance regarding the peoples of Iraq. Nevertheless, his descriptions do accurately portray the greatly declined social and cultural conditions in Iraq following centuries of warfare and subjugation.

OF THE PROVINCE OF MOSUL AND ITS DIFFERENT INHABITANTS OF THE PEOPLE NAMED KURDS AND OF THE TRADE OF THIS COUNTRY

Mosul is a large province inhabited by various descriptions of people, one class of whom pay reverence to Mahomet [Muhammad], and are called Arabians. The others profess the Christian faith, but not according to the Canons of the Church, which they depart from in many instances, and are denominated Nestorians, Jacobites, and Armenians. They have a patriarch whom they call Jacolit, and by him Archbishops, Bishops, and Abbots are consecrated and sent to all parts of [Asia], just as the Pope of Rome does in the Latin countries.

All those cloths of gold and of silk which we call muslins are

Marco Polo, *The Travels of Marco Polo*, translated and edited by Manuel Komroff. Garden City, NY: Garden City Publishing Company, Inc., 1926. Copyright © 1926 by Boni & Liveright, Inc. Reproduced by permission of Liveright Publishing Corporation.

of the manufacture of Mosul, and all the great merchants termed Mossulini, who convey spices and drugs, in large quantities, from one country to another, are from this province.

In the mountainous parts there is a race of people named Kurds, some of whom are Christians and others Mahometans. They are all an unprincipled people, whose occupation it is to rob the merchants. In the vicinity of this province there are places named Mus and Maredin, where cotton is produced in great abundance, of which they prepare the cloths called boccasini, and many other fabrics. The inhabitants are manufacturers and traders, and are all subjects of the king of the Tartars [eastern Asians]. We shall now speak of the city of Baudas.

OF THE GREAT CITY OF BAUDAS ANCIENTLY CALLED BABYLON AND OF THE VARIOUS SCIENCES STUDIED IN THAT CITY AND HOW IT WAS TAKEN

Baudas (Baghdad) is a large city, heretofore the residence of the Calif or Pontiff of all the [Arabs], as the Pope is of all Christians. A great river flows through the midst of it, by means of which the merchants transport their goods to and from the Sea of India; the distance being computed at seventeen days' navigation, in consequence of the windings of its course. Those who undertake the voyage, after leaving the river, touch at a place named Kisi, from whence they proceed to sea: but previously to their reaching this anchorage they pass a city named Balsara, in the vicinity of which are groves of palm-trees producing the best dates in the world.

In Baudas there is a manufacture of silks wrought with gold, and also of damasks, as well as of velvets ornamented with the figures of birds and beasts. Almost all the pearls brought to Europe from India have undergone the process of boring, at this place. The Mahometan law is here regularly studied, as are also magic, physics, astronomy, geomancy, and physiognomy. It is the noblest and most extensive city to be found in this part of the world.

The Calif, who is understood to have amassed greater treasures than had ever been possessed by any other sovereign, perished miserably under the following circumstances. At the period when the Tartar princes began to extend their dominion, there were amongst them four brothers, of whom the eldest, named Mangu, reigned in the royal seat of the family. Having subdued the country of Cathay [China], and other districts in that quarter, they were not satisfied, but coveting further territory, they conceived the idea of Universal Empire, and proposed that they should divide the world amongst them. With this object in view, it was agreed that one of them should proceed to the east, that another should make conquests in the south, and that the other two should direct their operations against the remaining quarters.

The Southern portion fell to the lot of Alaù, who assembled a vast army, and having subdued the provinces through which his route lay, proceeded in the year 1255 to the attack of this city of Baudas. Being aware, however, of its great strength and the prodigious number of its inhabitants, he trusted rather to stratagem than to force for its reduction, and in order to deceive the enemy with regard to the number of his troops, which consisted of a hundred thousand horse, besides foot soldiers, he posted one division of his army on the one side, another division on the other side of the approach to the city, in such a manner as to be concealed by a wood. Then placing himself at the head of a third, advanced boldly to within a short distance of the gate. The Calif made light of a force apparently so inconsiderable, and confident in the efficacy of the usual Mahometan ejaculation, thought of nothing less than its entire destruction, and for that purpose marched out of the city with his guards. But as soon as Alaù perceived his approach, he feigned retreat before him, until by this means he had drawn him beyond the wood where the other divisions were posted. By the closing of these from both sides, the army of the Calif was surrounded and broken, and he was made prisoner, and the city surrendered to the conqueror. . . .

OF THE NOBLE CITY OF TAURIS IN IRAK AND OF ITS COMMERCIAL AND OTHER INHABITANTS

Tauris is a large and very noble city belonging to the province of Irak, which contains many other cities and fortified places, but this is the most eminent and most populous. The inhabitants support themselves principally by commerce and manufactures, which latter consist of various kinds of silk, some of them interwoven with gold, and of high price. It is so advantageously situated for trade, that merchants from India, from Baudas, Mosul . . . as well as from different parts of Europe, resort thither to purchase and to sell a number of articles. Precious stones and pearls in abundance may be procured at this place.

The merchants concerned in foreign commerce acquire considerable wealth, but the inhabitants in general are poor. They consist of a mixture of various nations and sects, Nestorians, Armenians, Jacobites, Georgians, Persians, and the followers of Mahomet, who form the bulk of the population, and are those properly called Taurisians. Each description of people have their peculiar language. The city is surrounded with delightful gardens, producing the finest fruits.

The Mahometan inhabitants are treacherous and unprincipled. According to their doctrine, whatever is stolen or plundered from others of a different faith, is properly taken, and the theft is no crime; whilst those who suffer death or injury by the hands of Christians, are considered as martyrs. If, therefore, they were not prohibited and restrained by the powers who now govern them, they would commit many outrages. These principles are common to all the Saracens. When they are at the point of death, their priest attends upon them, and asks whether they believe that Mahomet was the true apostle of God. If their answer be that they do believe, their salvation is assured to them; and in consequence of this facility of absolution, they have succeeded in converting to their faith a great proportion of the Tartars.

The History of Nations
Chapter 3

Provinces and Protectorate: Iraq Under the Ottomans and British

The Ottoman Takeover

BY GEOFF SIMONS

After centuries of tumult and decline, Iraq was finally somewhat stabilized when it came under the control of the Ottoman Turks in the sixteenth century. Reigning from 1534 to World War I, the Ottomans built an impressive empire that lasted about four hundred years. The following excerpt from British author Geoff Simons's Iraq: From Sumer to Saddam *describes the Ottomans' rise to power, including their subjugation of Iraq. Simons is the author of over forty books on the Middle East.*

The Ottomans were a fierce Turkish warrior tribe that originated in the central and eastern Asian grasslands, the homelands also of the Scythians, Huns and Mongols. Like the Mongols they were great horsemen, and their skill with the bow gave them considerable military prowess. Many of the tribes were a racial mixture, some resembling the Chinese in skin colour and facial features, others the Caucasians of the southern steppe. In their westward trek in the seventh century the Ottoman Turks began to penetrate the borders of the Middle East, and within three hundred years they had become the dominant force in what was later Soviet Central Asia. In contact with the fringes of the Muslim empire some of the Ottomans adopted Islam and the caliphs increasingly relied on Turkish Mamluks ('slaves') to consolidate their power. The Mamluks established an Egyptian dynasty, defeated the Mongols, and eventually drove the residual crusaders from the Middle East. By 1366 the Ottomans had expelled the Byzantines from Anatolia and made Edirne (Adrianople) their new capital in the southern Balkans. Constantinople, the Byzantine capital, finally fell to the Ottoman forces on 29 May 1453 and Sultan Fatih ('Conqueror') Mehmet

Geoff Simons, *Iraq: From Sumer to Saddam*. New York: St. Martin's Press, 1994. Copyright © 1994 by Geoff Simons. Reproduced by permission of Palgrave Macmillan.

II occupied what was now the capital of the Muslim empire of the Ottomans. The scene was set for further Turkish conquests.

The Mongol conqueror Tamerlane (Timur, c. 1336–1405), a self-proclaimed descendant of Genghis Khan, had taken the throne of Samarkand by 1369 and thereafter led his Turks and Mongols in a series of expeditions that vastly expanded his empire. In one great campaign he fought against Persia and in 1387 had reached the Euphrates river. He then conquered the region of the Caucasus and invaded India in 1398, after which he again turned westward to attack the Egyptian Mamluks in Syria and to defeat the Ottoman Turks in Asia Minor. It was at this time, in 1401, that Tamerlane became yet another conqueror to attack Baghdad and to take the city. He died before launching a planned invasion of China, and his vast empire was divided among his heirs, the Timurids. After the death of Tamerlane's son Shah Rokh (1405–47), who managed to unite much of the eastern part of the empire, the whole region began to disintegrate into local dynasties (including what was to become the Mogul empire in India).

This turbulent period also saw a Persian national revival under the Safavids, a dynasty (1501–1736) founded by Ismail I who conquered most of Persia and added much of Iraq to his empire. In 1508 Shah Ismail took Baghdad and then Mosul, and the bulk of Iraq was united with his Persian conquests. Soon, however, the Safavids were forced to confront the expanding Ottoman empire. From its secure Anatolian heartland the Ottoman state was now spreading over three continents: Asia, Europe and Africa. Sultan Selim I, in a highly successful campaign (1516–17), had captured Syria, Palestine and Egypt; and soon his great successor, Suleiman the Magnificent (1520–66) was to invade Iraq as far as the borders of Persia and also penetrate into central Europe, adding Hungary and other regions to the empire.

Central and southern Iraq, including Basra and Baghdad, were still in the hands of the Safavids—who were even attempting to establish the Shia heresy in place of the orthodox Islam in the region that had once been the very heartland of the Abbasid caliphate. Orthodox teachers were persecuted and many Sunni shrines were desecrated, including those of the revered Muslims, Abu Hanifa and Abdul-Kadir Gilani. Suleiman, as leader of the orthodox Muslim world, could not remain indifferent to these activities; and in any case there were good economic reasons for an attack on the Safavids of Iraq. He believed that the Safavid control of both Iraq and Persia had hampered trade between the Far East and Europe, while the Portuguese had helped to block the trade routes through a Middle East that was now largely under Ottoman control. So in 1534 Sultan Suleiman, at the height of his powers, decided to punish the Safavids in Iraq. So would begin a Turkish Ottoman occupation of Iraq that would continue, with one brief interruption (1624–38), up to modern times.

The Iraqi Invasion

In April 1534 Suleiman despatched the Grand Wazir, Ibrahim Pasha to commence the conquest of Iraq. Thus within three months of the signing of the peace treaty with Austria, Ibrahim was marching out of Aleppo to confront the Safavids. At Tabriz a second army was brought up to support Ibrahim's force, Suleiman himself now taking control of the Ottoman armies. He then moved into Persia but it was a difficult journey: the winter was harsh and the Ottomans lost many men and horses and were forced to abandon guns, wagons and other equipment. This led Suleiman to focus his attention on Iraq, with its more congenial climate, and the Ottoman forces were led over the Zagros mountains and on to the Mesopotamian plains. At last the exhausted army reached Baghdad and what was left of the once great city was taken with little opposition. In fact the approach of the Suleiman force had encouraged the city's Sunni religious leaders to lead a popular uprising that massacred most of the Shia soldiers and religious heads that had been oppressing them. Most of Iraq fell to Suleiman within months, though parts of southern Iraq, including Basra, remained in the hands of local Bedouins, until in 1538 this region too was conquered. The threat of a Safavid advance through Iraq into Syria had been removed, and the lands of the old caliphate had been brought under the sultan's control. The orthodox Islam of the Sunnis had been rescued from Shi'ite persecution. Now Suleiman's supremacy in the Muslim world had been confirmed.

Suleiman made a state entry into Baghdad and decided to spend the winter in the city, restoring the orthodox institutions that had been emasculated by the Safavids and building the characteristic Ottoman tax and administrative system in the newly acquired territories. The Safavids managed to retain control in Azerbaijan, a few enclaves in eastern Iraq, and parts of the southern Caucasus; but their power had been drastically curtailed and Ottomans were secure enough to introduce a regular system of administration throughout the conquered land.

When Suleiman died in 1566 the empire soon began to decay under a series of vicious and incompetent sultans. In 1619 Bekr (the Su Bashi), a captain of the élite corps of Janissaries in Baghdad, staged a revolt and made himself master of the city. An Ottoman army was quickly despatched to re-establish order whereupon Bekr invited Shah Abbas I of Persia to take over Baghdad. Alarmed at this development the sultan offered Bekr the governorship of the city if he remained loyal to the empire, with the result that when Abbas arrived at Baghdad Bekr tried to refuse him entry. But then Bekr's son Mohammad betrayed him and opened the gates to the Persian army. Thus Abbas took Baghdad on 12 January 1624 and set about slaughtering all the Sunni inhabitants of the city; Bekr himself was tortured to death. Abbas also killed, by boiling in oil, all the Janissaries who had supported him, on the grounds that if they had betrayed the Ottomans they could just as well betray him. The Persians then advanced through the rest of Iraq, the Safavids pushing westwards into Anatolia, with only the regions of Mosul and Basra remaining in Ottoman hands. Soon however, with the inevitable swing of the pendulum, the sultans would regain control of Baghdad and the rest of Iraq.

Clashing with the Persians

There was an immense popular reaction in Istanbul to the fall of Iraq; the sultan Murat IV was able to survive only by juggling the political leadership, but his position was weakened. In 1625 the Ottomans again tried to retake Baghdad, but while they were able to defeat the Safavid army and lay siege to the city they were compelled to retire when Persian reinforcements arrived. On 26 March 1626 the Ottoman siege of Baghdad was lifted, but the sultan managed to retain northern Iraq, a suitable base for further campaigns against the Persian masters of Baghdad. In November 1638 Murat, at the head of a great army, reached the Iraqi capital; the Safavids put up a strong defence, lasting from 15 November to 25 December, but then the Persian governor was forced to surrender and all the Persians in the city were slaughtered. The Ottomans then sent troops over much of Mesopotamia to suppress the Sunni Muslims, wherever they could be found, and on

17 May 1639 a definitive peace was established between the Safavids and the Ottomans, resulting in the drawing up of borders between Iraq and Persia that have survived with little change up to modern times. Now the Ottomans had secured their hold on Iraq and the unimpeded trade routes to the Persian Gulf were restored. Murat returned to Istanbul and died soon afterwards on 8 February 1640—of gout, sciatica or excessive drinking.

There now began the long period of Ottoman decline, a process that was to last for the greater part of three centuries. The empire had been at its height under Suleiman[1] but after his death there were few territorial gains and the fragility of the Ottoman state became increasingly apparent. The war with Venice (1645–64) exposed serious weaknesses in the empire; and soon afterwards the Russo-Turkish war (1676–81) resulted in most of the Turkish Ukraine being lost to Russia. The long slow decay had begun, but it would take the First World War in the twentieth century to finally extinguish the Ottoman empire.

---

1. At his height Suleiman ruled all or part of Hungary, Yugoslavia, Albania, Greece, Bulgaria, Rumania, the Ukraine, the Crimea, Turkey, Iran, Iraq, Syria, Lebanon, Jordan, Egypt, Libya, Tunisia, and Algeria.

The Political and Social Roots of Modern Iraq

BY CHARLES TRIPP

During the period of Ottoman Turkish rule in Iraq (1534–World War I), the political, cultural, and social configurations that would contribute to making up the modern nation-state began to take form. These emanated from a bureaucratic organization set up by the Ottomans based in the major cities of Mosul, Baghdad, and Basra. Each city was the governing center of a separate province, but the three separate political entities began to forge a distinctive collective identity, especially during the later years of Ottoman rule. Charles Tripp is head of the Department of Politics at the School of Oriental and African Studies in London. The following excerpt from his book A History of Iraq *provides an overview of the social and political structures that emerged during Ottoman rule of Iraq.*

During the sixteenth and seventeenth centuries the lands that were to become the territories of the modern state of Iraq were gradually incorporated into the Ottoman Empire as three provinces, based on the towns of Mosul, Baghdad and Basra. The term *al-'Iraq* (meaning the shore of a great river along its length, as well as the grazing land surrounding it) had been used since at least the eighth century by Arab geographers to refer to the great alluvial plain of the Tigris and Euphrates Rivers, a region known in Europe as Mesopotamia. It was here that the Ottoman sultans were extending their own domains during these years and trying to check the ambitions of the Safavid [rulers] of Persia. Imperial and doctrinal rivalries between the Sunni Ottomans and the Shi'i Safavids touched the histories of the peoples of these frontier lands, requiring strategies of ac-

Charles Tripp, *A History of Iraq*. Cambridge, UK: Cambridge University Press, 2000. Copyright © 2000 by Cambridge University Press. Reproduced by permission of Cambridge University Press and the author.

commodation or evasion from their leaders and affecting them in a variety of ways. The political world that resulted was a complex and fragmented one. Centres of power existed in many cases autonomously, interacting under shifting circumstances that gave advantage now to one grouping, now to another, and in which the control of the central Ottoman government in Istanbul gradually diminished. Instead, initiative and power lay with those who could command the forces needed to defeat external and internal challengers alike.

The Pashas

At the summit of the systems of power in the three provinces stood the military elite of *mamluk* pashas [once a class of slaves who became military rulers] who acknowledged the sovereignty of the Ottoman sultan, but were increasingly beyond his control....

The *mamluk* pashas ruled over a tributary system. The main function of government was to maintain them and their entourage in an appropriate style by extracting the revenues which would enable them to service their clients and to defend the system against all challengers, internal or external. Thus, taxes were levied on rural communities within reach of the major towns and tribute was forthcoming from those tribal leaders who found it advisable to keep on good terms with the power that the most successful of these *mamluk* pashas could command. These funds were supplemented by the dues charged on goods in transit through Mesopotamia, increasing during the eighteenth century as trade development with the British East India Company, in particular.

The attitude of these pashas to the Ottoman Empire was formally correct.... However, they were less ready to accept material limitations on their rule. Appointees from Istanbul served on their staff, but only in subordinate positions. Imperial ... troops were stationed in Baghdad, but the pashas kept them under their direct command and ensured that their own elite force of *mamluks* could always subdue them. Tribute was sent to Istanbul, but irregularly....

The Cultural College of the Mesopotamian Provinces

Taken as a whole, the inhabitants of the three provinces of Mosul, Baghdad and Basra provided as broad a spectrum of social communal structures as anywhere in the empire. In the Kurdish-speaking areas of the north and north-east of Mosul and Baghdad provinces, dynastic, parochial and tribal identities and loyalties shaped the lives of the inhabitants. Also important was the influence of the Sufi orders—most notably the Qadiri and increasingly the Naqshabandi—which lent to the observance of Islam in these regions a distinctive character, strongly shaped by Kurdish shaikhs [religous leaders] and *sayyids* [descendants of the prophet Muhammad]. Also prominent in this region were the communities of Yazidis (Kurdish-speaking adherents of the syncretic religion of Yazidism), of Christians and of Shi'a, some Kurdish and some Turkoman. These features, as well as broader linguistic differences and geographical isolation, had led to the emergence of a number of local lordships and small principalities which enjoyed complex and shifting relations with each other and with the Ottoman and Persian Empires, the borders of which they straddled.

In the Arabic-speaking districts of Mosul province, the rural population was divided among sedentary and nomadic tribal groups, engaged in agriculture or pastoralism, with some profiting from the opportunities offered by the transit trade. Here too, strong tribal and local attachments coloured everyday life and helped to create distinct communities with particular identities and practices, linked by real or imagined bonds of kinship. These determined the relationship of individuals to the land and shaped the hierarchies of clans and families in the various settlements. Leadership was decided on this basis, but the size and remoteness, as well as the economic and military capacities, of the community in question would determine the power of the leader relative to that of the local Ottoman governor and the degree of autonomy he could therefore enjoy. For the majority of the members of such communities, any contact with the Ottoman state would be mediated by the leading family, encouraging worlds of difference to emerge in the views that people held of the histories of which they formed a part.

By contrast, Mosul itself was a much more directly integrated part of the Ottoman imperial system. Powerful local families, such as the Jalili, as well as prominent families of *ashraf* such as the 'Ubaidi, dominated certain quarters of the town. Reflecting to some degree the composition of the surrounding countryside, the population was predominantly Sunnik Arab, but there were also distinct communities of Turkomans and of Kurds, as well as of Jews and of Christians. The relative weight of these communities and their leading families was strongly influenced by the political hierarchies, the judicial system and the trading networks of the Ottoman Empire itself. Although families such as the Jalili tried to preserve a sphere of action free from the direct control of Istanbul, they, no less than the leaders of the *millet* communities [religious communities within the Ottoman Empire that enjoyed recognized autonomy] in the city, owed their prominence to their successful and distinctive engagement with the powers of the Ottoman state. As the nineteenth century was to show, they were equally vulnerable when the priorities of that state began to change.

Much the same could be said of the city of Baghdad. As a provincial capital, it had much in common with other great Ottoman cities. However, in several senses it was more remote from the controlling influence of Istanbul. The Georgian *mamluks* had introduced a distinctive and formidable military caste at the head of its social structure, dominating but separate from the respected hierarchies of the *ashraf*, led by the family of the al-Kailani. Furthermore, the proximity of Persia and the size of the Shi'i community in nearby al-Kazimiyya added a distinctive character to the city, as did the size and prominence of the long-established Jewish community, which constituted nearly 20 per cent of the population. The frontier nature of the province also left its mark through the steady influx of people from various parts of the empire. Whether they were Ottoman officials who came, stayed and intermarried with one of the established Baghdad families, or formed part of the inevitable trickle of immigrants from Baghdad's rural hinterland, or were traders who settled in the city, bringing with them their connections to Persia, the Gulf or India, the population of Baghdad underwent various forms of renewal—vitally necessary if the city was to survive the devastating man-made and natural disasters that afflicted its inhabitants during the seventeenth, eighteenth and early nineteenth centuries.

Baghdad, like Mosul, ruled over a province that was only nominally under the control of the authorities in the capital. As in the north, the lives of most of the rural population were shaped by the practices and values of the sedentary, semi-sedentary and nomadic tribes and tribal confederations to which they belonged. Only in the regions closest to Baghdad, more easily subject to the direct control of the administrative and political elite of the city, did tribal identities have less obvious political consequences. However the *mamluk* pashas could rarely impose their will on the more inaccessible, larger and more formidably armed tribes and tribal groupings, limiting their inability to extract tribute across the whole of the province of Baghdad.

A peculiarity of this province was the presence of the *'Atabat* (thresholds or doorways)—the collective name given to Najaf, Karbala, al-Kazimiyya and Samarra, four of the most venerated towns of the Shi'i Islam, long associated with the sacred history of the Caliph 'Ali bin Abi Talib and his descendants. These towns—particularly the more important centres of Najaf and Karbala—had always constituted a potential problem for the Ottoman authorities in Baghdad. They were centres of learning and scholarship of the Ja'fari school of law which the Ottoman state did not recognise. Consequently, the Shi'a generally ignored Ottoman institutions. They were inhabitants of the Ottoman state, but they scarcely engaged with it. Furthermore, the importance of these centres of Shi'i pilgrimage and learning for the Safavid and Qajar rulers of Persia meant not only a constant flow of pilgrims, traders and settlers from Persia itself, but also the close scrutiny of the Persian state, ever sensitive to real or imagined injustices by the Ottoman authorities against the shah's subjects who had settled there.

Finally, the influence of these towns and of the Shi'i *'ulama* on the tribesmen who gravitated to them and had begun to settle in the mid-Euphrates region was becoming ever more marked. The notorious Shi'i disdain for the pretensions of the Ottoman sultan-caliph and thus for the legitimacy of the Ottoman state accorded with the tribal suspicion and dislike of central state authority. This may explain in part the growing appeal of Shi'ism to the tribesmen of the region, large numbers of whom adopted the precepts of Shi'i Islam during the eighteenth and nineteenth centuries. Thus an increasingly large proportion of the inhabitants of Baghdad province saw little reason to associate themselves with, let alone pay taxes to, a state which seemed not only alien, but even doctrinally repulsive. Some of the *mamluk* pashas of Baghdad handled this problem adroitly and maintained good relations with the notables of the holy cities. Others, whether under the threat of Persian invasion, or in order to ingratiate themselves with Istanbul, or indeed out of their own prejudices as new converts to Sunni Islam, succeeded in deepening the divide between the Sunni and the Shi'a under their rule.

A similar set of tribal and doctrinal differences weakened the allegiance of most of the inhabitants of Basra province to the Ottoman state. In particular, the powerful tribal confederations of the Muntafiq and the Khaza'il and the substantial tribe of the al-Bu Muhammad dominated the lives of much of the population of the province, whether they were settled farmers, pastoralists or marsh-dwellers. The *mamluk* pashas in Basra had little or no influence in these regions, except on terms largely dictated by the tribal chieftains....

The society of Basra, as in Baghdad, was composed of a number of distinct groups, under the rule of the *mamluk* military caste. Overwhelmingly Arab and largely Shi'i in composition, its elite families were however predominantly Sunni. These were headed, in terms of status, by the family of the naqib al-ashraf, but they also included Ottoman officials and property owners and traders who had major interests in the local economy. This was based either upon the intensive cultivation of Basra's hinterland or on trading links with the Gulf and the Indian Ocean. The importance of the Indian trade, in particular, had been underlined by the opening of trading concessions by the British East India Company (as early as 1639), as well as by French and other European traders who were seeking to profit from and eventually to monopolise this trade during much of the period in question. This greater openness towards India, as well as towards the Gulf and eventually Egypt, with all that this implied in the eighteenth and nineteenth centuries, was to have a significant effect on Basra's society, as well as on the attitudes of its inhabitants towards the changes they were soon to experience.

The Reassertion of Ottoman Power

The significance of these differences among and within the three provinces became clearer with the Ottoman 'reconquest' in the early nineteenth century. The weaknesses of the empire vis-à-vis the European states and the worrying example of the growing power of the provincial governor of Egypt, Muhammad 'Ali Pasha, had set in train a reformist reaction in Istanbul. Under the rule of Sultan Mahmud II (1808–39) the central Ottoman government began to reassert its authority in outlying provinces, and reconstructed the military forces of the empire. The *Nizam-i Cedid* (New Order) implied the consolidation of power in the hands of the sultan and his government and left little room for semi-autonomous provincial governors. It was not long, therefore, before Istanbul turned its attention to Baghdad, Basra and Mosul. In 1831, when Da'ud Pasha, the *mamluk* governor of Baghdad, refused to comply with the sultan's edict that he relinquish his office, an army under the governor of Aleppo, 'Ali Rida Pasha, marched on Baghdad, capturing the city and Da'ud Pasha himself. With his capture the rule of the *mamluks* in Baghdad ceased abruptly.

'Ali Rida went on to occupy Basra, bringing *mamluk* rule in that city to an end and in 1834 central Ottoman authority was restored in Mosul, ending the hold of the Jalili family on the governorship. As a result, by the beginning of the period of the *Tanzimat* (the reforms) of Sultan Abdulmecid, the three provinces were under direct rule from Istanbul, opening them up to successive reforms in landholding, administration, conscription, law and public education. However, these reforms were implemented at different rates, depending upon the initiative and energy—and length of tenure—of the Ottoman governors sent out by Istanbul. For much of the period that followed, the norms and methods of the *mamluk* era prevailed in government and administration, just as the great majority of the *mamluk* families retained their wealth and status, providing many of the key officials of the New Order. In addition, the reassertion of central Ottoman control over the major cities did not automatically bring about a greater degree of control over the semi-autonomous tribes and tribal confederations of the countryside. Nevertheless, the direct and indirect consequences of the reforms had the effect of creating new interests and groups, some with an explicit commitment to the reforms themselves, others seeking to find a role as the reforming measures began to erode their hitherto secure status....

The principal instruments in the Ottoman attempt to reintegrate its Mesopotamian provinces into the empire were the reforms stemming from the Land Law of 1858 and from the Vilayet Law of 1864. The former sought to bring some regularity into the land tenure system of the empire, creating security of tenure (whilst reasserting state ownership of land) in the hope that this would encourage a more productive and settled agriculture, attracting investment and generating revenues for the imperial treasury. The second measure was the beginning of the administrative reorganisation of the empire. It was intended not only to demarcate the various provinces, but also to define the nature and shape of the state's authority vis-à-vis the provincial population and to spell out the exact functions and responsibilities of the provincial officials from the governor downwards.

With the arrival in Baghdad of the forceful and energetic Midhat Pasha as governor in 1869, decisive steps were taken to implement both the Vilayet Law and the Land Law. The Vilayet Law mapped out the territorial boundaries of the three provinces and established a new structure of administration from provincial down to village level, intending to bring the central administration systematically down to people who had hitherto been little touched by the apparatus of the state. More radically, at least in theory, it was also intended to involve them in the workings of the state through administrative councils which included not simply Ottoman officials, but also influential representatives of the population at large, both Muslim and non-Muslim.

Midhat Pasha was able to introduce these reforms with little difficulty since the initiative lay at this stage with the Ottoman authorities. The practical consequences were less clear-cut and took time to emerge. They were to be shaped by the personalities and the authority of the individuals involved, as well as by the changing fortunes of the advocates of decentralisation in Istanbul itself, who gradually lost out during the latter half of the nineteenth century to those who wanted to reassert close central control. During the second half of the nineteenth century, these were the factors which determined the nature of the three provinces' links to the centre and to some degree shaped the balance of power within the political worlds of Baghdad, Mosul and Basra.

Midhat Pasha's implementation of the Land Law was far from complete by the time he was recalled to Istanbul in 1872. Nevertheless, he began a process whereby the land tenure system was to be thoroughly revised, with far-reaching consequence for the majority of the population, who depended on the land for their livelihood. One of the main pillars of the land reform was the granting of title deeds *(tapu sanad)* to anyone who was in possession or occupation of land. The land remained the property of the state, but the registered owner of the title deeds would enjoy virtually complete rights of ownership. Across great tracts of the three provinces the Land Law introduced an institution akin to private property in agricultural land, initiating profound changes in structures of social power, the consequences of which were to be felt long after the demise of the Ottoman administration itself....

These transformations were, of course, gradual and drew different people into the state-directed reforms at varying rates. For certain families of urban notables and of Ottoman officials, the reform process satisfied both their material interests and their feelings of political propriety. For certain tribal chiefs, whether Arab or Kurdish, their welcome for the state's conferral of title deeds was unmatched by any sense of reciprocal obligation. Reluctance to pay taxes remained a constant irritant in relations between the state, based in the provincial capitals, and the countryside.... Sometimes this was due to the inability of the titleholder, even though from a shaikhly family, to extract the revenues from his tribesmen who had now, in the eyes of the law, become his tenants; sometimes, however, it was due to the delayed acceptance of any sense of obligation to the state that went beyond symbolic fealty to the sultan....

In the province of Baghdad, [reassertion of Ottoman power] was most advanced, in part because of the military strength of the Ottoman administration (Baghdad became the headquarters for the 6th Army Corps), but also because it was here that many of the tribal shaikhs had been drawn into a political game in which it was very much to their advantage to participate. The most prominent amongst them maintained agents and establishments in the city, supplying them with key intelligence and acting on their behalf to secure their interests at the court of the governor. It was in Baghdad that the centre of land registration lay, that decisions on changes of tenancy of *saniyya* lands [lands owned by the Ottoman ruler] were made and that public works central to the productivity of the lands in question—such as irrigation schemes or transport plans—were initiated. In exchange for this involvement by the shaikhs, which ensured a remarkable absence of rural disturbances in Baghdad province during the latter half of the nineteenth century, the Ottoman state honoured them, confirmed them in their positions and did little to undermine the principle of shaikhly domination in the countryside....

Provincial Political Reactions

The Young Turk revolution of 1908, which forced the sultan to reintroduced the Ottoman constitution and saw the emergence into the open of the Committee of Union and Progress (CUP), allowed many of the hitherto suppressed currents of political opinion within the three Mesopotamian provinces to find public expression, as they did elsewhere in the empire. The proliferation of clubs, groups and societies after 1908, as well as the explosion of journals and newspapers (an estimated sixty titles were published at various times in the three provinces in the years following the revolution of 1908), is testimony to the political engagement of growing numbers in Mosul, Baghdad and Basra. At the same time, of course, other forms of political activity by no means disappeared, indicating varying political trajectories and contrasting narratives, playing themselves out at different rates in the three provinces....

With ideas of a politics of participation came the growing realisation that in the new political order some might find themselves better positioned to participate effectively than others. Initially, these concerns fuelled the ongoing debate about the relative merits of decentralisation versus central control. The restoration of the constitution and the elections of the Ottoman Parliament in 1908 had raised expectations about the commitment of the new regime to the presentation of truly empire-wide interests and the possibility of meeting the varying claims of the provinces through some form of decentralisation. These hopes were dashed by the strong centralising policies of the CUP and it was not long before groups began to form which called for equality of all Ottomans, for the Arabic language to be given equal status to Turkish and for greater power to be devolved to the provinces.

As increasingly authoritarian CUP governments proceeded to entrench themselves in power in Istanbul, in the Arab provinces of the empire the frustrated calls for provincial autonomy fed into and reinforced emerging sentiments of Arab nationalism.

Turbulence in the Early Twentieth Century

BY PHEBE MARR

A series of events in the early twentieth century unsettled Iraq. A group of Ottomans known as the Young Turks overthrew the ruling sultan and imposed new authoritarian rule over the empire, suppressing the greater autonomy that had been emerging in Iraq. During World War I, Iraq became a battlefield between the British and the Ottomans. The British emerged victorious and took over Iraq, but after the war they were immediately faced with a serious Arab revolt against their rule. History professor Phebe Marr spent many years living and studying in Iraq. The following excerpt from her book The Modern History of Iraq *recounts the events that made the first two decades of the twentieth century so turbulent in Iraq.*

The last stage in the development of Ottoman relations with its Arab provinces was reached with the Young Turk revolution in 1908. Although the Young Turks were a mixed group of nationalists with a range of viewpoints on the future of the Ottoman Empire, their policies differed from those of [the deposed] Sultan 'Abd al-Hamīd in several important respects. One was their secular outlook. The first casualty of the revolution was 'Abd al-Hamīd's pan-Islamic policy. In fostering Islamic political unity and in emphasizing the dynasty's role as guardian of that unity during his thirty-two-year rule, 'Abd al-Hamīd had succeeded in tying a substantial portion of the *sunnī* community in Iraq—especially the 'ulamā' [high-ranking Islamic theologians], the older generation, and those with vested interests in the status quo—to Istanbul. The Young Turks, by contrast,

---

Phebe Marr, *The Modern History of Iraq*. Boulder, CO: Westview Press, Inc., 1985. Copyright © 1985 by Westview Press, Inc., a member of Perseus Books, L.L.C. Reproduced by permission.

aimed to separate religion and politics and make of the Ottoman Empire a unified nation-state based on secular Western models. Stress was placed, not on Muslim solidarity, but on the equality of all Ottoman subjects before the law, and on patriotism and loyalty to the new government. This shift was to have disruptive and ultimately fateful consequences for the empire.

Another difference lay in the Young Turks' brief introduction of the rudiments of a parliamentary system with the reinstitution of the 1876 constitution. After elections were held in 1908, the three Iraqi provinces sent seventeen delegates to Istanbul. Almost without exception, they represented the old, well-established families of the major cities. Nevertheless, the parliament that met in Istanbul provided the first experience of self-government to this group. It also brought something entirely unanticipated, the stirrings of Arab nationalism. It was not long before representatives of Arab background found that in language and customs, as well as in grievances, they had more in common with each other than with the new Young Turk rulers.

The impetus for Arab nationalism was the last, and most significant, contribution of the Young Turks to Iraq. As the Young Turks attempted to consolidate their rule in the face of European threats, they began to tighten their grasp on administration, to emphasize their Turkishness, and to clamp down on political freedoms of all sorts. The reaction in Iraq was not long in coming. Opposition took root, centered primarily on three issues: decentralization of administration, the use of Arabic in schools and in the administration, and the appointment to high office of the newly educated Arabs rather than Turks. Casting about for a new ideology by which to justify their aspirations, the young, secularly educated Arabs found it not in pan-Islam, but in Arab nationalism.

This new sense of nationalism took various forms. In the south of Iraq, the leading exponent of the movement was Tālib Pasha.... At a meeting in 1913 with a group of Arab representatives of the Gulf area of al-Muhammarah, Tālib put forth a program advocating the independence of Turkish Arabia and Iraq. Of far more significance in the long run were the new secret societies springing up in the central and northern towns of Iraq. The most important of these was al-Ahd (the Covenant), originally founded in Istanbul by an Egyptian army officer, 'Azīz 'Alī al-Misrī. Its membership was almost entirely drawn from Iraqi officers in the Ottoman army. Al-Ahd spread rapidly in

Mosul and Baghdad; by the outbreak of the war it was estimated to have at least 4,000 members, many of them the future ministers and prime ministers of Iraq.

However, too much should not be made of Arab nationalism among Iraqis prior to the war. All the evidence suggests that though the seeds of nationalism had been sown among a small educated group, Arab nationalism had as yet put down no deep roots among a population still wedded to tribe, clan, family, and above all, religion. Even among those committed to Arab nationalist goals, Ottoman values and ideals remained strong. Four centuries of Ottoman tradition had left their mark. The new generation of Iraqis, no matter how vociferously they might denounce the Young Turks, resembled nothing so much as an Arab version of the Young Turks themselves.

The British Takeover

The impact of British rule has been second only to that of Ottoman rule in shaping modern Iraq. In some respects the British left remarkably little behind them; in others they made a more lasting impression. Before the British mandate there was no Iraq; after it, a new state, with the beginnings of a modern government, had come into being. Along with the creation of the state, the British bequeathed Iraq its present boundaries and as a result, potential minority problems and border problems with its neighbors.

As state builders the British created or developed an impressive array of institutions—a monarchy, a parliament, a Western-style constitution, a bureaucracy, and an army. The bureaucracy and the army—both of which predated the British—still remain, but the monarchy and the Western-style democratic institutions have since been swept away. This is perhaps not surprising. Britain's stay in Iraq was one of the shortest in its imperial career. Moreover, for much of Britain's tenure in Iraq, its policy was vacillating and indecisive. Ultimately Britain did decide on a policy, one that would establish an Arab government capable of protecting Britain's interests at the least possible cost to the British taxpayer. To this end, they designed a constitutional structure that was less a system of government than a means of control. The British created an imposing institutional facade, but put down few deep roots.

In three respects, however, the British made a lasting, if unintended, impact. The first effect was to hasten, broaden, and deepen the drive for modernization already under way, and through development of oil resources, to provide the country with the revenues to finance this drive and accelerate Iraq's economic development. The second was the arabization of the administration, and the third was the creation of a nationalist movement whose leaders, placed in power largely by the British themselves, would do more to shape modern Iraq than the British.

The occupation that was to change the future of Mesopotamia came about less by design than by accident. Despite Britain's long-standing interests in the Gulf, the British had no intention of occupying the Tigris and Euphrates Valley at the outbreak of the First World War. However, when it became apparent late in 1914 that Turkey, Britain's traditional ally, would enter the war on the side of the Central Powers and was mobilizing at the head of the Gulf, Britain decided to occupy al-Fāw and Basra to protect its strategic interests and communications and its oil fields at the head of the Gulf. On 6 November 1914 the troops landed at al-Fāw and by 22 November they had moved up to Basra. Although British policy in Whitehall did not project beyond these defensive measures at the time, the lure of future political benefits to be gained by capturing Baghdad proved irresistible to the local commanders and the India Office; on their initiative, British troops began to move up the Tigris. In April 1916, they met with a humiliating defeat at al-Kūt, and had to retreat to the south once again.

By the end of 1916, however, the British position had changed. Not only was their military strength more secure, but secret agreements concluded with the [Islamic leader] Sharīf Husayn of Mecca and with the French had recognized Britain's right to establish special administrative arrangements in the Basra and Baghdad *wilāyah*s [provinces]. They were therefore anxious to secure their position on the ground, and in March 1917 they took Baghdad. By the end of that month the British had secured the Baghdad *wilāyah* and a portion of the Mosul *wilāyah*, including Kirkūk. A British column was on its way to Mosul city when the Armistice of Mudros was announced on 31 October 1918. In fact, British troops were then 14 miles (22.5 km) from the city and did not occupy it until 7 November. This occupation was to become a cause of contention between the British and the Turks, with the latter claiming that it was not included under the terms of the armistice.

With the fall of Mosul, the British wartime conquest of most of the Iraqi provinces was complete, but several key areas had not as yet been pacified. These included all of the Kurdish highlands bordering Turkey and Iran; the Euphrates from Baghdad south to al-Nāsiriyyah; and the two *shī'ī* cities of Karbalā' and al-Najaf. It is no accident that these were to be the most unstable areas of Iraq throughout the mandate and beyond.

While the conquest and occupation of the Iraqi provinces was taking place, the first rudiments of a British administration were being introduced. The administration imposed on Iraq was overwhelmingly the work of men seconded from the India Office and was modeled largely on Britain's imperial structure in India. The philosophy guiding this group was largely based on nineteenth-century ideas of the "white man's burden," a predilection for direct rule, and a distrust of the ability of local Arabs for self-government. This attitude deterred the appointment of local Arabs to positions of responsibility. Meanwhile, the British dismantled and supplanted the Ottoman administration as rapidly as possible. Mesopotamia was divided into political districts, each under the charge of a British officer, and administration at the highest levels was kept in British hands. A new civil and criminal code based on Anglo-Indian laws replaced the old Turkish laws; the Indian rupee became the medium of exchange; and the army and police force were increasingly staffed with Indians....

It was not long before the policies of the Indian school generated opposition both in Britain and Iraq. In March 1917 the British government issued a memo making it clear that an indigenous Arab government under British guidance was to be substituted for direct administration. As a response to the memo, the Anglo-Indian civil code was replaced by a return to Turkish courts and laws. However, little else was changed. New divisions and districts were created and staffed with British officers, and the number of British officials grew at the expense of Arabs. In 1917 there were 59 British officers in the civil administration; by 1920 there were 1,022. Less than 4 percent of the senior grades were occupied by Arab officials. By 1920, the local British bureaucrats in Baghdad had managed to frustrate the new policy directives, strengthening their hold on the country. The Foreign Office vacillated, waiting for the decisions of the slow-moving peace conference in Europe, and did not hand down a clear decision on Iraq's future government. When it came, the decision was made not by the British, but by the Iraqis.

The 1920 Revolt

The 1920 revolt, directed above all at the India Office policy, was sparked by the announcement in April 1920 that the Conference at San Remo had assigned a mandate for Iraq to Britain. Iraqi opposition to the British had been growing for some time inside and outside the country. In June 1919, a group of Iraqi officers in [King] Faysal's Syrian government had sent a memo to the Foreign Office asking for the immediate establishment of a national government in Iraq. In June 1920, an abortive revolt, led by one of these same officers, had taken place at Tal'afar, in the north of Iraq, with the aim of rousing Mosul.

Anti-British Sentiment

Inside Iraq, rising anti-British sentiment had been fanned by the nationalists in Baghdad, the *shī'ī* religious leaders of the holy cities, and disaffected mid-Euphrates tribal leaders. Though the motives of these groups were mixed, all were united by a desire to be free of British rule. A chief feature of the movement was the unprecedented cooperation between the *sunnī* and *shī'ī* communities; in Baghdad both used the mosque for anti-British gatherings and speeches, clearly mixing religion and politics. From Baghdad, nationalist propaganda spread south, stimulated by propaganda from the Iraqi offices in Syria. It met with a receptive reaction among the religious leaders of al-Najaf and Karbalā' and the still unsubdued tribes of the middle and lower Euphrates.

It was in the mid-Euphrates that the revolt began on 2 June 1920, when a shaykh who had refused to repay an agricultural debt was placed in prison at al-Rumaythah. His incensed tribesmen rose up against the British, and they were soon joined by others. Nationalist sentiments were aroused, and the revolt spread. By August, the mid-Euphrates south of al-Dīwāniyyah and al-Muntafiq had passed out of British control. The rebellion did not spread to the Tigris, where the British were firmly entrenched, nor to areas held by the Kurds, who were uninterested in Arab nationalism. But it did affect the districts north and east of Baghdad. It also spread to Kirkūk and to al-Dulaym, where Colonel Leachman, a British officer, was killed by members of the Zawba' tribe instigated by Shaykh Dārī. All in all, the insurgency lasted for about three months and affected about one-third of the countryside; none of the major cities and few of the urban nationalists were affected.

There are two distinct views on the 1920 revolt. The British have tended to see it as little more than a localized tribal insurgency fomented by nationalist agitation from Syria. The more accurate Iraqi view is that the revolt was a genuine nationalist rebellion, the first in a series of abortive attempts to overthrow unwanted British rule. Although it has often been claimed by the British that the revolt did not change British policy, that claim is not entirely borne out by the evidence. The uprising cost the British over 400 lives and up to 40 million pounds sterling. Even more important, the upheaval undid much of the work accomplished by the administrators in the previous five years and very nearly wrecked the British position entirely. Although the revolt did not achieve Iraqi independence or turn real authority over to the Iraqis, it did succeed in discrediting the India Office policy thoroughly, and it assured a much larger measure of participation by the Iraqis in their first national government. Perhaps the most significant outcome was to bring home to British taxpayers the expense of the India Office policy. It was their unwillingness to foot the bill that accounts for the indirect administration that Britain established in Iraq after the revolt.

On 1 October 1920, Sir Percy Cox landed in Basra to assume his responsibilities as high commissioner in Iraq. His new guidelines provided for the termination of military administration, the formulation of a constitution in consultation with the populace, and the establishment of a provisional government with an Arab president and council of state. For president, Cox selected the aging and venerable ʿAbd al-Rahman al-Kaylānī, Naqīb of Baghdad, whose virtues were his religious position, family background, and lack of experience in politics—which would leave ample scope for Cox to exercise real authority. The council members, drawn from the traditional upper classes, were religious leaders, landowners, and tribal shaykhs who could be expected to support the British. It was clear from the first, however, that this government was temporary. It was replaced after the Cairo Conference of 1921, at which several decisive steps were taken for Iraq's future. Among the most important was the decision to establish a monarchy in Iraq, with Faysal, the third son of the Sharīf Husayn of Mecca, as monarch.

The History of Nations
Chapter 4

The Emergence of Modern Independent Iraq

National Transition to Independence Under King Faisal

BY MAJID KHADDURI

The hope and promise of independence led many Arabs to support the British side against the Ottomans in World War I. When the war ended, the British and their allies did create several new Arab states out of what had been Ottoman provinces. However, they maintained a large political and military presence in many of those new states, including Iraq, which was effectively a British protectorate when it became a state entity in 1921. This continuing foreign presence caused considerable discontent among many Iraqis who favored full independence. It fell upon the first monarchal ruler of the country, the British-installed Faisal Husein, to guide Iraq through this period. In the following excerpt from his book Independent Iraq, *Majid Khadduri describes King Faisal's critical role in Iraq's modern history. Majid Khadduri is an Iraqi writer who has written extensively about the Middle East and has also been a professor of political science and international affairs at various American colleges.*

The winning of Iraq's independence, which seemed to the outside world in 1932 to be merely a happy combination of favourable circumstances—Britain's satisfaction with the Iraq Treaty, the attempt of the Great Powers [Great Britain and France] to demonstrate the possibility of change through peaceful means, and the League's [League of Nations] desire to increase its membership—was in fact the culmination of protracted negotiations between Iraq and Great Britain; and this was only one act in a larger movement of the challenge of Arab nationalism to European imperialism.

The Arab nationalist movement is a relatively recent phe-

Majid Khadduri, *Independent Iraq, 1932–1958: A Study in Iraqi Politics.* London: Oxford University Press, 1960.

nomenon in the Arab world. From the opening of the sixteenth century, when the Arab countries fell under the domination of the Turks, to the end of the nineteenth, the Arabs remained loyal subjects of the Ottoman Sultan. During the Hamidian period (1876–1909) pious Arabs found spiritual comfort in the autocratic shadow of a caliph who claimed to govern them after the fashion of the early Muslim caliphs. When, however, the Western idea of nationalism triumphed in the Balkans, it captured the imagination of other subject races of the empire. Nationalism, it is contended, may easily develop as a result of propaganda and bad administration; and this was nowhere more true than under Ottoman rule.

When the Young Turks seized power in 1908, enlightened Arabs, as other non-Turkish elements of the empire, were attracted by their policy which sought to transform Turkey into a modern constitutional State. But the Young Turks, who proved to be more nationalistic and less liberal than they professed, embarked upon a policy of Turkification which aimed at transforming all the racial elements of the empire into Turks. This led to an open rupture between Arabs and Turks. Until now the Arab nationalists, afraid of disrupting Islamic unity, had demanded an autonomous status under the Sultan; but the negative attitude of the Young Turks pushed the Arab nationalists to the more extreme demands which culminated in the revolt of 1916.

An Emerging Leader

The fathers of the Arab nationalist movement, important as they were, are too numerous to be mentioned here; when, however, the First World War broke out, leadership devolved upon Sharif Husayn of Hijaz. All of Husayn's sons played an important role in the prosecution of the Arab Revolt, but the one who played the most significant part was Husayn's third son, Faysal. Whether as a soldier in the desert, or as a national leader in Syria and Iraq, his ultimate aim was to espouse the general Arab cause.

Born fifteen years before the end of the nineteenth century, Faysal was destined to witness the shifting fortunes of the Ottoman Empire since the Hamidian period. He was brought up as a loyal subject of Sultan 'Abd al-Hamid, who ruled the empire as Caliph of all the Muslims and commanded the allegiance of pious Turks and Arabs. Thus Sharif Husayn, Faysal's father, with other notables of Mecca, could hardly question the sacred authority of their Padishah. In 1893 Sharif Husayn was invited to Constantinople, and remained there as the exiled guest of the Sultan for fifteen years. His sons, who received their education in the Ottoman capital, witnessed the rise of nationalism which eventually disrupted the Sultan's empire. During the decade in which the nascent Arab nationalist movement crystallized into a well-defined movement, Faysal emerged as the most promising Arab leader of those who distinguished themselves both in war and peace.

The story of Faysal as the chief champion of the Arab cause opens with the arresting picture of his dramatic capture of Damascus in 1918. Until then, as one of the military commanders, he was merely carrying out the orders of his father, with the help of General [Edmund] Allenby and the advice of T.E. Lawrence, in order to bring the holy war against the Turks to a successful conclusion. After his entry into Damascus, Faysal became the chosen leader of the Syrian nationalists who sought the restoration of the Umayyad capital as it had been in the glorious Arab past.

The young desert leader, who had just concluded his military career upon the cessation of hostilities with Turkey, was sent to Paris to represent his father at the Peace Conference and to plead for Syria's aspirations to independence. As a soldier who attained conclusive victories on the battlefield, Faysal, perhaps, expected to achieve similar conclusive results at the conference table. He was, however, shocked at the undisguised bargaining for what seemed to him to be unquestionable Arab rights. Though an ally of the victorious Powers, he realized that the Arab world, and more particularly Syria, had become a pawn in the diplomatic game of the Great Powers. He presented the Arab claims for independence before the Council of Ten, but secret arrangements, which reflected the ambitions of the Great Powers in the Arab world, ruined his case.

Faysal returned to Syria with an indelible memory of his brief diplomatic experience at Paris. He was not alarmed, for the soldierly spirit was still alive in him. In a speech which he made after his arrival at Beirut (30 April 1919), he conveyed to his people the result of his diplomatic mission. 'Complete independence', he declared, 'is never given; it is always taken'. His report was not encouraging, but the Syrians caught an echo of the words. Faysal urged his people to unite in order to be able to play their proper part in the determination of their future life. He contended that the fate of Syria, dependent as it was on the Great Powers, should not be determined entirely at their pleasure. This attitude eventually led to a quarrel with France, for neither Faysal nor France was prepared to share authority over Syria. But it was a fight between unequal partners. Within a few hours Faysal's forces were shattered at Maysalun (24 July 1920) and his throne at Damascus was for ever lost.

Just as the seat of the Arab Empire moved from Medina to Damascus and later to Baghdad, Faysal's political activities shifted from the capitals of Hijaz to Syria and finally to Iraq. The British suggested that he should accede to the throne of Iraq, but he would not accept it unless it was offered to him by the Iraqis themselves. Faysal, moreover, was not prepared to accept the new throne under a mandate. Winston Churchill, then Colonial Secretary, promised Faysal that Britain's relations with Iraq would be governed by a Treaty of Alliance. It was thus that Faysal not only obtained another throne for himself, but also won for Iraq more advantageous terms than Great Britain had been prepared to give without him. Iraq, it is true, had already been promised self-government, but Britain had not yet made up her mind what sort of a government should be set up. It was a happy coincidence that there was an available candidate for a vacant throne. No better choice could have been made. From the British standpoint, Faysal's Arab Government satisfied the angry clamours of the Iraqi nationalists; and for Faysal, Iraq afforded new possibilities of championing the Arab cause.

Faysal's Policy

Faysal's coming to Iraq did not bring that immediate full independence which he and the Iraqis had expected. Churchill's version of the treaty which he had promised Faysal to replace the mandate contained all the substance, though not the form, of that mandate. 'This is not the kind of treaty which Mr Churchill promised me in London', complained Faysal in an hour of despair. But Faysal's bitter experience in Syria had taught him the lesson never to clash with a Great Power in Iraq. He would never again yield to the advice of the extreme nationalists. The negative attitude of the Syrian extremists, he contended, had definitely resulted in a serious national loss. In Iraq Faysal thought it more prudent to accept what Britain was prepared to give, while he continued to press for further concessions under more favourable circumstances. He followed a policy aptly called in Arabic 'take and ask', or, in Western terminology, 'step by step'. This moderate approach to Anglo-Iraqi relations proved not only more advantageous to Iraq, but it also fitted well into the pattern of British colonial policy, which allowed dependencies to develop towards self-government by a slow and peaceful method.

Though hot-tempered and impatient, Faysal took a hopeful view of the treaty and ordered his ministers to sign it (10 October 1922). But the immediate reactions to the acceptance of the treaty were indeed grave and disastrous. Both Faysal and England fell into disfavour in the eyes of the Iraqi public. England was attacked for having deliberately denied Iraq her rightful independence, and Faysal was denounced as a traitor who had sold his country to save his skin. It took all his persuasive genius to convince the Iraqi public of the sincerity of his efforts and the soundness of his policy.

The treaty of 1922 taught both Faysal and Britain that it could not be regarded as a basis for a permanent Anglo-Iraqi friendship. The Iraqi nationalists were not prepared to accept any plan short of complete independence and the abrogation of the mandate. The treaty was revised in 1923 by a protocol which shortened its period from twenty years to four; and in 1926 and 1927 it was replaced by other treaties which, though they did not much advance Iraq's status towards full independence, demonstrated that Great Britain was quite prepared to grant Iraq her independence piecemeal.

In 1930 a final compromise was reached. The treaty of 30 June 1930 reconciled Iraq's national aspirations and Great Britain's fundamental interests. It was indeed Faysal's crowning effort, since it achieved for Iraq her much cherished independence but conceded to Britain her essential imperial interests. The treaty was denounced in Iraq by the extremists and in England by the imperialists. Sponsored, however, by General Nuri as-Sa'id, Prime Minister of Iraq, it was finally ratified by Parliament and came into force in 1932.

When Iraq was admitted as a member of the League of Nations, Faysal's name was so deservedly associated with the event that all those accredited representatives who spoke in the League Assembly congratulated him on 'the great work he has successfully accomplished'. General Nuri, Prime Minister of Iraq, endorsed all that had been said about his sovereign and declared that 'the homage which had been rendered to him in this great Assembly is the homage which he deserves'. Sir John Simon, British Secretary for Foreign Affairs, had probably interpreted the real sentiment of His Majesty's Government when he declared in the League Assembly that without Faysal's 'wise and energetic cooperation it would have been impossible, whatever might have been the good will on the side of the Power discharging its mandate, for the young State of Iraq in the space of no more than twelve years to qualify, as it has qualified, to take its place, as it now takes its place with the assent and approval of us all, in the comity of the League of Nations'....

The Foundation of the Iraqi Nation

Faysal's role in building up the Iraqi State can hardly be exaggerated. He came to the throne of Iraq, it will be remembered, with the help of the British; and, though his accession was approved by a national plebiscite, there were certain sections of the population that either did not want him or were not very enthusiastic for him. But Faysal steadily grew stronger with the years. He built up his own party and gained an increasing popular support for his administration and policy with each new step he attained towards independence. Though a young man, hardly thirty-six years old, Faysal ascended the throne of Iraq with the ripe experience of a decade crowded with events and episodes. His quarrel with the French in Syria taught him a great lesson; and his relations with the British in Iraq proved that he had become an abler diplomat and more far-seeing statesman than either his British or Arab friends had expected.

Faysal's greatest asset was his ability to hold a balance between the British and the Iraqi nationalists. He realized that British help and sympathy were essential both to protect Iraq against hostile neighbours and to bring the mandatory regime to an end. He genuinely believed in the value of British friendship, and contended that British and Iraqi interests were not essentially irreconcilable. It was thus that he was capable both of securing British sympathy for Iraq's national aspirations and of controlling the nationalist elements. He was, it is true, reproached at times for having encouraged the opposition parties in order to obtain more favourable terms in his treaty negotiations with Britain. But it is also true that he restrained nationalist extremists who were never satisfied with any treaty with Britain short of complete independence. . . .

Faysal, moreover, was able to win the confidence of the Iraqi nationalists. He gathered around him a number of able men ready to serve their country with devotion. Some of these men, originally from Iraq, had served in the Turkish army and then with him in Hijaz and Syria. When Faysal moved to Baghdad these men, together with a number of Syrian Arabs, moved with him. There was, it is true, a good deal of jealousy felt by other Iraqi politicians who were not originally with Faysal (and some of them, indeed, did not desert the Turks until the collapse of Turkey), who formed an opposition. But Faysal's personality and leadership soon dominated all those around him and he was respected, though not loved, by all. 'No-one could look at the Emir Feisal', Robert Lansing, Secretary of State of the United States, keenly observed, 'without the instinctive feeling that there was a man whom nature had chosen to be a leader of men, a man who was worthy to be a leader of men'.

Nor was Faysal capable only of controlling the townsmen. In a country like Iraq, where the tribal population had given much trouble to the Ottoman and British administrations in the past, the need for someone who could mediate between the tribes and the central authority was keenly felt. Faysal understood the tribal mentality and knew how to speak and behave like a Bedouin, having himself spent his early life and his war years in the desert. He won the confidence of the leading tribal shaykhs in Iraq, and acted as a link between the tribal and the town populations. But his policy towards the tribes was more positive than merely to demand their submission to authority; he fully understood their problems, and by the distribution of land and the reorganization of the irrigation system he sought the eventual settlement of the tribes and their accommodation to agriculture.

Gaining Hero Status

Occupying such a unique position in the life of his country, Faysal inevitably emerged as her unrivalled national hero. It is true that as a constitutional monarch he had limited powers; but in identifying himself with Iraq's need and aspirations, he played the role of the reformer and the benevolent monarch who could call and dismiss Cabinets at his own pleasure. He was indeed criticized for concentrating as much power as possible in his own hands; but this concentration of power, in a country where the old local divisions were still very strong, was probably necessary in order to ensure the progress of Iraq.... [Faysal] proved to be the only stable factor in the working of a European system of government imported into a country that had not yet had the time to create sufficient cohesion among its various racial-religious elements.

Internal Opposition and Factionalism in Postindependent Iraq

BY STEPHEN HEMSLEY LONGRIGG AND FRANK STOAKES

The establishment of full autonomy for Iraq did not eliminate the internal division and political opposition activity that arose during the years when Iraq was governed under the British mandate. The period that followed was marked by unrest and dissent among competing political factions, ultimately leading Britain to once again occupy Iraq during World War II. Following World War II, internal dissent within Iraq and opposition to its government reached new heights, with Arab-independence and anti-imperialist sentiments escalating. This period is described in the following excerpt from Iraq, *cowritten by Stephen Hemsley Longrigg, a British author who wrote several books about the Middle East during the 1950s and 1960s, and Frank Stoakes.*

King Faisal was succeeded by his son Ghazi [in 1933], at the age of twenty-one. With Faisal's guiding hand removed political leaders pursued their rivalries unchecked, invoked powerful and dangerous forces for political ends and were finally, in 1941, to involve the country in the conflict of the European Powers.

The first faction to use unconstitutional weapons successfully was the National Brotherhood. A month after Ghazi acceded he declined to dissolve an unco-operative Chamber at the request of Rashid 'Ali, who thereupon resigned (October 1933), to be followed by three cabinets under Jamil al-Midfa'i, with one of 'Ali Jaudat al-Ayyubi between. To regain office the Brotherhood had

Stephen Hemsley Longrigg and Frank Stoakes, *Iraq*. New York: Frederick A. Praeger, Inc., 1958.

recourse to tribal disaffection and Shi'i sectarianism on the Middle Euphrates, and thereby succeeded in unseating successively 'Ali Jaudat and Jamil al-Midfa'i and engineering their own return to power under the premiership of Yasin al-Hashimi (March 1935).

The Hashimi Government, resolute and enterprising, was in some ways the most successful of the period; with its tenure of eighteen months it was also the longest lived. When the tribal disturbances which had frustrated its predecessors refused to abate they were suppressed with ruthless rapidity by General Bakr Sidqi. Irrigation works were encouraged, industries planned, an Agricultural and Industrial Bank established, a labour code introduced, municipal development promoted and conscription enforced. The Hashimi Government's nationalism was immaculate: it maintained close relations with other Arab countries, proclaimed pan-Arabism, took a firm stand over Palestine and taught the same doctrine in the schools. But its clear intention to retain its position, its dictatorial attitude towards Parliament and its intolerance of criticism aroused resentment, particularly in the queue for office. Hikmat Sulaiman was especially incensed; he had sponsored the tribal intervention which brought the government to power and then been disappointed in its composition. He formed an alliance with two new political forces, left-wing reformists and the army. The reformists ranged from communism through orthodox to unorthodox socialism and were not primarily inspired by Arab nationalism; the more moderate of them were associated in the *Ahali* group, named after its newspaper. The younger army officers looked with distaste at the disputes of professional politicians, and with some envy at the part the army had played in Turkey and Persia. Their leader was the victorious general Bakr Sidqi. In October 1936, by prearrangement with Hikmat Sulaiman and the *Ahali* group, he moved military units against Baghdad and demanded the resignation of the Cabinet. The Prime Minister yielded and Hikmat Sulaiman formed a largely *Ahali* cabinet, with one of Bakr Sidqi's army associates as Minister of Defence and Bakr himself as Chief of Staff. Yasin al-Hashimi and Rashid 'Ali were banished, the former to die the following year in Damascus; Nuri al-Sa'id escaped to Egypt. He had a personal feud with the new government, for in their advance on Baghdad the officers had murdered his brother-in-law Ja'far al-'Askari, Minister of Defence in the Hashimi as in many previous cabinets and creator of the Iraqi army.

The alliance of Hikmat Sulaiman, *Ahali* and army did not last. The *Ahali*, concerned rather with agrarian reform than pan-Arabism, alienated tribal landlords and nationalists alike; and the officers, more disposed to Kemalist dictatorship than to democracy, were also hostile. Hikmat was forced to submit to majority opinion; he withdrew support from the *Ahali*, suppressed their organisation, and expelled some of the leaders and their communist associates from the country. By devout professions of pan-Arabism he propitiated the nationalists. He could not, despite appeasement, check tribal disorder, which the army continued to crush with severity; and for the first time there was serious labour unrest. The army itself became an embarrassment to him: it came increasingly to dominate the State machine and lost public sympathy through the excesses of General Bakr Sidqi's entourage. In August 1937 the General was assassinated by a disaffected military group, which thereupon attracted sufficient army units to its side to force the resignation of the government. Although the government had adduced the despotism of its predecessor as justification for its own *coup d'état*, it had itself respected civil liberties no more, had intervened no less in elections and administrative appointments, and had quelled tribal unrest with equal severity. Of its programme of reform and development, the reform was renounced and the development impeded by financial difficulties; it nevertheless undertook certain works of irrigation and communications. It was the first independent government to conclude agreements with other States: these were a treaty of alliance with Sa'udi Arabia in 1936, a treaty with Persia in 1937, which settled a long-standing dispute over the Shatt al-'Arab waterway, and in the same year the Sa'dabad Pact of mutual defence with Persia, Turkey and Afghanistan.

When Bakr Sidqi introduced the army into politics in 1936 he undertook to withdraw it once a new civilian government was established—a promise in which he was probably sincere. Withdrawal was, however, unwelcome not only to his personal followers but to other officers with dictatorial sympathies. The army, although internally divided, had become a powerful force; it had developed a mystique and considered itself the arbiter of national destiny. In the following four years (1937–41) it intervened time and again in politics, usually, however, from personal rather than political motives, and in conjunction with civilian politicians. The government of Jamil al-Midfa'i, which succeeded the régime of Hikmat Sulaiman and Bakr Sidqi, incurred the hostility of the latter's bitterest opponents, Nuri al-Sa'id and Rashid 'Ali. A third military *coup d'état*, in December 1938, resolved an internal army dispute and set Nuri al-Sa'id in the premiership, with Rashid 'Ali as head of the Royal Diwan. A fourth, in February 1940, returned Nuri to office in difficult circumstances and gave dominant influence in the army to four generals—the 'Golden Square'—who held key commands.

European Involvement

In April 1939 King Ghazi died in consequence of a motor accident and was succeeded by his infant son Faisal, for whom Prince 'Abdul-Ilah, Ghazi's first cousin, assumed the regency.

Hitherto the rivalry of the political leaders had been personal; after the autumn of 1939 it was drawn into the struggle of the European Powers. Extreme nationalist opinion had for some years past been courted by the Axis States, and would have liked their support in breaking the British connexion. Under pressure from the extremists, and himself no Anglophile, Rashid 'Ali, who succeeded Nuri al-Sa'id as premier in March 1940, hesitated to break with the potentially victorious Axis Powers. Iraq had indeed severed diplomatic relations with Germany in 1939; but the Rashidist cabinet had imposed conditions on the passage of British troops across the country, refused to break off relations with Italy, whose legation was a centre of anti-British activity, and permitted one of its members to make informal contact with [Nazi German ambassador to Turkey Franz] von Papen in Turkey, with the prospect of formal relations to follow. This policy involved the premier in disagreement with advocates of close co-operation with Great Britain, notably the Regent and Nuri al-Sa'id, and he became increasingly identified with extreme nationalists and Axis-sympathisers. The Regent eventually pressed him to resign and refused to dissolve a Chamber that was unfavourable to his cabinet. Rashid thereupon, in January 1941, invoked the dominant generals in a fifth military intervention; he was forced to resign, however, later in the month, when the Regent made government impossible for him by withdrawing from Baghdad. The generals now intervened once more, to impose a cabinet under General Taha al-Hashimi, in whom alone they had confidence, and again in April to unseat him, when they believed their confidence betrayed. On this occasion Rashid 'Ali renewed his alliance with them, in an attempt to coerce the Regent. The latter, however, escaped to Transjordan, where he was joined by Nuri al-Sa'id and other statesmen loyal to him. Rashid 'Ali, now the nominal head of a self-constituted military government, had Parliament unconstitutionally convoked and intimidated it into deposing the Regent and appointing an obscure member of the royal family in his place. He then formed a strongly nationalist civilian cabinet, which the British Government refused to recognise.

Just as he had drifted into leadership of extremist opinion Rashid now drifted into hostilities with Great Britain. In April 1941 the British Government made two requests for permission to land troops; this was on the first occasion granted conditionally, and on the second withheld until the first contingent should have left the country. When the troops were nevertheless landed, Iraqi forces were moved to a position commanding the British base at Habbaniya. On 2 May R.A.F. [Royal Air Force] aircraft attempted to dislodge them by bombing, and hostilities, thus commenced, lasted until the end of the month. During this period the Iraqi Government sought military aid from the Axis, and in fact received a number of aircraft before British reinforcements, advancing from Transjordan, made its position untenable. Had their campaign in Crete and preparations for invading Russia allowed the Germans to send more assistance, the British position in the Middle East might have been imperilled, for, although there is no evidence of pre-arrangement in detail between Rashid 'Ali and the Axis, his movement offered a conveniently open door. As it was, he and his government escaped before the British advance, an armistice was signed on 30 May and two days later the Regent returned from exile. The leading Rashidists were tried in absence, Rashid 'Ali himself and the four generals being sentenced to death. The generals were subsequently captured and executed; Rashid 'Ali continued to live in exile in Sa'udi Arabia and Egypt.

For the remainder of the war, under the premiership of Jamil al-Midfa'i (1941), Nuri al-Sa'id (1941–44) and the veteran nationalist Hamdi al-Pachachi (1944–46), Iraq co-operated fully with her British ally. She became a base for the military occupation of the Levant [the Middle East] and Persia, a channel of supply to Russia and, until the Axis pincers were withdrawn, a defensive position against possible attack through the Western Desert or the Caucasus [mountains]. . . .

Post-War Instability

The post-war history of Iraq displayed four main aspects. The first was the vastly increased wealth which accrued from her oil resources, and the possibility it afforded of extending her economy, consolidating her national strength and raising her standard of living. The second was the conflict between different conceptions of Arab unity in which she was involved, and her rivalry with Egypt for Arab leadership. The third was her alignment with the West in the cold war. The fourth was a new political division within Iraq herself, no longer so significantly within the ministerial group as between that group and upholders of a new form of nationalism opposed to many of that group's policies. The newer school combined a desire for neutrality between the world blocs (often, in effect, hostility to the West and benevolence to the East), a passionate desire for Arab unity and latterly an inclination towards Egypt and Syria, and—far more forcefully than pre-war nationalism—a desire for rapid and radical social reform. Finally, the attitude of Government and Opposition alike was marked indelibly by the war in Palestine and the establishment of Israel, which influenced every sphere of political life.

By the end of the war Iraqi nationalists were demanding the restoration of free political activity, which had been suspended in the interest of war-time security, and early revision of the Anglo-Iraqi treaty of 1930. The first was effected under the premiership of Taufiq al-Suwaidi (February–May 1946). Six parties were formed, representing equally the old and the new nationalism—or a standpoint rather left of the new nationalism. They set about the task of opposition so enthusiastically, with Press attacks and strike action, that the government of the ex-Mayor of Baghdad, Arshad al-'Umari, (June–November 1946) thought it expedient to curtail their activities. Succeeding premiers, Nuri al-Sa'id (1946–47) and Salih Jabr (1947–8)—the first Shi'i to hold this office—took stern measures against communist groups established illegally during and after the war, and closed the more extreme of the left-wing registered parties.

The programme of Salih Jabr's cabinet included treaty revision, and in January 1948 he signed a new treaty with Great Britain at Portsmouth. It was greeted with an outburst of political feeling. The opposition were incensed at governmental action against their parties and newspapers and complained of the conduct of elections.... They disapproved of the Portsmouth

Treaty, the conclusion of which, moreover, coincided with popular anxiety at an acute grain shortage and indignation at the continued export of grain. In the capital opposition to the treaty began with student demonstrations and labour strikes; these were reinforced by political parties and communist groups and soon turned to rioting, in which there were numerous casualties. The administration lost control, the government resigned and the treaty was repudiated. Disturbances continued in Baghdad and other towns during the premierships of the Shi'i divine Muhammad al-Sadr (January–June 1948) and Muzahim al-Pachachi (June 1948–January 1949), but were mastered under the martial law which accompanied the Palestine War [fought between displaced Arab Muslims and Israeli settlers]. Muzahim and his successor, Nuri al-Sa'id (January–December 1949) renewed the government's attack on communism: in 1949 four communist leaders were hanged. . . .

The Last Iraqi Monarch

King Faisal II came of age in 1953 and assumed sovereign powers on 2 May. In September he entrusted the premiership to the young Shi'i statesman Dr. Fadhil al-Jamali, an eloquent exponent of the Arab case in the United Nations. His cabinet was liberal in spirit, and contained two members of the United Popular Front and Iraq's most distinguished advocate of agrarian reform, 'Abdul-Karim al-Uzri. It attempted to reintroduce a land tax and to organise a comprehensive information service; it was the first post-war government officially to acknowledge the importance of public opinion. It received little support from the hard core of the opposition, which distrusted its western connexions and censured its attitude towards communist-exploited strikes. The phenomenal and well-nigh calamitous Tigris floods in the spring of 1954 provoked criticism of its measures for flood control, and, in consequence of this and lack of parliamentary support, it resigned in April with its projects unfulfilled.

Meanwhile a vast programme of national development had been undertaken which included defence against destructive flooding. Before the Second War Iraq's will to develop had been frustrated by lack of funds. The export of oil from 1934 onwards had, however, laid the foundation of prosperity. After the war oil revenues greatly increased in consequence of growing production and the new profit-sharing agreement of 1952, and 70 per cent of them was allocated to a Development Board created in 1950 to develop the country's economy and raise its standard of living. Plans were drawn up ... for systematic progress in most fields of national life; they provide for agronomy, flood control, industry, power, communications, town and country development, health, social security and education. It was the Vice-President of this Board, Arshad al-'Umari, who succeeded Dr Fadhil al-Jamali as premier, himself to give way in August 1954 to Nuri al-Sa'id.

This was General Nuri's twelfth premiership and, lasting nearly three years, was the longest in Iraqi history; it was also one of the most important. Nuri intended to effect the revision of the Anglo-Iraqi Treaty and—matters on which he believed the safety and well-being of the country to depend—to ensure defence against possible Soviet aggression and uninterrupted execution of the development programme.

The negotiations which were to lead to Iraq's membership of the Baghdad Pact had begun during the Jamali ministry. The Iraqi Government had been interested in the conception of a 'Northern Tier' which had appeared in the spring of 1953; and when it was announced, in February 1954, that Turkey and Pakistan were to consider closer collaboration and that Pakistan was to receive American military aid, the Jamali cabinet similarly applied to the United States for arms. In March King Faisal and Nuri al-Sa'id visited Pakistan and in October discussions were held in Turkey. A Turco-Pakistani treaty of friendly co-operation in April 1954 was followed in February 1955 by a Turco-Iraqi defence treaty, which was the nucleus of what came to be known as the Baghdad Pact; in the previous month Iraq had severed diplomatic relations with the Soviet Union. Pakistan acceded to the Pact in July and Persia in October 1955. In the new alignments both the British and Iraqi Governments had seen a solution to the problem of their joint treaty, unrevised in consequence of the riots of January 1948 and due to expire in 1957. In April 1955 Great Britain ratified her adherence to the Baghdad Pact and on that basis the two countries simultaneously concluded a new treaty of alliance by which the British bases were to pass under Iraqi command and British forces to be withdrawn.

General Nuri believed that the aims of external and domestic consolidation which he had set himself were endangered by party turbulence and communist conspiracy and would justify a considerable measure of control. Before entering on office he had dissolved his Constitutional Union Party, an example followed by Salih Jabr. In September 1954 he abolished all parties—of which those in opposition continued, however, to operate unofficially—and tightened the Press Law. Vigorous action was taken against communism and the allied Partisans of Peace, and a law was passed depriving convicted communists of Iraqi nationality. The agreements which constituted the Baghdad Pact were ratified without disturbance and the work of development proceeded briskly; but outward stability was purchased at the price of much bitterness on the part of frustrated intellectuals and adherents of the new nationalism, many of whom condemned the Pact and sympathised with the policies of [strongly pro-Arab, anti-Western Middle East nations] Egypt and Syria.

Pan-Arabism: A Decisive Force in Iraq's Destiny

BY MICHEL AFLAQ

Growing pro-independence sentiments among top military officials was one factor pressuring the pro-Western Iraqi government in the 1950s. Another was a sociopolitical movement called Pan-Arabism, which would prove to be critical to Iraq's development and history. Pan-Arabism's ideology combined advocacy for strong Arab unity and independence with socialist economic and political policies. Pan-Arabic beliefs were advocated in Iraq and other Arab countries by a political party known as the Ba'ath (Arabic for "resurrection"). Ironically, one of the most important people in the development of Pan-Arabism was a Greek Christian, Michel Aflaq. Aflaq's writings and speeches inspired large numbers of people to take up the cause of Pan-Arabism. The following excerpt is from a speech he gave at a Ba'ath Party gathering in February 1950.

Brethren: Let us free ourselves from traditional views, from the repetition of customary phrases and abstract words, and let us try to rise a little above the contingent problems of the day. Let us try to do all this in order to draw nearer to the truth concerning our one great problem, to the living and great truth of our cause, as it seeks true life, and as it finds its way by itself, by its own effort, in confidence and faith.

What is revolution? Shall we stop at political definitions? Shall our understanding be limited to political programs, and the schemes and suggestions they contain for organizing public life in its different aspects? Or are we to understand by revolution something truer and deeper? By revolution we understand that true awakening which it is no longer possible to deny or to doubt, the awakening of the Arab spirit at

Michel Aflaq, "Nationalism and Revolution," *Arab Nationalism: An Anthology*, edited by Sylvia G. Haim. Berkeley and Los Angeles: University of California Press, 1962. Copyright © 1962 by The Regents of the University of California. Reproduced by permission.

a decisive stage in human history. The reality of the revolution lies in this awakening, the awakening of the spirit which had been weighed down by stationary and vitiated conditions which, for a long time, prevented it from rising and radiating its influence. This spirit at last senses great danger, fateful danger, and rises up decisively.

This awakening, and its progress, cannot but be in a direction contrary to the conditions which have prevented its manifestation, have weighed it down, and have distorted its development, progress in a direction contrary to that of the existing conditions, of the vitiated, sickly, and artificial conditions. This opposition to the current is in order that what remains of the true spirit should awake, wherever it is found, come together, and coalesce. It is necessary to embark on such a progress, which is in contradiction to matter, which begins to live with every step it takes, which awakens and arouses attention, which revitalizes hidden or sleeping powers and restores to them seriousness, lucidity, the feeling of their independence, their value, and their influence. *Revolution, then, before being a political and social program, is that prime propelling power, that powerful psychic current, that mandatory struggle, without which the reawakening of the nation is not to be understood. This is what we understand by revolution.*

We do not then fight existing conditions merely because they are vitiated; rather, we fight them because we are compelled to fight, because we cannot but fight. The nation must discover in itself what remains of its true power, and we must extract from its depth the treasures of hidden vitality. We struggle and fight against the artificial vitiated political and social conditions, not only to remove and change them but so that the nation may recover its unity in this struggle also. The nation has denied its being as a result of its long sleep, and as a result of the distortion which it has undergone. It no longer knows itself, its parts no longer know one another, it has become mightily divided, and its parts and members have been scattered. It has sunk to a low level, being imprisoned in selfishness, in petty interests, in the habit of immobility and unadventurousness. At this level, no unity can be created in the nation, no focusing of that warmth necessary for acquaintance and friendship among the millions of Arabs. Fervor is then necessary, turmoil and movement at a high level are necessary, hardships to be overcome are necessary, a long march in which intellect and morality interpenetrate is necessary, trial and error and the correction of error are necessary. In this way, we may know one another and resume our relations, so that the nation may be unified in the path of struggle and hardships.

This is as far as the nation, taken as an entity, is concerned. As far as its individual members are concerned, revolution, which we have defined as opposition to the current, will alone reconstitute the Arab personality and will place on each individual the responsibility of his actions. It will liberate the intellect and make it independent, and make morality earnest and responsible; it will release the source of faith in the soul, because such a long and strenuous march does not find faith superfluous. On the contrary, its flesh and blood originate from so spiritual a source.

The Need for Revolution

Revolution, then, is a path, a path leading to the desired aim, to the healthy society which we seek. It is, however, not one of many paths, but indeed the only one. For this reason, even if present conditions were done away with, by some miracle, the nation which we desire and the aims which we seek will not be, and we will not be able to build the society we desire. The nation we seek, the society we want to build, depends on us, on our efforts, on our rectitude, on our awareness. It cannot descend from heaven; it cannot come in a mechanical fashion; it inheres in our intellect and morality. This path, therefore, is mandatory on us.

To oppose the current is, in our condition, the only criterion which distinguishes between truth and falsehood, between earnestness and make-believe. When we find ourselves ready to oppose the current, then will words, deeds, programs, and everything else become secondary, and the only tangible existing thing on which we can rely will be that we can find some who are ready to assume the responsibility and to go in a direction contrary to the existing situation in the Arab countries. Then, gradually, will come into existence and germinate the necessary virtues necessary to continue on this road and to build anew at the end of it. *Revolution is the opposition of truth to the existing situation*, because the nation has a truth in spite of its backwardness and mutilation, and this truth proclaims itself, however masterful the existing conditions. *Revolution is this proclamation, this assertion of the existence of truth. Revolution is the opposition of the future to the present*, because our aims, drawn from our depths and from our soul, have shone forth and have sped on to outdistance us, in order to beckon us on and to speed us on toward themselves; this is the future. Revolution, then, is the opposition of this future, which is the truth of ourselves and our aims, to the counterfeit present, to the present which is alien to our truth.

Brethren: the past is a real thing, and well established in the life of the nation. It would be in vain, it would show error and sterility of thought, to deny this eternal truth. We mean by the past that period of time when the Arab soul was realizing itself. What can we mean by the future, and what can this future be which beckons us on and drives us to struggle, if not that period of time in which our true soul is realized?

Our past, then, understood in this pure and true sense, we have stationed in the vanguard, a light to show us the way. We have not left it behind in order that we may bemoan the period when it existed and call upon it to help us while, passively immobile, we await its coming and expect it to descend to our present level. This is not the past. The past, considered as the reality of the Arab spirit, as the self-realizing reality of the Arab spirit, cannot come, cannot come back and come down and descend; rather, we must march toward it, onward in a progressive spirit. We must ascend to it, raise ourselves up to its level. We must walk a difficult and tiring road until we can grow in ourselves the virtues, the talents, and the capacities which will make us fit to understand it, to intermix and join up with it.

The progressive march, then, the ascendant march on the road of the revolution, is the only possible means for us to join up with our past, and this joining up cannot but be an ascent. It cannot be a descent or a degeneration; it cannot be immobility or persistence in immobility and passivity.

Side by side with this view of the past which places it in a distant future to evoke our energies in order to ascend and reach up to it after a struggle, and to deserve it nobly, there is the other view which reflects the black, ugly, heavy shadows of the present on that past. This, in consequence, is understood as a clinging to the present and an obstinate stand for preserving it and for sinking deeper into its faults and vices. How, then, can such a past provide spiritual release, an inventive intellect, upright and independent behavior, or a living and overflowing faith?

To hold on to existing conditions, to preserve them, to defend these conditions which threaten the Arabs with extinction; such is the past, it is [also] the present, the vitiated reality, the selfishness, and the servitude to material interests. As for the true past, it is our yearning for it which leads us to strive and work, to struggle and ascend. This is the free, spiritual, healthy past which the Arabs had. Such a past was an epoch in which the spirit was realized; that is, it was, itself, a revolution in which the intellect attained freedom and independence and youthfulness of feeling for life and the world; it innovated, organized, and was in harmony with the laws of life and nature. The human personality realized in it freedom, individuality, earnestness, and responsibility, and went on to engage in free actions, to take up heroic stands, to transcend the limits of egoism, to harmonize with the general will and with the whole. Then the spirit reached its pure source and was filled with fertility and renewal; it knew its eternal destiny and was filled with faith.

Our past was a revolution, and we will never reach its level or meet with it except through revolution. The new revolution, then, is a march, full of sharp awareness and of faith, toward those heights where contradictions are resolved and opposites are united, where the past meets the future and the nation is reconciled to itself in its creativity and in the accomplishment of its mission.

The "Arab Mission"

They ask us, Brethren, what do you mean by the mission, *the eternal Arab mission?* The Arab mission does not consist in words which we proclaim, it does not consist in principles to be incorporated in programs, it does not constitute matter for legislation. All these are dead, counterfeit things, because between us and the time when we may legislate out of the inspiration of our spirit and mission, there is a long distance and a high barrier. What, then, is this mission today?

It is our life itself, *it is to agree to experience this life with a deep and true experience, great and massive in proportion to the greatness of the Arab nation, in proportion to the depth of suffering undergone by the Arabs, in proportion to the great dangers which threaten its continued existence. This living and true experience will bring us back to ourselves, to our living realities; it will make us shoulder our responsibilities and will set us on the true path* in order that we may fight these diseases and these obstacles, these counterfeit conditions, in order to fight social injustice, class exploitation, and the eras of selfishness, bribery, and exploitation, in order to combat tyranny, the falsification of the popular will, and the insults to the dignity of the Arab as a citizen and a man; *for the sake of a free society in which every Arab will regain consciousness of himself, of his existence, his dignity, his thinking, and his responsibilities.* The experience in which our struggle takes place is that of the Arab nation dismembered into different countries and statelets, artificial and counterfeit; we struggle until we can reunite these scattered members, until we may reach a wholesome and natural state in which no severed member can speak in the name of all, until we can get rid of this strange and anomalous state. Then will it be possible for the Arabs to unite, for their spirit to be upstanding, their ideas clear, their morality upright; then will there be scope for their minds to create, for they will have become that wholesome natural entity, one nation. This wholesome and true experience, struggling against the existing conditions until we return to the right state, such is the Arab mission. A mission is what one part of the humanity presents to the whole of humanity. Nothing narrow or selfish may be called a mission; a mission has to have comprehensive, eternal, human significance. You may inquire what this mission will be like in tackling our problems. I would say to you that when the Arabs embark on this experience—and in reality they have already embarked on it, and will not go back—then such an experience will not only solve their problems, but they will emerge from it with a deep human experience which will create in them a personality instinct with the sufferings of human life, the knowledge of its secrets, the cure for its ills, and they will then present to the world and to humanity the fruit of this eternally memorable experience.

From Monarchy to Anarchy

By Sandra Mackey

Opposition to pro-Western forces in government finally reached critical mass in 1958, when a group of military officers led a coup d'etat and deposed the monarch and drove other officials supportive of British policies from power. This was only the first of three coups to take place between 1958 and 1968. In addition, during this period there were also other coup attempts as well as assassinations and assassination attempts. Sandra Mackey is a journalist and author who has written extensively about the Middle East. The following excerpt from her book The Reckoning: Iraq and the Legacy of Saddam Hussein *describes this especially tumultuous period in Iraq, with a special focus on the activities of the Iraqi Ba'ath Party, which would ultimately prevail in the long and bloody power struggles that ravaged the country during this time.*

For most Iraqis, the revolution of 1958 promised to break the last chains of imperialism and right the inequities of society. At six o'clock on the morning of July 14 when Baghdad Radio trumpeted, "Citizens of Baghdad, the Monarchy is dead! The Republic is here!" crowds in the streets erupted in rejoicing at the fall of the Hashemites [Iraqi monarchs]. In Iraq where it is too hot in summer to stage a revolution, it had all happened with lightning speed. The reason was that not a single army unit had injected itself between the monarchy and the Free Officers [group of high-ranking reform-minded military leaders].

Over the first few days of the new republic, only an early curfew that curtailed Baghdad's nightlife dampened the enthusiasm for the new order. The capital's buses plied their regular routes and men played backgammon at sidewalk tables while crowds of curiosity seekers pushed through [high-ranking member of the royal family's staff] Nuri al-Said's sacked house, where a broken

---

Sandra Mackey, *The Reckoning: Iraq and the Legacy of Saddam Hussein*. New York: W.W. Norton & Company, Inc., 2002. Copyright © 2002 by Sandra Mackey. Reproduced by permission of the publisher.

vermouth bottle sat on the pasha's bar. The city fathers of al-Hillah near ancient Babylon changed without protest the names of the major streets. King Faisal I became Revolution Street; King Faisal II, Freedom Street; and Prince Abdul al-Ilah was converted to the poetic-sounding Street of Awakening....

In the rejoicing no one cared to consider the comment of the departing British ambassador [Sir John Troutbeck]: "Iraqis have always been known for their turbulence and their latest revolution is unlikely to herald an era of tranquility, foreign alike to their history and their temperament."...

In the aftermath of the revolution, the leaders of the Free Officers, General Abd al-Karim Qasim and Colonel Abd al-Salam Arif, appeared committed to political and social reform that would address the endemic problems of Iraqi politics and society. Civilian rule was invested in a three-man council composed of an Arab Sunni, an Arab Shia, and a Kurd. The council in turn formed a cabinet remarkable for its broad inclusion of respected leaders of opposition to the monarchy. It all lent legitimacy and respect to what was in reality a military regime driven by anti-imperialism. General Qasim summed up the attitude of those who made the revolution: "If you tour any part of this country, you will see how extensive misery, poverty, and deprivation are in the life of the people. You will see the cottages [of the villages] ... moving skeletons.... The wealth of this country was robbed and wasted in the interest of imperialism and the foreigner."

Over the next weeks, the revolutionary government closed British military bases, purged the government of its Western advisors and contractors, promised Kurds a level of autonomy, lifted the restraints on radical ideological groups representing workers, and announced land reform that intended to release the peasants from their serfdom to the tribal sheikhs. Still, the new political, social, and economic paradigm left unresolved the problem of communalism, which had tormented Iraq since its inception. The Sunnis, Shia, and Kurds would continue to pursue their contradictory visions of Iraq while tribes and families within each community fought their own battles of interest and honor.... Iraq would enter a decade in which leaders exercised a total monopoly of state power and exhibited the characteristics once admired in tribal sheikhs: "fearlessness towards one's enemies, swift punishment to those judged wrong, and loyalty to kinsmen and supporters" [as stated by Robert A. Fernea]....

Violence and Instability on the Rise

Just past six o'clock in the evening on October 7, 1959, a Baathist hit squad, including a young party tough named Saddam Hussein, hid within the bustling commerce that daily clogged the narrowest point on al-Rashid street. The moment that Qasim's tan Chevrolet station wagon, en route to a reception at the East German embassy, rolled into sight, the assassins raced from beneath the Roman-style colonnade the British had built during the mandate. They halted, unleashed a barrage of bullets, and broke toward the warren of alleyways on the opposite side of the street. All they left behind was a dead guard and the bleeding general slumped in the backseat of his car. When the seriously injured Qasim finally left the hospital eight weeks later, a collection of Iraqi nationalists took to the streets shouting, "Long Live the Solidarity of the people, the Army, and the Government under the leadership of Abd al-Karim Qasim!"

Despite this show of support, Qasim was a man under pressure. His postrevolution government, characterized by maladministration rather than genuine reform, had produced little for the common man except the privilege to walk on the grass in public parks. The reasonably efficient bureaucracy of the monarchy had all but collapsed when much of the civil service was hauled before a kangaroo court and charged with "supporting imperialism and subverting Arab nationalism." The anemic political parties that provided a semblance of competitive politics lay on their death beds, victims of fear and intimidation. And the initial integration of Iraq's separate communities at the beginning of the revolutionary government never challenged, much less shattered, the dominance of the Sunnis. Qasim's one notable act—the adoption of land reform—withered away. The peasants who did receive the small amounts of land that were actually distributed found ownership a disaster. Too unskilled at management to coordinate care of the irrigation works and too illiterate to understand that land reform did not mean release from labor, the peasants had put down their tools on land no longer productive, drifting instead to the burgeoning slums of cities to work as day laborers.... With the support of dwindling numbers in the army, Qasim's regime degenerated into a cult of personality.

He became the "Sole Leader," the caliph of Baghdad, kept in power by a pampered segment of the army and a secret police force whose stringent security apparatus ensured his authoritarianism. Cultivating an image of devotion and martyrdom, he worked as many as twenty hours a day at the Ministry of Defense, where a giant illuminated portrait of himself hung on the front of the building. Around the clock, excerpts from his speeches burst like machine-gun fire from the government-held radio station. Like Saddam Hussein, Qasim was the self-created embodiment of the "great leader," always in uniform, towering above his people as a dictator claiming to embody the popular will. Emotionally unpredictable and lacking administrative talent, Qasim's modest accomplishments—demolition of some of Baghdad's worst slums, expanded availability of water and electricity, and increased primary education—faded as his political wounds deepened. The vultures circled. Leading the way were the pan-Arabists ready to devour Qasim and his Mesopotamian symbols of the Iraqi state....

For several days in early 1963, battles filled the streets of Baghdad as the remnants of the army loyal to Qasim, together with the Communists, battled against the pan-Arabist elements of the army and the Baath. The army's pan-Arabist officer corps neutralized the air force before moving on to take, one by one, all the placements of the government's defense. Simultaneously, the Baath militia swept the streets. Only Qasim's personal guard of fifteen hundred men and the people who had gained some little benefit from the postrevolution government—laborers, porters, and artisans from the mud huts east of the Tigris—fought for the general. By 12:30 P.M. on February 9, 1963, Qasim was a prisoner. A quick trial on charges of betrayal of the revolution condemned to death the general and the three officers who stayed at his side. Following the instant verdict, a contingent of revolutionaries including members of the Iraq Baath Party pushed Qasim and the others into the music studio of the government television station, sat them down, and shot them. Then they turned on the cameras. One body was sprawled backward on a spindly chair. Qasim lay on the floor. As if to prove the man who had tried to rule Iraq after the revolution was truly dead, a member of the execution squad grabbed the dead general's head by the hair and thrust it into the camera lens. Iraqis saw for themselves the glassy eyes and gold-capped teeth of their deposed leader. A short while later, the victors of yet another military coup appeared before a crowd of reporters gathered at a Baghdad hotel. They said simply, "We revolted against the cult of personality."

The new ruling tribunal, the National Council of the Revolutionary Command (NCRC), allocated power between the military and the Baath, the feeble rump of a party turned into a political force by its participation in the coup. At the time, the Baath still claimed only a thousand members. Its leadership included mostly Sunnis but also Shia and one Arabized Kurd. Its membership consisted largely of party functionaries, school teachers, and an occasional lawyer whose social class was determined by families who were peasants, workers, traders, or impoverished landlords. Lacking stature, respect, or power outside its membership in the army, the Baath accepted as president General Abd al-Salam Arif, Qasim's Nasserite [supporter of Egyptian leader and pan-Arab proponent Gamal Abdul Nasser] counterpart in the 1958 revolution and the person to whom the deposed leader had once referred as "my son, my friend, my brother." The quiet reserved army general Ahmed Hassan al-Bakr of the Baath assumed the premiership. Sixteen of the eighteen seats on the NCRC and twelve of the twenty-one seats on the cabinet also belonged to the Baath. Together the Nasserites of the army and the pan-Arabists of the Baath declared the country the "Iraqi region of the Arab homeland."

In the aftermath of the coup, a cadre of some two thousand Baath sympathizers from the Azamiyah quarter of Baghdad organized to defend the new government against any possible threat of a countercoup. Assuming the name of the National Guard, they were part of the hundreds of men sent out to round up the Communists. Identified by green arm bands, they carried mimeographed lists of members of the ICP [Iraqi Communist Party], complete with home addresses and auto tag numbers. Within a week, the regime had killed somewhere between five hundred and three thousand people whose Marxist ideology rejected pan-Arabism and whose members posed the only real challenge to the new regime. Tariq Aziz, who was in the leadership of the Baath at the time, has said, "To understand why so much blood flowed in those days you have to remember Iraq's history is not one in which political dissent has been allowed.". . .

By March . . . the government was spiraling toward anarchy. Although every faction carried its burden of blame, it was the Baath's National Guard that terrorized the streets. In the wake of the coup, the Baath militia had swollen by several thousand. New recruits were no longer idealistically inclined students but were,

MONARCHY MURDERS

The revolt that finally deposed the Iraqi monarchy after years of tension between pro-Western Iraqi forces and strong Arab nationalists was brief and limited in its targets, but it was not without gruesome violence. An article in Time *magazine describes the critical action that led to the Free Officers' taking power.*

The revolt burst on Iraq at 5 o'clock Monday morning. Major General Abdul Kareem el-Kassim, 42, who had been ordered to lead his men into Jordan to bolster King Hussein against a coup, led them instead into sleeping Baghdad. Silently, and without firing a shot, his soldiers took over the key points of the city.... By the time the troops began heading for the palace of 23-year-old King Feisal, an excited mob was at their heels.

The unsuspecting young King and his uncle, Crown Prince Adbul Illah, 46, were getting ready to fly to Istanbul.... Seeing the gathering crowd, they went outside the palace. According to the rebels, the palace guard fired into the crowd, [killing] 14. The soldiers returned the fire. Feisal was killed, along with Crown Prince Abdul Illah, the Crown Prince's mother, two nurses and two palace guardsmen....

The rebels later said they had not wanted to kill [Feisal], descendant of the Prophet. Fearing public revulsion against his murder, the killers kept his death a secret, wrapped him in a carpet and smuggled his body away to be buried. But the Crown Prince, who had ruled the country for 14 years as Regent, and was widely disliked, was another matter. His assassins threw his body out a window, let the mobs drag him through the streets and string his body up in public.

"Iraq: In One Swift Hour," *Time*, July 28, 1958, pp. 25–26.

as one Iraqi Communist leader said, "adolescents befuddled by jingoistic propaganda, declassed elements and all sorts of riffraff" who sought personal power. Knocking on doors in the middle of the night, they seized suspected Baath enemies. During the day, they swaggered through the streets intimidating civilians, taking from them what they wanted. Most of all, they exercised the power of arrest. Those seized were thrown into prison or the torture chambers of the Qasr al-Nihayah, the "Palace of the End." Used for detention and interrogation since the end of the monarchy, it became the Baath's Bureau of Special Investigations, where enforcers, including a young Saddam Hussein, wielded the Baath's instruments of torture....

On November 18, 1963, a collection of army officers, including some disaffected Baathists, sent tanks to secure strategic points in Baghdad. Specifically targeting the Baath organization, they fired rockets into the headquarters of the National Guard and dispatched soldiers to round up the Baath leadership. Barely qualifying as a coup, the military action purged the Baath from government. The generals, led by the deposed Arif, now ruled alone in an atmosphere in which the street power of the Communists had been tamed, the pretensions of the National Guard leveled, and the anarchy of the Baath ended. It was now Arif's turn to decide if Iraq would join the Arab world or keep itself apart.

In his usual dark suit and tasteful tie, [Iraqi military revolutionary leader] Abd al-Salam Arif looked more like a civilian than a solider. But almost everything about the general defied easy classification. He was a conservative Iraqi in a tumultuous time. He was an Arab nationalist. Even though the ideology of Arab nationalism struggled with Islam's power within the culture, he was a deeply religious Sunni Muslim. One thing about Arif was clear. He was a military man determined to preserve the authority of the army. Declaring his Arab nationalist credentials above all else, Arif abolished the Akkadian sun and the star of Ishtar as official symbols of Iraq. Likewise, the emblems of Mesopotamia that had frequented postage stamps of the Qasim regime disappeared, replaced by images commemorating anniversaries of the Arab League and pan-Arab conferences and celebrating Arab themes connected to Sunni Arab culture. On May 3, 1964, the Arif government issued a provisional constitution declaring Iraq to be "a part of the Arab nation."...

The fragility of the regime revealed itself on September 4,

1964, when the Baath attempted to regain power in another coup while Arif's rivals in the army tried to shoot down his plane as it took off from a military base. Although both actions failed, Arif's tenure as the head of Iraq was about to end. Before he could either succeed or fail in ruling his discordant country, he died when his helicopter crashed in a sandstorm in southern Iraq on April 13, 1966.

His brother, General Abd al-Rahman Arif, took over Iraq's military government. The second Arif president devoted himself more to upholding the power of the army than to promoting Arab nationalism or union with Egypt. Despite their failure to address Iraq's internal needs, the older and younger Arif brothers did succeed in keeping the country intact and sovereign....

The Backlash of National Shame

Tangled in a war of wills since the Suez crisis of 1956, Israel and its Arab neighbors once more inched toward war.... On June 6, 1967, as dawn broke ... Israeli fighter planes streaked out over the calm waters of the Mediterranean, doubling back toward land to lay waste to the Egyptian Air Force, the Royal Jordanian Air Force, and Syria's fighter planes, which were sitting on the country's lone airfield north of Damascus. The Arab states, including Iraq, hastily sent their armies into battle. One by one, the Israelis destroyed them. Egypt lost the Sinai; Jordan forfeited Jerusalem and the West Bank of the Jordan River; Syria sacrificed the Golan Heights; Iraq lost nothing. Sharing no contiguous borders with Israel, Iraq's lone armored brigade and three infantry brigades sent in the name of Arab nationalism never left Jordan....

As the public resentment over Iraq's failure to contribute sufficiently to the 1967 war between Israel and the Arabs swelled, the Baath Party beat the drum of Arabism. Railing against the cowardliness of the Abd al-Rahman Arif government, the Baath sent demonstrators into the streets. Thousands more responded emotionally to Baath rhetoric that hit the raw nerve beneath the humiliation of what was being called the Six Day War. Riddled by corruption, branded with incompetence, deaf to demands for parliamentary government, Arif and his dwindling corps of army officers huddled behind the facade of authority. Iraq, which had averaged two coups or attempted coups every year since the revolution, was about to witness another.

At three o'clock on the morning of July 17, 1968, the telephone rang in the bedroom of the sleeping Abd al-Rahman Arif. When the startled president answered, the voice of a high-ranking Baath officer in the Iraqi army tersely announced, "I am speaking from the Ministry of Defense. Tanks are now proceeding toward the palace." Suddenly, five rifle shots outside the window split the air. The president meekly surrendered, drank a cup of tea with those deposing him, accepted transportation to the airport, and boarded an Iraqi airliner to join his ailing wife in London. The coup, planned and executed by the Baath, was over. Coincidence struck a haunting chord: the Baath had ended military rule almost ten years to the day after the army erased the monarchy in 1958.

In retrospect, the monarchy, despite its serious shortcomings, had governed Iraq better than any government that followed. When it fell, it took most of the educated class with it. In place of the king and the educated elite, the military stepped in as the guardians of government. Under the batons of generals, the people of Iraq found that they had traded feudalism and imperialism for authoritarianism, insecurity, and economic regression. At the end of a chaotic decade of military government in which the competing ideologies of the 1958 revolution waged battle, Iraq passed into the iron grip of the Baath Party. Over the next decade, the Baath, through political organization more than military fiat, would drive fragmented Iraq toward the dictatorship of Saddam Hussein.

THE HISTORY OF NATIONS
Chapter 5

The Reign of Saddam Hussein

The Making of Hussein's Persona and Character

BY EFRAIM KARSH AND INARI RAUTSI

Saddam Hussein became president of Iraq in 1979, although he held important government positions for many years prior to his presidency. Hussein's early life and his formative experiences indoctrinated him to become a militant proponent of Arab unity and independence and an opponent of foreign intervention in his home nation. Being surrounded by abject poverty for much of his early life, Hussein also came to hold socialist economic views. In the following excerpt, Efraim Karsh and Inari Rautsi, two academic Middle Eastern experts based in England, recount Hussein's early life experiences and his time as an outlaw and underground activist. The authors conclude that these experiences influenced and shaped Hussein as a government leader. This excerpt was taken from Karsh and Rautsi's book Saddam Hussein: A Political Biography.

In 1394, as the Tartar hordes of Timurlane swept over Mesopotamia, they took the trouble of stopping at a small provincial town on the Tigris river, some hundred miles north of Baghdad, where they erected a pyramid with the skulls of their victims. The name of the town was Tikrit, and its choice as the site for demonstrating Timurlane's ferocity was not accidental. A small garrison protected by a formidable fortress, Tikrit had been a center of defiance to external invaders, leading the eighteenth-century English historian, Edward Gibbon, to define it as an "impregnable fortress of independent Arabs." This was the place where Saladin, the legendary Muslim military commander who defeated the Crusaders in the renowned battle of Hittin and liberated Jerusalem from Christian rule, had been born in 1138. Ex-

Efraim Karsh and Inari Rautsi, *Saddam Hussein: A Political Biography*. New York: The Free Press, 1991. Copyright © 1991 by Efraim Karsh and Inari Rautsi. Reproduced by permission.

actly 800 years later, it was to become the birthplace of a modern Iraqi ruler, aspiring to don the mantle of his great predecessor: Saddam Hussein. . . .

Childhood Amid Turmoil

The Iraq of Saddam's early years was marked by profound political instability, compounded by the gathering storm in Europe and the eventual outbreak of a general war. Resenting the continuation of British presence and influence in Iraq—despite its formal independence the country remained tied to Britain by a bilateral treaty signed in 1930, which gave the latter preferential political status and two military bases on Iraqi territory—the militant Iraqi nationalists looked forward to the triumph of Nazi Germany and its allies. A Nazi victory, they believed, would dislodge Britain from the Middle East and render Iraq, and the other Arab lands of the Middle East, truly independent. As the Germans went from strength to strength, anti-British sentiments soared and Baghdad became one of the main regional centers for pro-Axis activities. A showdown between the nationalists, who enjoyed widespread support within the army, and the British seemed only a matter of time.

In April 1941 London approached Baghdad with a request to allow the landing and transfer of British troops through Iraqi territory in accordance with the 1930 Treaty. Iraq's pro-Nazi Prime Minister, Rashid Ali al-Kailani, who had come to power earlier that month through a military coup, viewed the request as a de facto occupation of Iraq. Yet, mindful that the real agenda behind the British demand was his own overthrow, he took care to profess his readiness to abide by the bilateral treaty. The British, nevertheless, did not take any chances, and in late April began landing their troops in southern Iraq. At this point Rashid Ali ordered his army to move on the British air base at Habbaniya, near Baghdad, and appealed for German support. In the ensuing hostilities the Iraqi army was decisively beaten by a British expeditionary force, and Rashid Ali and some of his supporters fled the country. The authority of the monarchy was restored by British bayonets. Many participants in the uprising were jailed and some of them executed by the old-new government.

These events had a profound effect on Saddam's life. His uncle and foster father Khairallah, an army officer and ardent Arab nationalist, participated in the ill-fated uprising and was subsequently dismissed from the military and jailed for five years. The young boy was thus forced to move to the small village of al-Shawish, near Tikrit, to live with his mother who had meanwhile remarried. Her new husband was Hasan Ibrahim, a brother of Saddam's late father. In the following years he was to ask his mother time and again where his uncle was, only to be given the routine answer: "Uncle Khairallah is in jail." In Saddam's own account, his empathy with Khairallah had a crucial impact on the development of his nationalist sentiments in that it fueled a deep-seated hatred of the monarchy and the foreign power behind it, a feeling which he was to harbor for years to come. As he would write later: "Our children should be taught to beware of everything foreign and not to disclose any state or party secrets to foreigners . . . for foreigners are eyes for their countries, and some of them are counterrevolutionary instruments [in the hands of imperialism]."

The move from Tikrit to al-Shawish was quite traumatic for Saddam. . . .

Unlike Khairallah, who as a military officer enjoyed a relatively high social status, the Ibrahims were considered "local brigands." Saddam was thus condemned to a lonely existence. He had no friends among the village boys, who often mocked him for being fatherless, and he used to carry an iron bar to protect himself against attacks. . . .

To make things worse, nobody in the family showed great interest in Saddam, who had to look after himself from his first days in the village. His stepfather, "Hasan the liar" as he was known locally, was a brutish man who used to amuse himself by humiliating Saddam. His common punishment was to beat the youth with an asphalt-covered stick, forcing him to dance around to dodge the blows. He prevented Saddam from acquiring education, sending him instead to steal for him; the young boy was even reported to have spent some time in a juvenile detention center. Saddam learnt from firsthand experience, at a very early age the cruel law of *homo homini lupus* (man is a wolf to man). Its corollaries of suspicion and distrust of one's closest associates, a need for total self-reliance, and for intimidating others so as never to be seen as prey were to guide his thoughts and acts from that time forward.

A Fortuitous Move

Had Saddam spent his entire youth at his mother's secluded village, he would most probably have become an undistinguished

Iraqi peasant. However, to his great excitement, in 1947, shortly after his uncle's release from prison, he left his mother and stepfather and returned to Khairallah's home in Tikrit where he began attending school. Studies were quite burdensome for the young boy, who at the age of ten did not know how to spell his name. He would rather amuse his classmates with practical jokes, such as embracing his old Koran teacher in a deceptively friendly hug and then inserting a snake beneath his robe. Yet, Khairallah's constant encouragement and guiding hand kept Saddam going through these difficult years. Another source of support was provided by Khairallah's son, Adnan, three years Saddam's junior and his best friend, who would later become Minister of Defense. In the fall of 1955, having graduated from primary school, Hussein followed his uncle to Baghdad where he enrolled at the Karkh high school. He was then 18 years old.

Those were days of national fervor and the cafés of Baghdad were alive with intrigue and conspiracies. In 1955 Iraq joined Britain, Turkey, Iran and Pakistan in forming a regional defense organization, known as the Baghdad Pact. In taking this step, the Iraqi Prime Minister, Nuri Sa'id, was motivated by wider objectives than the containment of the "Soviet threat" which, ostensibly, constituted the raison d'être for the new security system. Faced by mounting public pressure for a unilateral abrogation of the 1930 Treaty with Britain, but reluctant to jeopardize Iraq's relations with its main international ally, Sa'id sought a magic formula that would allow him to have his cake and eat it too: to project himself as a staunch nationalist who freed his country from foreign influence, while keeping British support for Iraq intact. The Baghdad Pact, he reasoned, could offer such a solution by creating a multilateral framework that would put Anglo-Iraqi relations on a new footing, amenable to both Britain and Iraq. Besides, if joined by other Arab states, such as Jordan and Syria, the Baghdad Pact could give Iraq a springboard for outshining Egypt, its traditional rival for leadership of the Arab World. Since the ancient struggle for regional hegemony between Mesopotamia and Egypt, the relationship between Iraq and Egypt had been a competitive one.

These expectations turned sour. By the time the pact was established, it was already evident to Sa'id that he had lost the battle over the minds and souls of the Arab masses to the young and dynamic Egyptian President, Gamal Abd al-Nasser. In September 1955 Nasser dealt a blow to the West by concluding a large-scale arms deal with the Soviet Union (known as the "Czech deal" since Prague was the official signatory to the agreement), which gave Moscow a doorway to the Middle East, hitherto an almost exclusive Western "preserve." (It was the Western great powers that had defeated the Ottoman Empire in the First World War and carved up the Middle East between them in a series of League of Nations mandates in accordance with the Sykes-Picot Agreement of 1916.) Ten months later Nasser publicly snubbed Great Britain by nationalizing the Suez Canal. The British response was not slow in coming: in October Egypt was attacked by an Anglo-French-Israeli war coalition. Even though the Egyptian army was defeated by the Israelis and suffered significant losses at the hands of the British and the French, and although it was the United States (and to a lesser extent, the Soviet Union) that saved the day for Nasser by forcing the invading forces to relinquish their gains, in Arab eyes Nasser was the hero of the Suez Crisis; the person who had taken on "world imperialism" single-handedly and managed to emerge victorious.

While Nasser was steadily establishing himself as the standard-bearer of the anti-imperialist struggle and the embodiment of Arab nationalism, the Iraqi leadership was increasingly viewed as a "lackey of Western imperialism," a reactionary regime out of step with the historic march of Arab destiny. Hence, not only did Iraq fail to attract other Arab partners to the Baghdad Pact, finding itself in glaring regional isolation, but the formation of the pact met with considerable domestic disapproval. The left-wing factions resented Iraq's involvement in what they viewed as direct aggression against the USSR. The nationalists, for their part, considered the pact a submission to Western imperialism and a betrayal of the cause of pan-Arabism.

Public dissatisfaction in Iraq reached its peak in the fall of 1956 when widespread riots engulfed Baghdad in reaction to the regime's passivity during the Suez Crisis. One of the many people who roamed the streets during those heated days was Saddam, who felt in his element in this turbulent environment. The political milieu was not daunting to him; indeed he was well suited to it. His uncle's example had inspired him to political activism and his lack of close, emotional ties in his early childhood had taught him to scheme and manipulate to survive. Finding anti-government activity far more gratifying than studies, he plunged wholeheartedly into the seething streets of the capital.

In early 1957, at the age of 20, he joined the Ba'th Party....

Precisely what drove Hussein to join the Ba'th Party at such a low ebb in its development is difficult to say. In later years he was to argue that the Party's commitment to the idea of Arab nationalism was particularly appealing to him. Yet such inclinations could have been readily satisfied within the other, more prominent, nationalistic parties. It is true that Ba'thi radicalism provided an outlet for the unbounded energies and discontentments of the young Tikriti, but so could have the rest of the radical factions that abounded at the time in Iraq. The main reason for Hussein's preference for the Ba'th over the seemingly more promising alternatives seems therefore to be less romantic and more prosaic, less related to his ideological predilections than to his relations with his uncle and foster father, Khairallah Talfah.

Khairallah probably had the most influence on molding Saddam's character. It was he who played the role of father to the boy and was his object of male identification. As both model and mentor, he nurtured the nationalistic sentiments of the young Saddam. He introduced Saddam to people who were to play a key role in his rise to power, including the future President, Ahmad Hasan al-Bakr, Khairallah's cousin and close friend throughout the 1940s and 1950s. Following in his uncle's footsteps, Hussein applied to the prestigious Baghdad Military Academy, but failed the entrance examinations. His unfulfilled desire to don an officer's uniform was to haunt Saddam Hussein for nearly two decades until in 1976, while number two in the Iraqi leadership, the man who had never served in the Iraqi military had the rank of General conferred upon him by his then superior, President Bakr.

In Hussein's eyes, Khairallah, who became headmaster of a local school following his expulsion from the army, was an intellectual "who understood the value of going to school." What kind of values the uncle managed to instill in his nephew is not entirely clear. To judge by Khairallah's public and political behavior in future years, however, it would seem that his home provided a useful workshop in which Saddam took his first lessons in manipulation and intrigue, vital tools for survival in the devious corridors of the Iraqi political system....

A Youthful Militant

That Saddam Hussein was a man of action rather than of letters, an operator rather than an intellectual, was evident from his earliest days of political activity. A low-ranking new member of the Ba'th, Saddam's initial assignment was to incite his high-schoolmates into anti-government activities. This he did with great enthusiasm, rallying the students (as well as some local thugs) into an organized gang that struck fear into the hearts of many inhabitants of his Baghdad suburb of Karkh by beating political opponents and innocent passers-by. In late 1958, at the age of 21, Saddam was implicated in the murder of a government official in his hometown of Tikrit and thrown into jail. He was released six months later, apparently due to insufficient evidence against him. However, shortly after this initial notoriety, he was given, together with several other young and relatively obscure Ba'thists, his most important party assignment until then: participation in an attempt on the life of Iraq's ruler, General Abd al-Karim Qassem.

Relations between the Ba'th and Qassem, who headed a group of "Free Officers" in overthrowing the Hashemite monarchy in a bloody coup on July 14, 1958, were initially warm. The Ba'thists wholeheartedly embraced the coup. They did not hesitate to participate in Qassem's cabinet and to capitalize on the nationalist fervor which swept the country in order to expand their narrow popular base and to consolidate their organization. Yet relations quickly soured as the two parties found themselves hopelessly polarized over the key political issue facing Iraq at the time: whether or not to join the Syro-Egyptian union called the United Arab Republic (UAR), established in February 1958. This was a political union of Egypt and Syria, with Nasser as its President and Cairo as its capital. Yemen joined in 1958 to form a federation called the United Arab States. The union was, however, short-lived, for Syria withdrew in 1961, soon followed by Yemen.

While the Iraqi Ba'thists, like their Syrian counterparts, pressed for a speedy merger with Egypt, which they viewed as a major stride toward the ultimate unification of the "Arab nation," Qassem was vehemently opposed to such a move. His position was essentially pragmatic. He would not transform Iraq into yet another part of an Egyptian-dominated wider state....

Anxious to shore up his position against what he perceived as an imminent threat to his leadership, Qassem swiftly took on the "unionists.".... Simultaneously, as a result of its support for the union, the Ba'th Party rapidly lost its newly acquired influence in military and political institutions, with many Party members being thrown into the overcrowded prisons. In his struggle against the "unionists," Qassem chose to rely on the communists, whose influence consequently grew. In a desperate bid to stem this mounting tide of communist influence, in March 1959 non-Ba'thist Arab nationalist officers staged an abortive uprising in the northern city of Mosul. Qassem's retribution was prompt and ominous. One of the bloodiest episodes in Iraq's modern political history ensued. The communist militias were given a free hand in Mosul to take revenge. Rapes, murders, lootings, summary trials and executions in front of cheering mobs followed. Hundreds lost their lives, most of them Arab nationalists.

The horrors of the Mosul massacre forced the Ba'th underground. They were now convinced that Iraq's salvation lay with the killing of Qassem. Despite the growing deterioration in Qassem's relations with the communists, following yet another massacre carried out in Kirkuk, this conclusion remained unchanged. Hence, in the early evening hours of October 7, 1959, a group of young Ba'th activists, including Saddam, ambushed Qassem's car on his way home from his office and shot him at close range. Wounded, but narrowly escaping death, the shaken dictator ordered a nationwide clampdown on the Ba'th Party from his hospital bed. Although the ensuing purge severely disrupted the Party's organization and curbed its activities, the defiant stand of many Ba'thists in the public trials which were held put them in the national spotlight and exposed the still-small party to widespread recognition and respect.

The abortive attempt on Qassem's life became a major landmark in the evolution of the Iraqi Ba'th, as well as in the life of Saddam Hussein. Suddenly he emerged from complete obscurity to become one of the country's most wanted men....

Escape and Exile

Saddam managed to cross the border to Syria where he was very warmly received by the Ba'th leadership, then part of the joint leadership of the United Arab Republic. Michel Aflaq, a founding father of the Party and its chief ideologue, reportedly took a personal interest in the young political exile and promoted him to the highest rank of Party membership, full member.... In 1964, largely due to Aflaq's efforts on his behalf, he was elected to the Iraqi Party's highest decision-making body, the Regional Command....

In February 1960, after a pleasant stay of three months in Damascus, Saddam left for Cairo, still the undisputed center of pan-Arabism.... The Egyptian capital abounded with political activists and exiles of all sorts, and Saddam quickly integrated into this vibrant community. Together with his close friend Abd al-Karim al-Shaykhli, who had also participated in the abortive attempt on Qassem's life, he joined the local Egyptian branch of the Ba'th Party. Within a short while Saddam became a member of its Regional Command. Yet, his foremost preoccupation in the Egyptian capital had less to do with revolutionary activity than with the advancement of his formal education. In 1961, at the age of 24, he finally graduated from high school in Cairo, and a year later he enrolled for law studies at the University of Cairo....

The Egyptian period in Hussein's life ended in February 1963 when the Ba'th Party in Iraq, together with sympathetic military officers, managed to overwhelm Qassem and to seize power. Like the ascendancy of the deposed regime, five years earlier, the Ba'thi takeover was excessively bloody. Qassem and some of his close associates were immediately executed and his supporters, the communists in particular, combatted the army and the Ba'thi militia, the National Guard, in the streets of Baghdad for several days. By the time they had laid down their weapons, between 1,500 and 5,000 people had perished. This, however, did not end the bloodshed. Having established themselves in power, the Ba'thists turned to settle scores with political opponents. Thousands of leftists and communists were arrested and tortured. Hundreds were executed.

Coming Home to Chaos

Saddam, nevertheless, had nothing to do with these events. Upon arriving in Baghdad he found himself very much an outsider. At the time of his escape from Iraq he had been too junior in the Party to build up a power base, and his three years in Egypt had kept him isolated from its development. Hussein's major credential, participating in the attempt on Qassem's life, failed now to buy him a ticket to the Party's inner circle. The frustrated young man had, therefore, to linger on the fringes of the newly installed Ba'thi administration and to content himself with the minor position of a member of the Party's central bureau for peasants. Without delay, he began building up his position within the Party by joining the faction co-headed by his fellow Tikriti and blood relative Brigadier Ahmad Hasan al-Bakr, who now served as

Prime Minister of Iraq, and Colonel Salih Mahdi Ammash, the Defense Minister.

Hardly had the Ba'th gained power when it was torn by a bitter ideological struggle between two main rival camps. The first, a leftist and militant group headed by the Party's Secretary-General, Ali Salih al-Sa'di, preached a fundamental, rapid transformation of the Iraqi socio-political system to a socialist state. It was opposed by a dovish, right-wing faction that advocated a more gradual evolution to socialism and supported collaboration with non-Ba'thist military officers. Among its members was the-then Commander of the Air Force, General Hardan al-Tikriti. Bakr's faction struck a middle course between these two extremes with a certain bias toward the right-wing camp. This centrist faction lacked the ideological commitment and political zeal of the other two camps. It did not share their willingness to commit political suicide for a theoretical position. Practical and pragmatic to the core, Bakr and his associates worked assiduously to reconcile the rival wings. They knew that the Party's only hope lay in its unity. Either it stuck together or it would hang together.

They were fighting a hopeless rearguard action. Not heeding words of moderation, the extremist factions continued their relentless infighting. In a special session of the Party's Regional Command on November 11, 1963, the leftist group was expelled from the Party. Secretary-General Sa'di and four of his closest aides were arrested during the session, driven to the airport and flown to exile in Spain. This coup sparked off a wave of violence in Baghdad, bringing the capital to the verge of civil war. The National Guard, Sa'di's political instrument, raged in the streets, killing and looting. In a desperate attempt to mediate a compromise solution, a high-ranking Syrian delegation headed by Michel Aflaq rushed to Iraq, only to realize that reconciliation was no longer feasible and that the only way out of the crisis was to purge the Party of the two extremist camps. Within a day, the visiting members of the National Command expelled the right-wing group from the Regional Command, and its leaders found themselves on a plane to Beirut.

By way of filling the ensuing power vacuum in the Iraqi leadership, the National Command in Damascus stepped on the scene and assumed responsibility over the Iraqi branch. This proved a fatal mistake. With the Iraqi Ba'th leadership effectively removed and the National Command's interference in Iraqi politics viewed by the public as a blatant violation of their country's sovereignty, the Party's national standing plummeted to its lowest point. This in turn enabled President Abd al-Salam Aref, who had been installed in his position by the Ba'th as a titular figure, to move against his previous benefactors. In November 1963, after nine turbulent months at the helm, the Ba'th found itself outside the corridors of power.

Their ouster was a traumatic event in Ba'thist history. The general feeling was one of a great loss, of a missed historic opportunity. A soul-searching process began amid an acrimonious exchange of accusations and a strenuous jockeying for positions. Yet, just as the general good does not necessarily benefit every single individual, so a collective adversity does not bode ill for all. For Saddam Hussein, the Party's setback was a blessing in disguise, a major turning point in his career which would transform him within a few years into one of the most powerful figures in the Party.

As a junior member in the centrist faction of the ruling Ba'thi administration, Hussein's chances for rapid promotion had been virtually nil, given the prior balance of forces within the Party. Once the Ba'th had been thrown into disarray, however, new promising avenues were opened to the young and ambitious Tikriti. By the mid-1960s Bakr's camp had developed into the dominant power within the Ba'th. Bakr himself was elected in 1964 as a member of the National Command and a year later he became Secretary-General of the Iraqi Regional Command. And, in his train, Saddam followed. He quickly gained Bakr's trust, becoming his close confidant and, ultimately, his right-hand man.

The reward for his fidelity followed soon after. In February 1964 the Seventh Congress of the National Command sought to invigorate the debilitated Iraqi branch by establishing a provisional Regional Command that excluded those involved in the Party's fall from power. Due to Michel Aflaq's efforts, and Bakr's support, Hussein was appointed Secretary of the new organ. When the permanent Regional Command was re-established later that year, the two introduced their young protégé into this institution as well.

Becoming Emboldened

From his first moments in the Party's supreme decision-making body, Hussein was adamant on assuming responsibility for security affairs. If there was one single lesson he drew from his experience, it was that in the violent Iraqi political world there was no substitute for physical force; that physical force was indispensable both for coming to power and staying there, as well as for subordinating any and all political factions to one's will. It was armed force which had enabled Qassem to overthrow the monarchy in 1958 and which then accounted for his own destruction five years later....

Hence, if the Ba'th were to return to power, it would have to be achieved through military means....

As one of the few senior Party members outside prison during Aref's purge of the Party, Hussein faced an agonizing decision: either to try to escape to Syria and continue the struggle from there, or to stay in Baghdad and run the likely risk of being caught and arrested. Choosing the second alternative, he defied the National Command in Damascus which instructed him to leave for the Syrian capital. The reasons for this decision are not difficult to gauge. Fleeing Iraq at the time when most of the Ba'th leaders, including Bakr, were rotting in jail was likely to be interpreted as an act of cowardice which could tarnish Hussein's prospects within the Party. Masterminding the Ba'thi campaign against the regime, on the other hand, contained the seeds of future glory and involved far smaller risks than those he had already run during the attempt on Qassem's life a few years earlier. No death penalty awaited Hussein this time. The gravest punishment he faced was to join his colleagues behind bars which could only "martyr" him on "the altar of the revolution."

Given this balance of risks and opportunities, Hussein's decision to remain in Baghdad seemed reasonable. Like the numerous risky decisions he was to take in subsequent years, this move was anything but impetuous; rather it was made after a careful consideration of the costs and benefits involved. As in many of Hussein's future actions, the calculated risk paid off, though not without paving a certain price: in mid-October 1964 Hussein's hideout was surrounded by security forces, and, after an exchange of fire, he ran out of ammunition and was forced to give himself up.

Hussein's account of his two years in Aref's prison is conspicuously reminiscent of the prison term served by another young revolutionary whom the Iraqi leader has unabashedly admitted admiring: Joseph Stalin. He "imposed upon himself a rigid discipline, rose early, worked hard, read much, and was one of the chief debaters in the prison commune." This routine enabled

Hussein to sharpen his skills and assert his leadership over fellow political prisoners. More importantly, he managed to maintain close contacts with Bakr, who had already been released, by transmitting and receiving messages hidden under the robe of his baby son, Udai, who was brought by [his wife] Sajidah on her weekly visits to the prison. Hussein had already established himself as Bakr's closest aide, the "fixer" who would handle all bureaucratic and organizational problems, the single-minded strategist whose determination to reinstate the Ba'th in power would not be sidetracked by ideological or moral niceties. The extent of Bakr's confidence in his younger associate was best illustrated when he later appointed Hussein Deputy Secretary-General of the Iraqi Regional Command.

Like many other stories relating to his underground days, Saddam's road to freedom from behind bars was to become part of the Saddam legend. According to the escape plan which was devised by Saddam, together with two other Ba'thist friends, Abd al-Karim al-Shaykhli and Hasan al-Amiri, the three were to persuade the guards accompanying them to court to stop at a certain Baghdadi restaurant for lunch. Two of them were then to go to the washroom, which opened directly to the street, and to get away by a special car that would be waiting for them. The third was to engage the guards and try to persuade them to desert. The scheme was executed as planned. Amiri remained behind while Saddam and Shaykhli left the room, rushed into a car which was waiting outside with the doors open, and were driven away by Sa'dun Shakir, Saddam's cousin and an active Ba'thist. . . .

Hussein concentrated on reconstructing the Party's organization in Iraq, but not before purging the remaining leftists in the ranks of the Ba'th. He completed the formation of the Party's security apparatus (which he personally headed), laid the foundations for a new party militia, and expanded the Party's network of branches throughout Iraq. Above all, together with Ahmad Hasan al-Bakr and a narrow circle of associates, he began to calculatingly weave a tangled web which was to close on President Aref a couple of years later.

The Ba'thist conspiracy was largely facilitated by a rather lenient attitude on the part of the Iraqi authorities toward the Party's activities. In April 1966 the Iraqi President, Abd al-Salam Aref died in a helicopter crash and his brother, Abd al-Rahman Aref, assumed the Presidency. A weak and colorless character, . . .

Aref sought to improve his position by using the carrot rather than the stick. Repression of Ba'thist activities eased significantly, and on several occasions the President even sounded out the Party's readiness to collaborate with the regime. This, in turn, enabled the Ba'th to consolidate its power base and to wait patiently for the right moment for a renewed bid for power.

Ruthless Rule Yields Social Progress

BY SAMIR AL-KHALIL

The Ba'ath Party seized power briefly in 1963 and again in 1968. After the 1968 coup, the party avoided the mistakes of 1963 and effectively consolidated its power. Although he was not initially part of the central leadership and did not officially become the head of state of Iraq until 1979, Saddam Hussein was instrumental in the Ba'ath takeover. He also played a critical role in the Ba'ath's solidifying and extending its power over the nation.

Samir al-Khalil is the pseudonym of Kanan Makiya, an Iraqi expatriate journalist who wrote an insider exposé of the Ba'ath regime and the rule of Saddam Hussein titled Republic of Fear: The Inside Story of Saddam's Iraq. *The following excerpt from that work describes the harsh and ruthless measures taken by Hussein and the Ba'ath in imposing their rule, but it also identifies improvements in Iraqi society that took place under the Ba'ath regime. In particular, the excerpt reviews progress in the education and literacy levels of the population and the greater socioeconomic status enjoyed by women.*

The seriousness with which the Ba'th treat their ideological assertions materializes in its most deadly form in their organization of youth. Primary school children are organized in the Pioneers; boys and girls between the ages of ten and fifteen in the Vanguards (*tala'i'a*); and youth between fifteen and twenty in the Youth Organization (*futuwwa*). These are not the boy scouts; they contribute to the revolution and the Ba'th party. The 1974 congress of the ABSP [Arab Ba'th Socialist Party] summed up the party's ambitions in this regard:

Samir al-Khalil, *Republic of Fear: The Inside Story of Saddam's Iraq.* New York: Pantheon Books, 1989. Copyright © 1989 by The Regents of the University of California. Reproduced by permission.

What has so far been achieved in this domain represents only a beginning. It falls far short of the Party's ambitions and the needs of the new phase.... The Party itself must exert great and urgent efforts to promote the activities of youth organizations. They must come to embrace a majority of our young people, boys and girls, and contribute actively to cultivating Pan-Arab and socialist principles among them, inspiring them with the vision and educating them in the ways that will allow them fully to participate in revolutionary construction, national defence and Pan-Arab tasks.

Within a few years of the eighth congress [held by the Ba'th party in 1974], most Iraqi youth were passing through the youth organizations. Members take oaths, wear uniforms, and are organized in a hierarchy that resembles that of the Ba'th party. The Vanguard, founded in 1973, is probably the most important among the three; it has national, regional, and local congresses that elect a "Central Office," which in turn elects a "Core Committee." None of these organizations, held together under the umbrella of the General Federation of Iraqi Youth, are formally party bodies. They belong to the state. The party has its own youth front organization called the Partisans. But as members gather in their weekly cell meetings held at school, they are instructed in party ways and general principles of "the transformation process" by the highest-ranking party members or sympathizers available. They are asked to write reports and provide other information. Although membership is not compulsory, the fear of nonconformism makes it so. Ten-year-olds on up have been organized in this way for many years now in Iraq. Their injection with Ba'thist ideas started many years before that, when they first entered school at the age of five or six.

Government Intrusiveness

Ba'thism's radicalism lies in its willingness to harness the power accumulated through this kind of organization to break down cherished boundaries taken for granted by society. Consider the chilling implications of these words by Saddam Husain on the private, hitherto inviolable world of the Arab family:

To prevent the father and mother dominating the household with backwardness, we must make the small one radiate internally to expel it. Some fathers have slipped away from us for various reasons, but the small boy is still in our hands and we must transform him into an interactive radiating centre inside the family through all the hours that he spends with his parents to change their condition for the better. We must also keep him away from bad influences.

... The unity of the family must not be based on backward concepts, but on congruence with centralizing mores derived from the policies and traditions of the revolution in its construction of the new society. Whenever there is a conflict between the unity of the family and these mores, ... it must be resolved in the favour of the new mores. ...

You must surround adults [the word used is *tatwia*, which has the sense of closing all avenues of escape] through their sons, in addition to other means. Teach the student to object to his parents if he hears them discussing state secrets and to alert them that this is not correct. Teach them to criticize their mothers and fathers respectfully if they hear them talking about organizational and party secrets. You must place in every corner a son of the revolution, with a trustworthy eye and a firm mind that receives its instructions from the responsible centre of the revolution. ... Teach him to object, with respect, to either of his parents should he discover them wasting the state's wealth which he should let them know is dearer to him than his own; for he would not have personal property if the state did not have its wealth, and this property belongs to society. ... Also teach the child at this stage to beware of the foreigner, for the latter is a pair of eyes for his country and some of them are saboteurs of the revolution. Therefore, accompanying foreigners and talking with them in the absence of known controls is forbidden. Plant in the child's soul a vigilance not to give the foreigner anything of state or party secrets. Also he must warn others, young and old alike, in a respectful way, that they also should not talk in front of foreigners. ... The child in his relationship to the teacher is like a piece of raw

> marble in the hands of a sculptor who has the power to impart aesthetic form, or discard the piece to the ravages of time and the vagaries of nature.

To dismiss these passages as the musings of a demented albeit powerful personality abstracts from the long history of a movement that has consistently laid stress on this conception of education....

Although compulsory education laws had been passed after 1958, not until the 1970s were all Iraqi children attending school. The content of education was changed with the same vigour.

> The next five years must be devoted to building an educational system compatible with the principles and aims of the Party and the Revolution....
>
> In the next phase there can be no question of putting up with the slow development of this domain in the last period. Time is not on the side of the Revolution....
>
> New syllabuses must at once be prepared for every level from nursery school to university, inspired by the principles of the party and the Revolution.... Reactionary bourgeois and liberal ideas and trends in the syllabus and the educational institutions must be rooted out. The new generation must be immunized against ideologies and cultures conflicting with our Arab nation's basic aspirations and its aim for unity, liberty and socialism. [ABSP, *Political Report*] 171–72.

From an illiteracy rate of 99.5 percent in the last years of the Ottoman rule, to 81.7 percent in 1957, the rate for the early 1980s can be inferred at significantly less than 50 percent. This turnaround was largely due to measures taken after 1968, which coincided with underlying demographic trends. Among illiterate adults, however, Ba'thist resolve was also very striking. In May 1978 the "Comprehensive National Campaign for Compulsory Eradication of Illiteracy" was promulgated by the RCC [Revolutionary Command Council]. The Minister of Education and representatives from the Ministry of Defence, internal security forces, the ABSP, and the mass organizations formed a Supreme Council, which was replicated at the governate and local council levels. This method of organizing the campaign was linked to party resolutions dating back to 1963 and also to the "historical decisions" taken at the eighth regional congress of the ABSP in 1974, which specified the involvement of the army and the internal security forces in the campaign.

All illiterates between the ages of fifteen and forty-five had to attend assigned adult education classes. A time limit of twenty-one months (reduced from thirty-six) was set for the eradication of illiteracy in this category—technically unfeasible and an operational nightmare, but typically Ba'thist. Laws stipulated that those who failed to attend would become ineligible for employment in the public and private sectors, for any government licenses, and for all bank loans. They also faced imprisonment and a fine. By 1981 around 2 million people had passed through a designated programme either in one of the 1,779 Anti-Illiteracy Centres or in one of the 21,853 People's Schools established throughout the country. In 1965 there had been a mere 368 adult literacy centres in Iraq. By 1979, UNESCO was giving the Supreme Council an award for having "harnessed in a remarkable way the country's full energies in promoting a far-reaching literacy campaign."

A Stampede to Education

For a while the country was gripped by a feverish campaign. Hundreds of thousands of people were enrolled using various public buildings, "floating schools" in the southern marshes region, and "travelling schools" in remote villages and nomadic areas. The mass media, trade unions, and state organizations were all mobilized. Special programmes were broadcast on radio and television. Daily literacy lessons were televised. Prisoners were informed that educational achievement under incarceration would be taken into account in the remission of sentences. Significantly, the majority of those enrolled in the literacy programs were Shi'ites because of the higher rates of illiteracy known to prevail in the south. Needless to say, education at all levels and of all categories was free. This 1974 exemption from costs applied to books and all other educational material.

A later administrative regulation issued by the president's office attempted to sort out the responsibilities and lines of authority of the various officials who were by now falling over each other trying to get the campaign to meet its stated objectives. It listed the registers that each centre must keep, and the files that had to be opened on each student. Article 12 imposed the criterion on all teachers in the campaign that they "be bound by the principles of the ABSP" in the execution of their duties.

The 1978 legislation combatting illiteracy defined an illiterate as a person who could not read and write and as someone who "did not reach the civilized level." One reached this level "provided" that these skills "enable him to undertake the duties and rights of citizenship." The knowledge gained "should be continuous and developing" and bound up "with the movement of society and aims of the Arab nation in Unity, Freedom and Socialism."

These and other measures created a new audience held in thrall to Ba'thist ideological productions whose chief characteristic was that it had never existed before. Terror campaigns to weed out that "old generation" of intellectuals associated with another world's inbuilt elitism (if by no means ever advocates of it) were thus combined from the outset with laying down the groundwork for a society made up of mass consumers of ideological artifacts....

The Status of Women

In 1965, 12 percent of adult literacy centres were for women, although female illiterates outnumbered males by more than two to one. A national breakdown for 1980 is not available. However, *al-Jumhuriyya* [an Iraqi daily national newspaper] reported that out of one batch of 762 people's schools, 416 were for women and 31 were mixed. By the fourth grade the proportion of women increased, presumably because the men were dropping out faster (the illiteracy centres and people's schools that follow on from them have their own grading system). Moreover, nursery and childcare facilities were available in many of the new centres.

The entry of women into the educational system as a whole is another noteworthy Ba'thist accomplishment. In 1970–71, there were 318,524 girls in primary school, 88,595 at the secondary level, and 9,212 at the university level. For the 1979–80 school year the absolute numbers were respectively as follows: 1,165,856, 278,485, and 28,647.

By 1980 women accounted for 46 percent of all teachers, 29 percent of physicians, 46 percent of dentists, 70 percent of pharmacists, 15 percent of accountants, 14 percent of factory workers, and 16 percent of civil servants. It has even been claimed that in the Ministry of Oil in 1980, 37 percent of the design staff and 30 percent of the construction supervisors were women. The State Organization of Buildings is another government department technically staffed by many women. Women's participation in senior management, however, was 4 percent overall in 1980 and showed no sign of rising. Generally the total participation of women in the nonagricultural labour force rose from 7 percent in 1968 to 19 percent in 1980.

The labour and civil service laws promulgated to bring about these trends include equal pay and opportunity measures, preferential hiring regulations in government departments, paid maternity leave, childcare facilities at the workplace, and a reduced retirement age for working women.

As in the case of youth, women are organized in a General Federation for Iraqi Women. It has 18 branches, 1 in each province of Iraq, 265 subsections based on major towns, 755 centres that incorporate villages with more than 200 families or quarters of cities with more than 6,000 people, and an additional 1,612 liaison committees that extend to all remaining villages and quarters. Conferences and elections determine a General Council out of which a Central Council of thirty-eight members is elected and an Executive Bureau chosen. In short women were not only learning to read, entering higher education, and forging ahead in the labour force, they were, like everyone else, being thoroughly organized.

These important changes in the social role of women ought to be considered alongside the 1978 amendments to the Code of Personal Status introduced by the Ba'th. The preamble states that the new code is based on "the principles of the Islamic *shari'a* [Islamic law], but only those that are suited to the spirit of today." The break with tradition as it affected women occurred in two important areas: first, authority was given to a state-appointed judge to overrule the wishes of the father in the case of early marriages; second, the new legislation nullified forced marriages and severely curtailed the traditional panoply of rights held over women by the men of the larger kinship group (uncles, cousins, and so on). The intent of the legislation as a whole was to diminish the power of the patriarchal family, and separate out the nuclear family from the larger kinship group whose hold over the lives of women was considerably weakened....

In the 1977 law regulating women's entry into the armed

forces, no mention was made of any military functions. However, enrolled women were considered completely subject to all military regulations, with the exception of "what does not conform with her nature." The law stipulated that a woman may be appointed as an officer if she carried a university degree in a health-related field (medicine, dentistry, pharmacy). Her rank descended from a low-set level on a scale carefully correlating health-related qualifications to military title (for example, a nursing qualification of not less than two years' study attracts the rank of sergeant second-grade). Clearly the army was absorbing women because of their dominant position in the health services. Much the same story applies to women's entry into the popular militia forces, which started in 1976. By 1982 some 40,000 women had been enrolled.

These nonetheless bold legislative steps must be set against the surprising mildness of the reforms in those areas that most directly affected women as individuals: polygamy, divorce, and inheritance. Here male dominance in the spirit of Islamic law held sway, albeit with some reforms to the letter of the *shari'a* in the case of adultery (no longer called *zina* in the new code, but *khiyana zawjiyya*—marital treachery)....

Ba'th Achievement

A regime of terror actually presided over an across-the-board increase in the standard of living in Iraq, and it significantly improved the lot of the most destitute layers, furthering the levelling of income differentials that began after 1958. The changes are impressive: the prices of most basic necessities were stabilized by state subsidy; the minimum daily wage greatly increased over the rate of inflation, which was kept low; new labour laws provided complete job security; the state became an employer of last resort for all graduates; free education and health care was provided; and per-capita national income increased from 195 Iraqi dinar (ID) in 1970 to 7,564 ID in 1979.

The Iran-Iraq War

BY SANDRA MACKEY

Once Saddam Hussein took full control of the Iraqi government, he showed that he would be militant not just domestically but in international matters as well. In 1980 Hussein provoked a major war with neighboring Iran, a war that would last until 1988 and prove to be one of the most destructive in history. As costly as the war was for Iraq, some observers claim that Iraq emerged from the conflict as the beneficiary. Though there was still dissent and division within Iraq, the Ba'ath Party's campaign to win public support through improved social conditions was successful enough to produce widespread support for the war. And the threat of a foreign power overpowering Iraq, which became real during the conflict when Iran launched several successful offensives into Iraq, helped bring diverse factions within Iraq together for the sake of defending their homeland. Even the Shia Muslims in the south, who had often been strongly opposed to the Sunni-dominated central government in Baghdad, proved loyal to Iraq during the war, despite the fact that Iran was ruled by Shia Muslims who urged their Iraqi brethren to rise up against Hussein's Ba'ath regime. The following excerpt from Sandra Mackey's book The Reckoning: Iraq and the Legacy of Saddam Hussein *chronicles and analyzes the Iran-Iraq War. Sandra Mackey's credits as a journalist include commentary on the Middle East for CNN.*

The Iran-Iraq War ranks as the longest conventional war of the twentieth century. Often called the First Gulf War, it killed at least a million people, wounded another 2 million, engaged almost 40 percent of the adult male population of both countries, and cost roughly $1,190 billion in economic terms. The societal costs remain incalculable, as both belligerents—one employing chemical weapons, the other child soldiers—cast aside humanity in the name of war.

For the revolutionaries of Iran, the war was waged for Islam and the protection of the soil of Iran. For Iraq, it was a war fought to protect the rule of Saddam Hussein and the territorial

Sandra Mackey, *The Reckoning: Iraq and the Legacy of Saddam Hussein.* New York: W.W. Norton & Company, Inc., 2002. Copyright © 2002 by Sandra Mackey. Reproduced by permission of the publisher.

integrity of the fragile Iraqi state. In an uneven contest of competing identities, [Iran's Ayatollah] Khomeini carried into battle 2,500 years of Iranian cultural continuity. Hussein threw into the conflict a country void of any clear sense of itself, claiming a history of only half a century. Iran, emotionally and militarily crippled by the tumult of the Iranian revolution of 1979, survived against Iraq's far superior war machine precisely because the Iranians were called to defend the hallowed territory of their historic homeland. Iraq survived because five decades of nation building using the bricks of education, economics, and culture had persuaded the majority of the Arab Shia that their identity resided more with Arab Iraq than with Shia Iran....

Historic Hostility

The roots of conflict between Iraq and Iran run deep. They germinated in the Persian conquest of Mesopotamia in the fourth century B.C. and took root in the competition for control of Mesopotamia between the Sunni Ottoman Empire and the Shia dynasties of Persia. They grew through centuries of endless disputes over borders, land, navigation rights, and sovereignty. And they became entangled in the issues of ethnicity, religion, and culture that pitted Semitic Arab against Aryan Persian, Sunni against Shia. In 1969, a new phase of conflict erupted when Iran's Muhammad Reza Shah launched his own version of the Persian Empire by challenging Iraq's exclusive claim to the Shatt al Arab. Less than two years later, on March 1, 1971, when Britain began its much-heralded withdrawal of its naval forces from "east of Suez," the Iranian king jumped into the resulting vacuum of power. Intent on snatching hegemony in the Persian Gulf away from all would-be rivals, he granted diplomatic recognition to the government of the island state of Bahrain with its majority Shia population and revived Iran's claim to the forlorn but strategic islands of Abu Musa and Greater and Lesser Tunbs. Desolate spots of land, they are located at the mouth of the Strait of Hormuz, Iraq's sole outlet from the Persian Gulf to the Indian Ocean. Charging Iran with denying Iraq access to the open seas, Baghdad severed diplomatic relations with Iran. But protest did little to quell the shah's expansionist appetite. For reasons of geography, ethnicity, and economics, Muhammad Reza's ambitions posed a direct threat to Iraq's increasingly important oil industry. In the northern Kurdish region, which produced nearly 65 percent of Iraq's crude oil the year the Baath resumed power, Iran's position along the common border enabled Tehran to weaken Baghdad by goading Kurdish unrest almost at will. Feeding the Kurdish insurrection of 1971–75, Iran, in essence, conducted a surrogate war against Iraq that ended with the Algiers Agreement of 1975. Over the next four years, each side scrupulously upheld its side of the diplomatic bargain. But with the 1979 Iranian revolution that ended the reign of Muhammad Reza Shah, all previous problems between Arab Iraq and Persian Iran were revived. Added to the bitter mix was Iranian incitement of religious revolution among the Shia of Iraq against the secular Baath government sitting in Baghdad. To Saddam Hussein, this was the poisonous seed that produced the Iran-Iraq War.

In a sense, the war between Iraq and Iran began with two Persians: Muhammad Reza Shah and Ayatollah Ruhollah Khomeini. Their contest to determine whether Iran lived as a secular state under the rule of a king, or a theocracy in which the most renowned *mujtahid* [exalted Islamic jurist] acted as the final arbiter of political power, unfolded largely outside the purview of Iraq. As in the plot line of a grand drama, Khomeini became a mullah in 1926, the same year the Pahlavi dynasty mounted the throne of Iran. For the next three decades, the stern Shia cleric built a reputation as a teacher and Islamic scholar. By the 1950s, he had achieved recognition among the Shia as an exceptional legal talent. In 1963, Ayatollah Khomeini's religious influence crossed into the realm of politics. When Muhammad Reza Shah announced his White Revolution, a program of reforms that included the distribution of clerical lands to the peasants and the emancipation of women, Khomeini sternly warned the Muslim community of the imminent dangers the shah posed to the Koran. From the religious center of Qom in that year of 1963, Khomeini pointed his finger at the Peacock Throne and spoke the prophetic words, "Oh Allah, I have performed my first duty and if you allow me to live longer and permit me, I shall shoulder other tasks in the future."

Moral authority waged with words met secular authority enforced with armed might when the soldiers of Muhammad Reza Shah attempted to silence dissent by storming the revered Faiziyeh Theological School in Qom where Khomeini taught. In the collision, two students died armed with nothing but their Korans. Forty days later, Khomeini led thousands in the traditional Shia mourning ceremonies for the dead. One symbolic act followed another until days of rioting during June 1963 engulfed Mashhad, Isfahan, Shiraz, and Qom. In 1964 when Khomeini again sent his followers into the streets—this time to denounce a military agreement between Iran and the United States—the shah dispatched the ayatollah into exile. Turning expulsion into allegory, Khomeini left for Turkey in November, cloaked in the imagery of the Prophet driven from Mecca by the Quraysh. Nearly a year later, he arrived in Najaf, the great theological center of Shia Islam in Iraq. He stayed for the next fourteen years, watching with great interest events in Iran as well as Iraq's own contest with Muhammad Reza Shah.

Ignited by the popular demonstrations of 1963, the forces demanding political reform of the monarchy and protection of Iranian nationalism from the influences of the United States gathered against Muhammad Reza Shah. By the mid-1970s when the shah was vigorously pursuing his empire in the Persian Gulf, much of the opposition to the Pahlavi king had gathered around Khomeini. Already sixty-three years old, Khomeini lived in a simple house located in a narrow alleyway behind Imam Ali's shrine in Najaf. Like the Prophet, he ate a meager diet, slept on an ordinary rug spread on the floor, and spent his days engaged in prayer and study. Through this asceticism and regimentation, he labored to hold himself aloof from any hint of corruption bred of materialism and worldly power. In the context of the Shia psyche, Khomeini reigned as the symbol of righteousness holding Islam's sword above an unjust ruler.

From Iraq, Khomeini preached rebellion against "the corrupt" Muhammad Reza Shah. In Iran, his network of clerics and theological students received the ayatollah's words, mimeographed them on cheap paper, and covertly distributed them through the shrines, mosques, bazaars, and lower-class urban neighborhoods. Bit by bit, Khomeini and his followers built support for revolution. Seeking to still the voice of rebellion, Muhammad Reza Shah in October 1978 exerted pressure on his old nemesis Saddam Hussein to force Khomeini out of Najaf. Fearful of the cleric's presence in the midst of his own Shia population, Hussein complied. That left an angry Khomeini to pack his family and his entourage for sanctuary in France. Still, opposition to the shah mounted. By the end of 1978, the streets of Pahlavi Iran had become conduits for massive protests, which the sympathetic soldiers of the lower ranks of the army refused to put down. In the rising anarchy, a tearful Muhammad Reza Shah arrived at Tehran's Mehrabad airport on the morning of January 16, 1979, to fly into exile. Fifteen days later, on February 1, the black turbaned Ayatollah Ruhollah Khomeini crept down the steps of a charted Air France jetliner to lay claim to the revolution for Islam.

Fundamentalist Revolution Threatens Iraq

By March 1979, Khomeini's message of Islamic revolution was reaching beyond the borders of Iran. Carrying the weight of the ayatollah's religious and political credentials, it implied that all governments considered "corrupt" by Khomeini and his foot soldiers of God would be overthrown by Islamic subversives among their own people. In Baghdad, Saddam Hussein and the secular Baath shuddered when Hassan Ahmed al-Bakr's cable to Khomeini expressing hopes of regional peace was answered by the terse phrase, "Peace is with those who follow the righteous path." The men of Baghdad knew that the theology and ideology of the Iranian revolution called to the downtrodden Shia of Iraq. Nonetheless, the imagery of revolution in the name of Islam surpassed the reality, for religion had never burrowed as deeply in Iraqi society as it did in Iranian society. Furthermore, Iraq lacked the socioeconomic infrastructure that had empowered an Islamic revolution in Iran. Still, the regime in Baghdad recognized all too well that the Iranian revolution provided a powerful catalyst for the Iraqi Shias' long smoldering resentment against Baghdad. Even more, the revolution in Iran drove home to the Baath of Iraq the ugly truth that any repressive political order could unravel if enough people defiantly pulled at the strings of authority.

As Tehran radio broadcast its Islamic rhetoric to southern Iraq, the Shia listened to the powerful theological theme of the just society, which resonated for a community already mounting a clandestine challenge to the Baath from the ramparts of religion....

Islamic Political Opposition

At the end of the [Iraqi] monarchy, the immediate threat to religion had resided in atheistic Communism. Yet in the decade of instability following the 1958 revolution, the clerics succeeded in stealing numbers of Shia out of the camp of Marxism. Already disillusioned by the meager fruits of the revolution, these recruits of religion came with the bitter taste of Communism's failure to secure a new order capable of redistributing economic and political power. With the ascension of the Baath in 1968, the Shia religious establishment once more went on the offensive against a threat to the faith. This time it was against a political party wed to a secularism that aggressively suppressed all competing groups and ideologies. In response, the Baath in the summer of 1968 attacked the anemic institutions of Shiism that had survived the repeated bleedings of previous governments. Locks closed the gates of the theological college in Najaf, strict censorship descended on religious publications, and imprisonment and deportation further reduced the already depleted ranks of the *ulama* [the clerical authority figures] and religious students. As if to pour salt into the wounds, the Baath authorized for the first time in Iraqi history the sale of alcohol in the Shia shrine cities. Propelling everything was the Baath's determination to impose secularism on Iraq.

Ideologically the Baath had always held Islam responsible for the perceived backwardness of the Arabs. But more important to the Iraqi Baath's attitude toward religion was the raw politics of power. Baath secularism invited the Shia Arabs to belong to the Iraqi state while at the same time depriving the Shia of the potent political weapon of religion that they had always exercised in Shia Iran. This is what drove the Baath's Mesopotamian theme of Iraqi culture. But the Shia clerics would not be seduced by contrived cultural identity. Instead, they damned the government's glorification of Mesopotamia's ancient pre-Islamic cultures as paganism, ignorance, and barbarism. And they called their people back to Islam, for it was through the faith that the clerics would recover their exalted position and the deprived Shia masses would find the just society of Shia theology....

Religious Devotion Turns Violent

On April 1, 1980, an Islamic militant believed to be attached to al-Dawah [a radical Shia Islamic movement in Iraq] lurked at the entrance of the old Mustansiriyah school in the heart of Baghdad. When Tariq Aziz, deputy prime minister and member of the Revolutionary Command Council, arrived to open a student conference, the messenger of political Islam rushed forward and hurled a grenade. Although Aziz escaped death, the attempted assassination of one of the pillars of the Baath regime gave Saddam Hussein the pretext to stomp the life out of the Shia political movement.

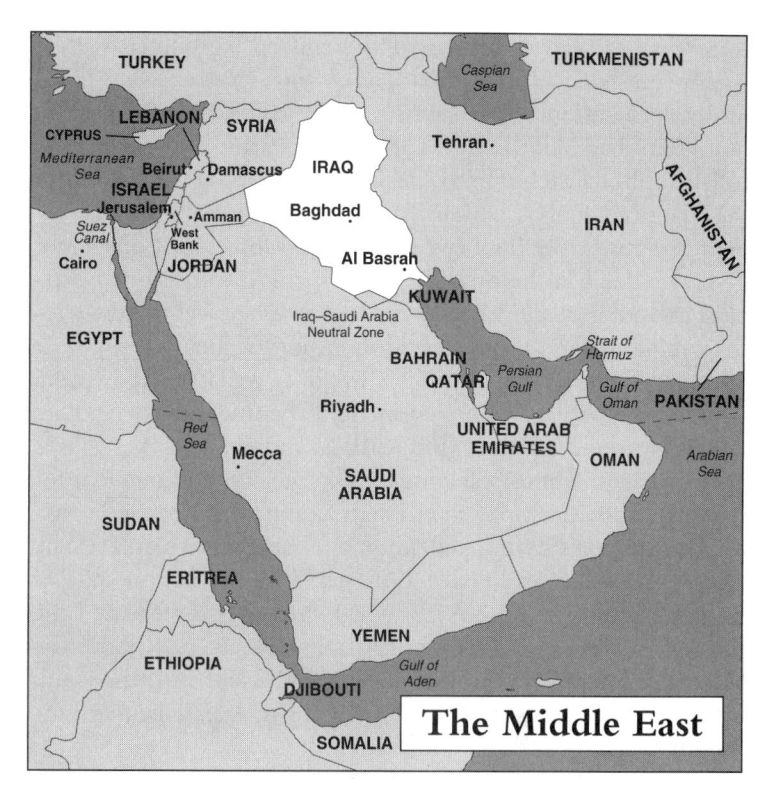

The white four-wheel-drive Toyotas of the security services rolled forth to collect thousands of Shia out of their strongholds. In Najaf, uniformed deputies of the Baath regime rousted [Muhammad Baqir] al-Sadr [a prominent Shia Islamic dissident] and his sister Amina Bint al-Huda from their house. They were thrown into the dungeons of the Baath's security system where, the Shia believe, the guardians of the regime sexually assaulted and then killed Bint al-Huda, the "daughter of righteousness," in the presence of her brother. Then the masters of torture turned on al-Sadr, the unwilling symbol of Shia resistance. After setting fire to the cleric's beard, they eliminated him from the scene of political protest by driving nails through his head. Man by man, death took the leadership of al-Dawah and other militant Islamic groups. Every Iraqi tainted by even the remotest connection with Iran—by birth, marriage, or name—faced the threat of expulsion. Since the ranks of Shia clerics were already so thin, there were no reserves ready to move into the trenches of Shia politics cleared by Hussein. That left the Shia without leaders other than the clerics appointed by Baghdad, a group characterized by their detractors as the *ulama al-hafiz*, service *ulama*. Thus, under persecution and co-option, the organized power of militant Islam died. All that was left was the warning voice of Ayatollah Ruhollah Khomeini speaking to the Iraqi military from the Islamic Republic of Iran: "I have given up hope on the upper echelons of the Iraqi law enforcement forces. But I have not given up hope in the officers, NCO's [noncommissioned officers] and soldiers and I expect them to rise heroically and to destroy the foundations of oppression ... so that they will not bear the shame of the Ba'th Party." He might as well have quoted the Koranic injunction "O believers, fight the unbelievers who are near to you, and let them find hardness in you."

Suddenly the historical conflict between Iraq and Iran that for centuries had encompassed ethnicity, culture, religion, and territory focused on Hussein and Khomeini. One was a secular Arab, the other a religious Persian. One stood for the nation-state of Iraq encased within the Arab world; the other represented the idea of an Islamic empire incorporating all Muslims under the leadership of the paramount *mujtahid*. Hussein and Khomeini faced off in a cataclysmic battle of words waged with the symbols of ethnicity, piety, and identity.

In a speech at Nineveh on April 15, 1980, Saddam Hussein drew the sword of Arabism against the offending Iranian clerics: "Iraq is once again to assume its leading Arab role. Iraq is once again to serve the Arab nation and defend its honor, dignity and sovereignty. Iraq is destined once again to face the concerted machinations of the forces of darkness." Khomeini roared back, vowing to consign the nefarious Saddam to "the trash heap of history." Khomeini's deputy, Hussein Ali Muntazari, took up his leader's message, charging that the regime of "butcher Saddam Hussein" was opposed to Islam: "I am confident that the noble blood of the martyrs of Islam will boil in the Islamic Iraqi people.... This blood will continue to boil until Saddam Hussein's regime is completely overthrown."

As the venom flowed, Hussein calculated the strength of Iran. Peering across the border, he saw a country in the throes of not one but two revolutions: the uprising against Muhammad Reza Shah and the subsequent contest between the clerics and the secularists for the right to claim the revolution. In the tumult, it looked as if every street corner in Iran from north to south, east to west, hosted a rival government. He also saw the shah's formidable military force stripped to its bones by foot soldiers turned revolutionaries and officers hanged by ropes as a precaution against a coup. Finally he saw, with accuracy, revolutionary Iran as a pariah state isolated from the international community. In the political upheaval, military disintegration, and diplomatic quarantine of his stronger neighbor, Hussein's ambitions exploded. The Iraqi president coveted complete control of the Shatt al Arab, which he equated with power in the Persian Gulf. And domination of the Gulf would give substance to Hussein's aspiration to transform Iraq into a force within the mythical Arab nation. But above everything else, Hussein gazed on the opportunity to insulate Iraq's Shia from the contagion of the Iranian revolution by eliminating the threat at its source.

Pointed Provocation

On September 17, 1980, Saddam Hussein sat down before the cameras of Iraqi television. He picked up the 1975 Algiers Agreement in which Iraq surrendered to Iran sovereignty over the Shatt al Arab and tore it to bits. Triumphantly he declared to his countrymen, "This Shatt shall again be, as it has been throughout history, Iraqi and Arab in name and reality, with all rights of full sovereignty over it." Five days later, at dawn on September 22, fifty thousand Iraqi troops hit four strategic junctions along the 730-mile-long Iran-Iraq border. While the infantry thrust forward into Iranian territory from the bleak mountain ranges of northern Kurdistan to the swamplands of oil-rich Khuzistan, Iraqi planes pounded Iran's airfields and military installations. In the Persian Gulf, the supertankers hauling black crude oil from the producers to the consumers dropped anchor to wait out what everyone assumed would be a short war between two predominately Shia countries—one Arab and one Persian. They were wrong. The Iran-Iraq War would prove to be a long, incredibly costly conflict of eight years fought in four bloody stages: the Iraqi advances of 1980–81; the Iranian counterattacks of 1982–84; the entrenchment of 1985; and the grand offensives of 1986–87, fought to end a war in which neither side could win and neither side was willing to surrender....

Physically and emotionally, the first two years of the war proved relatively painless for Iraq, especially Baghdad. The men who gathered in the neighborhood coffeehouses to smoke and play dominoes could shut their minds to the war that raged along the Shatt al Arab because this was the will of Saddam Hussein. Consumer goods, except for cigarettes and butane gas, crowded the shops, delivered by a government intent on ensuring plenty. That same government addressed personal tragedy by bestowing on the families of soldiers lost at the front enough money to buy a piece of land, a new house, and a car. This was a period in which Hussein traveled the country, stopping at random in Mosul, Basra, tribal areas of the Sunni triangle, and the Shia marshes. He visited Christian churches, nodded to the Yazidi devil worshipers, and prayed in mosques maintained by Sunnis and Shia. Constantly on the move, he visited schools, pinned badges on graduating firemen, and inaugurated water mains in obscure villages. Like the star that he was, he dressed the part, once turning up at a farm in a peasant's sheepskin vest and carrying a shepherd's staff. At Baghdad University, he was a young graduate in a cap and gown; at the race track, a desert horseman; in the oil fields, the chief engineer in a specially designed construction hat. Unique in the memory of most Iraqis, Hussein's campaign of public relations followed a preordained plot line: cultural diversity was acceptable; the central government was committed to the development of all its people regardless of religion or ethnicity; and every person in Iraq was first and foremost a citizen of the unified Iraqi state.

War's Ravages

But there was another side of the war. Soldiers in prodigious numbers were bleeding and dying on the southern front. Most of them were Shia, the enrolled and conscripted foot soldiers of the army. So it was that day after day, processions of battered taxis sped along the roads from the battlefield bearing flag-draped coffins on their roofs for delivery to the families of the fallen. Unspoken blame fell on Saddam Hussein. Then on July 11, 1982, the president entered a building in a mixed Sunni-Shia town forty miles north of Baghdad. Without warning, a group of armed men laid a barrage of gunfire on the structure, pinning Hussein inside. Two hours elapsed before heavily armed reenforcements from the army were able to rescue him. It was the second assassination attempt in four months. Amid escalating reports of unrest and attempted coups, Hussein retreated into the presidential palace. He has rarely been seen in public since.

Meanwhile the war went into its second phase. Iran's "Army

of Twenty Million," recruited from the streets and villages of revolutionary Iran, sent boys twelve, thirteen, and fourteen years old walking across minefields to clear the way for assaults against Iraqi lines. No such dedication to the war expressed itself on the Iraqi side of the border, where the Shia foot soldiers and Sunni draftees possessed neither the morale nor the motivation of their Iranian counterparts. It made a difference to the entire Iraqi war effort. With his forces driven out of Iranian territory, and unable to push back east, Hussein reduced his conditions for peace to a cease-fire and a return to the status quo ante bellum. Khomeini refused. Speaking directly to Iraq's Shia, he told them, "We are related by race, traditions, and religion.... No other government or nation in the world except Iran has the right to be concerned about Iraq's future."...

A Mounting Toll

By 1984, the conflict with Iran ate at Iraq like a cancer. In the south, Basra, which once nestled "in a belt of gardens under palm trees soft and woolley as green velvet," was bombed and burned. Sand bags stacked ten high failed to conceal the scars of the seesaw battles that had marred with bullets and shrapnel almost every wall in the center of the city. On the perimeter, houses stood deserted; on every street corner, young men swathed in bandages leaned on their crutches. To the north at Karbala, more and more caskets entered the main gate of Hussein's shrine. They were followed by grim processions of black-clad women shrieking with grief while solemn men in the time-honored rituals of death slapped themselves on the cheeks as they chanted dirges of mourning. Yet the bulk of the Shia, the sinew of Hussein's war machine, remained in the trenches to fight and to die for Iraq.

Although the Shia carried the brunt of battle, all Iraqis suffered the economic effects of the war. Before the invasion, Iraq had exported 3.3 million barrels of oil a day. But with the Persian Gulf mined by Iranian revolutionaries operating out of little more than inflated rafts and the pipeline through Syria shut off by Hafiz al-Assad, Iraq now struggled to put 700,000 to 800,000 barrels a day on the market. Most of the $35 billion in foreign reserves that were on hand when the war started were gone. So were the gold reserves. In four years, Iraq had been transformed from a capital surplus nation to a debtor nation living on transfusions of money from two major donors—Kuwait and Saudi Arabia—both of whom harbored their own fears of the Iranian revolution. To cope, the government cut the generous payments to the families of those killed on the battlefield and banned the import of luxury goods, including cars, watches, television sets, and some clothing. Government edict collected gold wedding jewelry. And raging inflation crippled the middle class that had been so carefully nurtured by Baath economic policies. As the value of the dinar slid from $3.30 toward $.90, an Iraqi could no longer boast, "We have been spoiled with the good life, a lot of money and no poverty."...

The Conflict Widens

In July 1986, the war entered its fourth phase as military action dramatically shifted from land to sea. Attempting to strangle the Islamic Republic economically by shutting its oil exports off from Iran's main oil terminal at Kharg island, Iraq sent its superior planes and missiles out over the Persian Gulf. Since Iraqi shipping in the Gulf had already been shut off in 1984, Iran retaliated by hitting the ships of Iraq's Arab allies. Suddenly Hussein's war touched the Gulf states. Saudi Arabia hunkered down, but Kuwait screamed for help. The United States, reacting both to the imperative to keep oil flowing out of the Gulf and to bottle up an Iranian government bent on driving the West from the Islamic world, put a flotilla in the Gulf to keep navigation open. Tensions and insurance rates skyrocketed. But the "tanker war" failed to break Iran. From Tehran, Khomeini vowed to fight as long as Hussein ruled Iraq....

The Final Offensives

On February 29, 1988, [Iraq sent] seventeen Soviet Scud missiles crashing into Tehran. For the next four and a half months, one attack after another tore at Iranian morale as bombs hit the revered Friday Mosque in Isfahan and the shrine city of Qom. Chemical weapons recaptured the vital Fao Peninsula, location of the oil-exporting facility on the Shatt al Arab whose conquest in 1982 had marked Iran's greatest victory on Iraqi soil. In the onslaught, the mullahs of Tehran concluded that the Islamic Republic possessed neither the time nor the resources to defeat Hussein, his Arab backers, and Western suppliers. Concluding that the interests of his nation exceeded the goal of exporting Islamic revolution, Khomeini made a decision "more deadly than drinking hemlock." He accepted UN Security Council Resolution 598. In what was simply a cease-fire, the resolution ended Khomeini's vendetta against Iraq's Baath and ensured Hussein's survival in the face of militant Islam. After eight long years, the guns stilled in the Shia south. . . .

For Iraq's Arabs, a fragile sense of nationalism, nurtured by the successive governments of Iraq from the monarchy through the Baath, crawled out of the bloody battlefield of the Iran-Iraq War. The Sunnis, largely protected from the carnage, never considered surrender to the Persian foe. The Shia, whose allegiance to the Iraqi state Hussein had questioned in 1980, had proved, in the end, unwilling to sacrifice their frail nation to their sectarian brothers in Iran. The reasons were ethereal—language, Arab tribal identity, and cultural affinity—and they were tangible—a half-century of national education, the largess of the oil economy, the deportation and assassination of the Shia clerical leadership, and the abiding fear of Hussein's police state. All combined to bring the Sunnis and Shia out of eight grueling years of brutal warfare with a renewed sense of Arabism and a refined vision of the Iraqi state. Each group along the sectarian divide acknowledged the nation-state of Iraq within its existing boundaries.

The War over Kuwait

By George H.W. Bush

Under Saddam Hussein's leadership Iraq fared well in its war against Iran, proving itself a formidable power in the region. This was due largely to substantial military, financial, and intelligence assistance it received from a wide variety of nations. This alliance included most of the western powers, the Soviet Union, and the bulk of the Arab nations. However, the benefits Iraq realized from these international relations were virtually wiped out when Hussein provoked another war. In 1990, Iraq invaded and conquered its southern neighbor Kuwait, which had been one of its strongest allies in the Iran-Iraq War. Hussein cited long-standing territorial disputes with Kuwait as his reason for the invasion. Kuwait had also been pressing Iraq over debts on credit Kuwait had extended Iraq during its war with Iran. President George H.W. Bush responded to Iraq's aggression by forging an international military coalition to drive Hussein's armies out of Kuwait. As this coalition initiated action against Iraq in Kuwait on January 16, 1991, President Bush addressed the people of the United States and the world with the following speech, laying out his rationale for military action against Iraq and stating his hopes and objectives for the international force that had been gathered to oppose Hussein.

Just 2 hours ago, allied air forces began an attack on military targets in Iraq and Kuwait. These attacks continue as I speak. Ground forces are not engaged.

This conflict started August 2nd when the dictator of Iraq invaded a small and helpless neighbor. Kuwait—a member of the Arab League and a member of the United Nations—was crushed; its people, brutalized. Five months ago, Saddam Hussein started this cruel war against Kuwait. Tonight, the battle has been joined.

This military action, taken in accord with United Nations res-

George H.W. Bush, televised address to the American people, January 16, 1991.

olutions and with the consent of the United States Congress, follows months of constant and virtually endless diplomatic activity on the part of the United Nations, the United States, and many, many other countries.

Arab leaders sought what became known as an Arab solution, only to conclude that Saddam Hussein was unwilling to leave Kuwait. Others traveled to Baghdad in a variety of efforts to restore peace and justice. Our Secretary of State, James Baker, held an historic meeting in Geneva, only to be totally rebuffed.

This past weekend, in a last-ditch effort, the Secretary General of the United Nations went to the Middle East with peace in his heart—his second such mission. And he came back from Baghdad with no progress at all in getting Saddam Hussein to withdraw from Kuwait.

Now the 28 countries with forces in the Gulf area have exhausted all reasonable efforts to reach a peaceful resolution, and have no choice but to drive Saddam from Kuwait by force. We will not fail.

Objectives

As I report to you, air attacks are underway against military targets in Iraq. We are determined to knock out Saddam Hussein's nuclear bomb potential. We will also destroy his chemical weapons facilities. Much of Saddam's artillery and tanks will be destroyed. Our operations are designed to best protect the lives of all the coalition forces by targeting Saddam's vast military arsenal.

Initial reports from General Schwarzkopf are that our operations are proceeding according to plan. Our objectives are clear: Saddam Hussein's forces will leave Kuwait. The legitimate government of Kuwait will be restored to its rightful place, and Kuwait will once again be free.

Iraq will eventually comply with all relevant United Nations resolutions, and then, when peace is restored, it is our hope that Iraq will live as a peaceful and cooperative member of the family of nations, thus enhancing the security and stability of the Gulf.

The World Cannot Wait

Some may ask: Why act now? Why not wait? The answer is clear: The world could wait no longer. Sanctions, though having some effect, showed no signs of accomplishing their objective.

Sanctions were tried for well over 5 months, and we and our allies concluded that sanctions alone would not force Saddam from Kuwait.

While the world waited, Saddam Hussein systematically raped, pillaged, and plundered a tiny nation, no threat to his own. He subjected the people of Kuwait to unspeakable atrocities—and among those maimed and murdered, innocent children.

While the world waited, Saddam sought to add to the chemical weapons arsenal he now possesses, an infinitely more dangerous weapon of mass destruction—a nuclear weapon. And while the world waited, while the world talked peace and withdrawal, Saddam Hussein dug in and moved massive forces into Kuwait.

While the world waited, while Saddam stalled, more damage was being done to the fragile economies of the Third World, emerging democracies of Eastern Europe, to the entire world, including to our own economy.

The United States, together with the United Nations, exhausted every means at our disposal to bring this crisis to a peaceful end. However, Saddam clearly felt that by stalling and threatening and defying the United Nations, he could weaken the forces arrayed against him.

While the world waited, Saddam Hussein met every overture of peace with open contempt. While the world prayed for peace, Saddam prepared for war....

Saddam was warned over and over again to comply with the will of the United Nations: Leave Kuwait, or be driven out. Saddam has arrogantly rejected all warnings. Instead, he tried to make this a dispute between Iraq and the United States of America.

A New World Order

Well, he failed. Tonight, 28 nations—countries from 5 continents, Europe and Asia, Africa, and the Arab League—have forces in the Gulf area standing shoulder to shoulder against Saddam Hussein. These countries had hoped the use of force could be avoided. Regrettably, we now believe that only force will make him leave.

Prior to ordering our forces into battle, I instructed our military commanders to take every necessary step to prevail as quickly as possible, and with the greatest degree of protection possible for American and allied service men and women.... I'm hopeful that this fighting will not go on for long and that casualties will be held to an absolute minimum.

This is an historic moment. We have in this past year made great progress in ending the long era of conflict and cold war. We have before us the opportunity to forge for ourselves and for future generations a new world order—a world where the rule of law, not the law of the jungle, governs the conduct of nations....

Our goal is not the conquest of Iraq. It is the liberation of Kuwait. It is my hope that somehow the Iraqi people can, even now, convince their dictator that he must lay down his arms, leave Kuwait, and let Iraq itself rejoin the family of peace-loving nations.

Thomas Paine wrote many years ago: "These are the times that try men's souls." Those well-known words are so very true today. But even as planes of the multinational forces attack Iraq, I prefer to think of peace, not war. I am convinced not only that we will prevail but that out of the horror of combat will come the recognition that no nation can stand against a world united, no nation will be permitted to brutally assault its neighbor.

No President can easily commit our sons and daughters to war. They are the Nation's finest. Ours is an all-volunteer force, magnificently trained, highly motivated. The troops know why they're there. And listen to what they say, because they've said it better than any President or Prime Minister ever could. Listen to Hollywood Huddleston, Marine lance corporal. He says, "Let's free these people, so we can go home and be free again." And he's right. The terrible crimes and tortures committed by Saddam's henchmen against the innocent people of Kuwait are an affront to mankind and a challenge to the freedom of all.

Courageous Troops

Listen to one of our great officers out there, Marine Lieutenant General Walter Boomer. He said: "There are things worth fighting for. A world in which brutality and lawlessness are allowed to go unchecked isn't the kind of world we're going to want to live in."

Listen to Master Sergeant J.P. Kendall of the 82nd Airborne: "We're here for more than just the price of a gallon of gas. What we're doing is going to chart the future of the world for the next 100 years. It's better to deal with this guy now than 5 years from now."

And finally, we should all sit up and listen to Jackie Jones, an

Army lieutenant, when she says, "If we let him get away with this, who knows what's going to be next?"

I have called upon Hollywood and Walter and J.P. and Jackie and all their courageous comrades-in-arms to do what must be done. Tonight, America and the world are deeply grateful to them and to their families.

And let me say to everyone listening or watching tonight: When the troops we've sent in finish their work, I am determined to bring them home as soon as possible. Tonight, as our forces fight, they and their families are in our prayers.

May God bless each and every one of them, and the coalition forces at our side in the Gulf, and may He continue to bless our nation, the United States of America.

Hussein's Quest for Nuclear Weapons

BY KHIDHIR HAMZA WITH JEFF STEIN

One issue concerning Iraq that gained massive worldwide attention following Iraq's wars with Iran and the international coalition backing Kuwait was Iraq's development and use of weapons of mass destruction. Weapons of mass destruction are generally categorized as biological, chemical, and nuclear weapons. Khidhir Hamza is an Iraqi nuclear physicist who was recruited to work on developing nuclear weapons for Hussein's government. Hamza fled Iraq in 1994 for his own safety and also to warn the world about Hussein's attempts to acquire nuclear weapons for Iraq. This excerpt from his book Saddam's Bombmaker, *written in collaboration with English translator Jeff Stein, an American journalist based in Washington, D.C., provides a personal inside look at how Hussein set up a potentially viable nuclear weapons program that could gravely threaten both the Middle East region and the world at large.*

One day [in the early 1970s] I was having lunch in the [Iraqi Atomic Energy Commission] cafeteria with a few colleagues, discussing, as we often did, the future of atomic energy. [Atomic Energy Secretary general] Dr. al-Mallah strutted in, accompanied by a diminutive, friendly-looking man named Husham Sharif, who had just been appointed ... director of the Nuclear Research Center.

Sharif, it was immediately clear, was a courteous and cultured fellow.... He was also a longtime fixture in the Baath Party, with a direct pipeline to Saddam. Unfortunately, he was saddled with a civil engineering degree, a weak hand for dealing with nuclear scientists. Sharif, however, knew what Saddam wanted, and if Saddam was pleased, then everybody could be at ease.

Sharif and al-Mallah asked me to their offices for a cup of tea. When I arrived, they engaged me in some pleasant, aimless ban-

Khidhir Hamza with Jeff Stein, *Saddam's Bombmaker: The Terrifying Inside Story of the Iraqi Nuclear and Biological Weapons Agenda.* New York: Scribner, 2000. Copyright © 2000 by Khidhir Hamza. Reproduced by permission.

ter about my work. Then al-Mallah gave me an odd instruction. He asked me to return to my office, retrieve my briefcase, and go to the gate, where a car and driver would pick me up.

"Speak to no one," he said.

I started to ask what it was about, but he raised a spindly hand. "We just want to talk to you in private, at my house," the secretary general said. "Some things are more easily discussed away from the office."...

Diabolical Discussion

At first, it was just shop talk: projects and gossip, the usual stuff when colleagues gather after work. The subject shifted to international developments in nuclear power, upcoming conferences, scientific research. Oddly, however, the mood was rather tense, even glum. Al-Mallah and Sharif kept returning to the theme that Iraq's nuclear program was in the doldrums. Budgets were flat, even declining. Nothing new was going on. The leadership, the code word for Saddam, didn't seem to have much interest in what we were doing.

Then Sharif abruptly turned to me and changed the subject. Had I read the new book called *The Israeli Bomb?* It was written by Fouad Jabir, an American of Palestinian origins.

Of course I had. It was the talk of the Arab intelligentsia. Its theme, which of course I'd heard advanced in a Washington apartment, was that the Arab world faced a bleak future as long as Israel was building nuclear bombs and the Arabs had none. Unless we could create a "balance of terror," we faced permanent, second-class citizenship, with all its political and cultural ramifications. Something had to be done.

I continued eating, uncomfortable with the direction the conversation was taking. The dream of every Baathist, I well understood, was to unify the Arab world and triumph over the Israelis.

"What do you think of Jabir's book?" Sharif suddenly asked me directly.

I was on the spot. I took my time before answering. I knew this was a test, but I didn't care.

"It's a ridiculous study," I said offhandedly, "by somebody who obviously knows nothing about atomic energy and bombs."

The smiles left their faces. They'd obviously swallowed the book whole.

Al-Mallah tried another tack. "We thought it was a very thorough study of the Israeli atomic bomb program," he said.

I shook my head.

"It looks that way," I said, "until you begin to analyze it more closely." I couldn't resist a small jibe. "But you guys must have accepted it without question, because I saw no less than fifty copies in the AE [Atomic Energy] library."

I chuckled, but I'd gone too far. They expected more deference.

"First," I explained seriously, "the idea that Israel has a huge arsenal of nuclear bombs right now is ridiculous on its face," I said. "The Dimona reactor could not produce that much plutonium in such a short time." (Israel had manufactured about a dozen nuclear bombs, according to current reports.)

They nodded slowly.

"Second, in order to compile such an arsenal, they'd have to test at least one or more of them. They're going to make sure the design actually works, because the cost of manufacturing bombs is so huge . . ." I raised my hands in exasperation.

"The cost of making so many bombs is so huge that nobody, certainly not the Israelis, is going to make such an investment—not before they test one and are assured it works. And we have no evidence that they've done this."

They were listening respectfully. Well, I thought, this is what they're paying me for, what they sent me to MIT and brought me back to Iraq for. I might as well tell them the truth.

"It is a good, politically motivated story," I said lightly, "but technically, it's nonsense."

Al-Mallah seemed to break out of a trance. "You mean Israel has no atomic bombs?" he nearly shouted.

"I did not say that," I said softly. "They are in the development stage. So, yes, it's possible they could have a few bombs. But my guess is that they have winnowed their designs to a few workable possibilities, optimizing their budget. They probably have a couple of design versions actually manufactured. But nothing's been tested."

Sharif now came to life. "Don't you expect the Americans or sympathetic Europeans would have helped them select a reliable design? One they don't need to test?"

I nodded. "Maybe," I said. "Maybe. But without testing it's still highly unlikely that they would go into full-scale production. Even if they had, where could they have obtained all this plutonium to make so many bombs? They'd need a ton of the stuff."

"They could have stolen it from American factories," al-Mallah declared.

"No way," I answered. "Not in those quantities."

Al-Mallah's wife had appeared at some point with more coffee and sweets, put them on the table, and withdrew.

Sharif looked pensive, al-Mallah troubled. Obviously they weren't prepared for my skepticism about the book.

Sharif tried another tack. "If we accept your theory that the Israelis may not have more than a few bombs," he said, "it still means they are way ahead of any of us. It still means that they have the bomb and a production system. And once they assure themselves, one way or the other, that their design is reliable, they can go straight into production, full blast."

Perhaps, I thought. But not likely.

"In any case," Sharif continued, "even if we accept your analysis, what do you suggest we do? We at AE are the only authority in the country in this matter and we have been approached by the political leadership and asked for an opinion."

An opinion. Now we were getting to the crux of the matter.

"What exactly were you asked to advise on?" I hedged.

"Well, is it not obvious?" countered Sharif. "Isn't it? Do or die, that's what we face, isn't it? Or do you think there's another way to handle this?"

Well, there it was, out on the table: an Iraqi bomb. The leadership wanted to see if we could build one—or more. And they wanted to know if I would go along. . . .

"You guys are authorized to go in that direction?" I asked.

Sharif folded his hands on the table and looked directly at me. "We are Atomic Energy. We need no authorization to make proposals. But if you are worried about wasting your time and energy, I can tell you that I'm confident that if we made a proposal to match the Israeli program, we would have very receptive ears from the highest authority."

It would bail out our floundering program, he went on, renew Saddam's interest in our work.

"If you remember, we could not even send you to a scientific conference earlier in the year because we had no money," he said. "We've reduced our staff and equipment purchases because nobody is interested in atomic energy up there." He meant the presidential palace. "If this continues, we'll be effectively dead, scientifically speaking. The military angle is all they are interested in. If we give them something like this, everything will change overnight."

Sensing my resistance, he threw me an out. "If we had a real live nuclear program, even the peaceful part of the program would benefit."

Now both men seized that angle, clumsily enthusing over the fabulous amounts of money that would flow to AE for nuclear power, nuclear medicine, nuclear research if we got a bomb program going. Anything was possible with Saddam's backing. But the only thing that would get his attention was a bomb.

I parried again.

"Are you going to send your proposal through normal channels?" I asked, remembering the problems I'd had with the computer purchase.

They laughed and looked at each other. "No, it will be going straight to the top," Sharif said. "But again, all we need for now is a plan, something grand but not too detailed. Something that will interest the leadership." He smiled. "And something they can understand."

We all fell silent.

"You can do this, can't you, Hamza," al-Mallah finally said. "Put something on paper." That was an order.

My mind spun. This was deep water. Just this "innocent" conversation had entangled me in state secrets. If I said the wrong thing, Sharif and al-Mallah could have me killed right now, out back. Or by a red truck in an "accident" on the way home. My wife was pregnant with our first child. I wanted to live. I had to put the best face on the situation right now.

I started to nod my acceptance.

"Okay," I said solemnly. "I will do it."

Al-Mallah brightened. Sharif smiled broadly.

"Wonderful!" they both said. "Wonderful!"

I smiled back weakly. I had just taken a first step into a very dark tunnel. . . .

Laying the Plans for Destruction

There was no how-to book on making a bomb, although the basic principles had been well known for over half a century. Beginning in the 1940s, each country had gone its own way, starting with Germany (the Nazis abandoned the effort as impractical). Their work was picked up by the United States, the Soviet

Union, England, France, China, and Israel. India, Pakistan, and South Africa would follow. Every nation had the same goal: to split atoms in a way that mocked a sunburst on Earth.

The Americans, of course, were the first to master the bomb, with a successful test in the New Mexico desert in July 1945. Incredibly, I found their Manhattan Project reports on a dusty shelf in the AE library, under a placard reading, "This is a gift from the United States Atomic Energy Commission." Apparently they were donated to Iraq in 1956 under the so-called Atoms for Peace program. Later, when the Kennedy administration learned the Soviets were offering Iraq a nuclear reactor, it offered an American reactor, but a communist faction in the regime forced the government to refuse it in favor of the inferior Russian model. In any event, I was sure that if U.S. officials knew how valuable its Manhattan Project reports would be to us years later, they would have kicked themselves.

After a few days at al-Mallah's, we decided to follow the path of the Israelis. They'd bought a small research reactor from the French in 1956 and clandestinely turned it to their purposes. We'd do the same, acquiring a medium-size, research-oriented nuclear reactor, along with uranium fuel. But Iraq had its own source of uranium, too, in sulfur deposits in the desert and veins in the northern mountains. The fission of the uranium in the foreign fuel would produce small neutron particles, some of which, in turn, would be reabsorbed by our own uranium in the reactor, producing plutonium.

The task was daunting. We'd also need a clandestine fuel reprocessing unit to separate the plutonium. Normally, at least eleven pounds were needed to make a single atomic bomb. The trick would be getting our own uranium in and out of the reactor unobserved by the international inspectors and their cameras, and hiding the reprocessing operation. The International Atomic Energy Agency (IAEA) had the right to inspect its signatories' nuclear facilities every six months. Israel, India, and Pakistan had never signed. We had.

The enormity of it all nearly had us laughing. But all that was far, far down the line. For now, al-Mallah thought, we at least had enough material to write a report for Saddam.

We wrote a forty-page plan, which was both conservative and optimistic. We made no pledges. We made no guarantees. We promised Saddam only the possibility of a bomb, and then only if he provided the necessary hundreds of millions of dollars in support. Foreign sources would have to be induced to provide the necessary technology. And all along we'd have to get around international safeguards and inspections.

It was a very tall order. Leaping all those hurdles was, I reflected, a remote possibility. But in the meantime, al-Mallah crowed, the money would start flowing like water....

Hussein's Clever Maneuvering

What's the IAEA? Saddam demanded. His memo landed on our desks like a mortar.

The International Atomic Energy Agency, headquartered in Vienna, had been organized by the United States and other members of the nuclear club to monitor the proliferation of atomic reactors, which, pushed by the major plant manufacturers, had been spreading rapidly to Iran, Israel, India, Pakistan, South Africa, and other countries who might use them to make a bomb. There were reactors in South Vietnam and the Philippines. Even Taiwan, nominally leashed by the United States, was secretly toying with the idea of making a bomb from the byproducts of nuclear reactors. Iraq had a small Russian reactor that was not really adequate for producing fuel for a bomb.

Members of the IAEA pledged to open their atomic programs to international inspection. Iraq's pro-West royalist government, which had also signed the 1961 Nuclear Nonproliferation Treaty, had joined the IAEA at its inception.

Eventually, we figured out the answer Saddam wanted and gave it to him: The IAEA was essentially a U.S.-dominated international spy agency, whose purpose was to prevent countries like Iraq from getting the bomb. His response: Get inside it and turn it to our purposes.

A tall order. Under the indifferent watch of our ambassador in Vienna, Iraq's involvement in the IAEA was nonexistent. Our first priority would be to mount a strenuous campaign to get Iraq onto the IAEA's board of governors, which held elections for half of its twenty-two seats every year. At the same time, we wanted to get an Iraqi appointed as a nuclear inspector. That way we'd have our own spy on the inside, as Saddam wanted. But we had to get to Vienna and work the rooms.

In September 1973, we flew to Vienna, the cradle of Haydn and Mozart, Franz Joseph and Prince Metternich. Supposedly, the ambassador had paved the way for our plan. But when we arrived, no political work had been done, and we didn't even have hotel rooms. To our furious complaint, the ambassador responded with a diffident shrug. Obviously, he hadn't grasped the fact that we were sent by Saddam. The next day he was removed as head of our delegation.

Our new chief flew in from Baghdad. Thin and intense, Dr. Husham al-Shawi was the regime's Oxford-educated minister of education, a portfolio obtained by virtue of his leadership of an Arab nationalist group aligned with Saddam.

The change was electric: Al-Shawi was brisk and authoritative, quickly grasping our difficulties and issuing instructions in his clipped British style. It was also clear that he was closely following Saddam's script. Over the following days he studied Saddam's cables like a schoolboy, making sure he missed nothing and understood every word.

At first glance, we faced impossible odds. Our rival, Iran, with

Israel Targets Iraq's Weapons

In 1981, Israel raided an Iraqi nuclear reactor that Israel claimed was being used to produce materials for nuclear weapons. Israeli prime minister Menachem Begin gives his reasons for launching the attack in this excerpt from an interview conducted shortly after the raid.

Shimon Schiffer: Mr Prime Minister, when was the decision taken to attack the nuclear reactor in Iraq and what were the Cabinet's considerations in the matter?

Menachem Begin: The decision to attack Iraq's nuclear reactor, which is intended to produce atomic bombs, was adopted many months ago. But there were hindrances. There were also various considerations and there were a number of delays—until we arrived at a situation where it was clear to us that if we did not act now we might perhaps miss the propitious time. That is to say, either in July or in September, this reactor, according to the reliable information we had received, would be, as one puts it, hot. In such plans to buy twenty nuclear power stations, had been campaigning for the board's Middle East seat for a year and was backed by the United States. It appeared to have the votes locked up, even among Arab delegations, including the Saudis, who apologized profusely but informed us that diplomatic niceties made it impossible to change their votes. The Soviet bloc was also in the Iranian column. Al-Shawi immediately apprised Saddam.

To our utter shock, within a few days a parade of delegations began showing up at the embassy to announce, in solemn tones, that they were changing their votes. Of course, we were curious. We learned that Saddam had simply called his foreign minister on the carpet and let him know his job was riding on the IAEA vote. Midnight cables had gone out to Iraqi ambassadors in each target country and summonses were issued to foreign ambassadors in Baghdad. The message was as subtle as an oncoming train: With oil prices high and supplies tight in the wake of the Arab oil embargo, Iraq was ready to cut prices to its special

---

circumstances, no Israeli Government could have, our Cabinet wouldn't have, adopted a decision to bomb the reactor, because it would have been torn open and deadly radioactivity would have enveloped the city of Baghdad and it would have hit tens, perhaps hundreds of thousands of innocent men, women and children. . . . And then we would have had to stand by passively, from afar, and know that atomic weapons were being produced, of the type that were dropped on Hiroshima at the end of the second world war, which caused hundreds of thousands of people to be hit. With three, four or five such atomic bombs, Saddam Husayn, an incomparably cruel person who, with his own hands, murdered his best friends in order to seize control of Iraq, wouldn't have the slightest hesitation in dropping those bombs on concentrations of our population and he could liquidate the country; certainly its infrastructure; certainly the better part of its army.

Menachem Begin, interviewed by Shimon Schiffer of the Israeli Home Service on June 8, 1981.

friends. We also had huge standing orders for their nuclear and other technologies. Friends would be rewarded, enemies punished. Overnight, the vote started swinging our way.

It was the talk of Vienna. But then the Americans got angry. Four U.S. presidents, going back to a CIA coup that returned Shah Reza Pahlavi to the Peacock Throne, had backed Iran. Teheran was the linchpin of U.S. security interests in the Middle East, second only to Israel. The United States was not about to allow the upstart Iraqis to push the Iranians aside. Soon enough, as I was sitting in the Iraqi delegation's seat at the IAEA assembly, I felt the full heat of Washington's frustration. An American diplomat approached me, his face twisted in anger.

"We know what you're doing," he said, wagging a finger. I looked around. This was very undiplomatic behavior. Nearby delegates saw the commotion and glanced our way.

"You should save yourselves the trouble and just quit," the American continued, oblivious to the stir he'd caused, "because we are on to you, and we will never—never—let you win." With that he turned on his heel and stalked away.

All in all, the incident was fairly amusing, but when I told al-Shawi about it, he frowned. He fidgeted in thought for a brief moment, and then announced crisply, "It means that we cannot pursue that seat now." Directly challenging Washington would be a mistake, he said. We had to consider alternatives.

As if on cue, a super-delegation of several South American countries showed up. They suggested we drop our fight with Iran, which was tearing the assembly apart, and instead accept a "floating seat" traditionally reserved for an African or Asian country. The seat was now held by Egypt, but its term was up. If we agreed to take it, the assembly would approve.

It was obvious that Washington had put the South Americans up to the scheme, but we decided to play ball. A floating seat was a seat, after all.

The next day, however, we learned we'd been double-crossed. An Iraqi source in the IAEA told us that Egypt in fact intended to hold on to its seat.

Now our necks were really on the block. Saddam had made it perfectly clear that we were not to come back to Baghdad empty-handed. In our desperation, we decided to call Egypt's bluff.

As soon as I spotted the Egyptian ambassador at the evening banquet, I approached him very discreetly. Arm-twisting was supposed to be off-limits during the dinner.

"As you know, Mr. Ambassador, we've been offered the floating seat," I said quietly, "but if you still want it, we'll step aside. It's not our intent to pick a fight with our Egyptian brothers."

The ambassador's eyes narrowed, but he was on the spot. There was no way he could admit Egypt's double-dealing. So he drew himself up, managed a smile, and assured me there wouldn't be a problem. "We have no intent to pursue that seat," he said. "To the contrary, I have strict instructions from my government to campaign for you."

"Thank you, Mr. Ambassador," I responded. "That's very kind of you. I'm sure Iraq will remember this selfless act." With that I smiled and withdrew.

On election day we split the delegates among us. I took two aisles, al-Mallah took two, and another member of our team took two. We told the delegates that Egypt had withdrawn its nomination and wanted its votes thrown to Iraq. In the end, we moved just enough votes to win (and not long after, to get an Iraqi appointed as a nuclear inspector). After the tally, I happened to pass the Egyptian ambassador, who looked at me with murder in his eyes. The U.S. ambassador was nowhere to be seen.

We flew home relieved, like a football team that had won on the last play. Nothing those delegations could have done would have equaled Saddam's fury. And sure enough, classified information began to flow from our spy inside the IAEA. Saddam had been right.

The History of Nations
Chapter 6

The U.S. War on Iraq and Its Aftermath

Iraq Poses a Threat to World Peace

BY GEORGE W. BUSH

After the September 11, 2001, terrorist attacks, U.S. president George W. Bush consistently spoke out against the Iraqi regime, claiming that it provided assistance to international terrorist groups and that its programs to develop weapons of mass destruction posed a threat to the security of the United States and the rest of the world. Bush held out the possibility of renewed military action against Iraq as a means of dealing with the threats posed by that country. In a speech delivered in Cincinnati, Ohio, on October 7, 2002, President Bush sought to clarify and galvanize support for his position on confronting Iraq. That speech is excerpted here.

Tonight I want to take a few minutes to discuss a grave threat to peace, and America's determination to lead the world in confronting that threat.

The threat comes from Iraq. It arises directly from the Iraqi regime's own actions—its history of aggression, and its drive toward an arsenal of terror. Eleven years ago, as a condition for ending the Persian Gulf War, the Iraqi regime was required to destroy its weapons of mass destruction, to cease all development of such weapons, and to stop all support for terrorist groups. The Iraqi regime has violated all of those obligations. It possesses and produces chemical and biological weapons. It is seeking nuclear weapons. It has given shelter and support to terrorism, and practices terror against its own people. The entire world has witnessed Iraq's eleven-year history of defiance, deception and bad faith.

We also must never forget the most vivid events of recent history. On September the 11th, 2001, America felt its vulnerability—even to threats that gather on the other side of the earth. We resolved then, and we are resolved today, to confront every

George W. Bush, address at the Cincinnati Museum Center–Cincinnati Union Terminal, Cincinnati, Ohio, October 7, 2002.

threat, from any source, that could bring sudden terror and suffering to America.

Members of the Congress of both political parties, and members of the United Nations Security Council, agree that Saddam Hussein is a threat to peace and must disarm. We agree that the Iraqi dictator must not be permitted to threaten America and the world with horrible poisons and diseases and gases and atomic weapons. Since we all agree on this goal, the issue is: how can we best achieve it?

Many Americans have raised legitimate questions: about the nature of the threat; about the urgency of action—why be concerned now; about the link between Iraq developing weapons of terror, and the wider war on terror. These are all issues we've discussed broadly and fully within my administration. And tonight, I want to share those discussions with you.

A Merciless Regime

First, some ask why Iraq is different from other countries or regimes that also have terrible weapons. While there are many dangers in the world, the threat from Iraq stands alone—because it gathers the most serious dangers of our age in one place. Iraq's weapons of mass destruction are controlled by a murderous tyrant who has already used chemical weapons to kill thousands of people. This same tyrant has tried to dominate the Middle East, has invaded and brutally occupied a small neighbor, has struck other nations without warning, and holds an unrelenting hostility toward the United States.

By its past and present actions, by its technological capabilities, by the merciless nature of its regime, Iraq is unique. As a former chief weapons inspector of the U.N. has said, "The fundamental problem with Iraq remains the nature of the regime, itself. Saddam Hussein is a homicidal dictator who is addicted to weapons of mass destruction."

Some ask how urgent this danger is to America and the world. The danger is already significant, and it only grows worse with time. If we know Saddam Hussein has dangerous weapons today—and we do—does it make any sense for the world to wait to confront him as he grows even stronger and develops even more dangerous weapons?

In 1995, after several years of deceit by the Iraqi regime, the head of Iraq's military industries defected. It was then that the regime was forced to admit that it had produced more than 30,000 liters of anthrax and other deadly biological agents. The inspectors, however, concluded that Iraq had likely produced two to four times that amount. This is a massive stockpile of biological weapons that has never been accounted for, and capable of killing millions.

We know that the regime has produced thousands of tons of chemical agents, including mustard gas, sarin nerve gas, VX nerve gas. Saddam Hussein also has experience in using chemical weapons. He has ordered chemical attacks on Iran, and on more than forty villages in his own country. These actions killed or injured at least 20,000 people, more than six times the number of people who died in the attacks of September the 11th.

And surveillance photos reveal that the regime is rebuilding facilities that it had used to produce chemical and biological weapons. Every chemical and biological weapon that Iraq has or makes is a direct violation of the truce that ended the Persian Gulf War in 1991. Yet, Saddam Hussein has chosen to build and keep these weapons despite international sanctions, U.N. demands, and isolation from the civilized world.

Iraq possesses ballistic missiles with a likely range of hundreds of miles—far enough to strike Saudi Arabia, Israel, Turkey, and other nations—in a region where more than 135,000 American civilians and service members live and work. We've also discovered through intelligence that Iraq has a growing fleet of manned and unmanned aerial vehicles [UAVs] that could be used to disperse chemical or biological weapons across broad areas. We're concerned that Iraq is exploring ways of using these UAVs for missions targeting the United States. And, of course, sophisticated delivery systems aren't required for a chemical or biological attack; all that might be required are a small container and one terrorist or Iraqi intelligence operative to deliver it.

And that is the source of our urgent concern about Saddam Hussein's links to international terrorist groups. Over the years, Iraq has provided safe haven to terrorists such as Abu Nidal, whose terror organization carried out more than 90 terrorist attacks in 20 countries that killed or injured nearly 900 people, including 12 Americans. Iraq has also provided safe haven to Abu Abbas, who was responsible for seizing the *Achille Lauro* and killing an American passenger. And we know that Iraq is continuing to finance terror and gives assistance to groups that use terrorism to undermine Middle East peace....

Iraq could decide on any given day to provide a biological or chemical weapon to a terrorist group or individual terrorists. Alliance with terrorists could allow the Iraqi regime to attack America without leaving any fingerprints.

LINKING HUSSEIN WITH TERRORISM

In a presentation to the United Nations Security Council on February 5, 2003, U.S. Secretary of State Colin Powell set out to substantiate controversial claims that Iraq had ties with al-Qaeda, the terrorist organization headed by Osama bin Laden.

Early Al Qaeda ties were forged by ... secret Iraqi intelligence high-level contacts with Al Qaeda. We know members of both organizations met repeatedly and have met at least eight times at very senior levels since the early 1990's. In 1996, a foreign security service tells us that bin Laden met with a senior Iraqi intelligence official in Khartoum and later met the director of the Iraqi intelligence service....

Iraqis continued to visit bin Laden in his new home in Afghanistan. A senior defector, one of Saddam's former intelligence chiefs in Europe, says Saddam sent his agents to Afghanistan sometime in the mid-1990's to provide training to Al Qaeda members on document forgery. From the late 1990's until 2001, the Iraqi embassy in Pakistan played the role of liaison to the Al Qaeda organization....

Ambition and hatred are enough to bring Iraq and Al Qaeda together, enough so Al Qaeda could learn how to build more sophisticated bombs and learn how to forge documents; and enough so that Al Qaeda could turn to Iraq for help in acquiring expertise on weapons of mass destruction.

Colin Powell, address to the UN Security Council, February 5, 2003.

The War on Terror

Some have argued that confronting the threat from Iraq could detract from the war against terror. To the contrary; confronting the threat posed by Iraq is crucial to winning the war on terror. When I spoke to Congress more than a year ago, I said that those who harbor terrorists are as guilty as the terrorists themselves. Saddam Hussein is harboring terrorists and the instruments of terror, the instruments of mass death and destruction. And he cannot be trusted. The risk is simply too great that he will use them, or provide them to a terror network.

Terror cells and outlaw regimes building weapons of mass destruction are different faces of the same evil. Our security requires that we confront both. And the United States military is capable of confronting both.

Many people have asked how close Saddam Hussein is to developing a nuclear weapon. Well, we don't know exactly, and that's the problem. Before the Gulf War, the best intelligence indicated that Iraq was eight to ten years away from developing a nuclear weapon. After the war, international inspectors learned that the regime has been much closer—the regime in Iraq would likely have possessed a nuclear weapon no later than 1993. The inspectors discovered that Iraq had an advanced nuclear weapons development program, had a design for a workable nuclear weapon, and was pursuing several different methods of enriching uranium for a bomb.

Before being barred from Iraq in 1998, the International Atomic Energy Agency dismantled extensive nuclear weapons–related facilities, including three uranium enrichment sites. That same year, information from a high-ranking Iraqi nuclear engineer who had defected revealed that despite his public promises, Saddam Hussein had ordered his nuclear program to continue.

The evidence indicates that Iraq is reconstituting its nuclear weapons program. Saddam Hussein has held numerous meetings with Iraqi nuclear scientists, a group he calls his "nuclear mujahideen"—his nuclear holy warriors. Satellite photographs reveal that Iraq is rebuilding facilities at sites that have been part of its nuclear program in the past. Iraq has attempted to purchase high-strength aluminum tubes and other equipment needed for gas centrifuges, which are used to enrich uranium for nuclear weapons.

If the Iraqi regime is able to produce, buy, or steal an amount of highly enriched uranium a little larger than a single softball, it could have a nuclear weapon in less than a year. And if we allow that to happen, a terrible line would be crossed. Saddam Hussein would be in a position to blackmail anyone who opposes his aggression. He would be in a position to dominate the Middle East. He would be in a position to threaten America. And Saddam Hussein would be in a position to pass nuclear technology to terrorists.

Some citizens wonder, after 11 years of living with this problem, why do we need to confront it now? And there's a reason. We've experienced the horror of September the 11th. We have seen that those who hate America are willing to crash airplanes into buildings full of innocent people. Our enemies would be no less willing, in fact, they would be eager, to use biological or chemical, or a nuclear weapon.

Knowing these realities, America must not ignore the threat gathering against us. Facing clear evidence of peril, we cannot wait for the final proof—the smoking gun—that could come in the form of a mushroom cloud. As President Kennedy said in October of 1962, "Neither the United States of America, nor the world community of nations can tolerate deliberate deception and offensive threats on the part of any nation, large or small. We no longer live in a world," he said, "where only the actual firing of weapons represents a sufficient challenge to a nation's security to constitute maximum peril."

Understanding the threats of our time, knowing the designs and deceptions of the Iraqi regime, we have every reason to assume the worst, and we have an urgent duty to prevent the worst from occurring.

The Old Approach Has Failed

Some believe we can address this danger by simply resuming the old approach to inspections, and applying diplomatic and economic pressure. Yet this is precisely what the world has tried to do since 1991. The U.N. inspections program was met with systematic deception. The Iraqi regime bugged hotel rooms and offices of inspectors to find where they were going next; they forged documents, destroyed evidence, and developed mobile weapons facilities to keep a step ahead of inspectors. Eight so-called presidential palaces were declared off-limits to unfettered inspections. These sites actually encompass twelve square miles, with hundreds of structures, both above and below the ground, where sensitive materials could be hidden.

The world has also tried economic sanctions—and watched Iraq use billions of dollars in illegal oil revenues to fund more weapons purchases, rather than providing for the needs of the Iraqi people.

The world has tried limited military strikes to destroy Iraq's weapons of mass destruction capabilities—only to see them openly rebuilt, while the regime again denies they even exist.

The world has tried no-fly zones to keep Saddam from terrorizing his own people—and in the last year alone, the Iraqi military has fired upon American and British pilots more than 750 times.

After eleven years during which we have tried containment, sanctions, inspections, even selected military action, the end result is that Saddam Hussein still has chemical and biological weapons and is increasing his capabilities to make more. And he is moving ever closer to developing a nuclear weapon.

Clearly, to actually work, any new inspections, sanctions or enforcement mechanisms will have to be very different. America wants the U.N. to be an effective organization that helps keep the peace. And that is why we are urging the Security Council to adopt a new resolution setting out tough, immediate requirements. Among those requirements: the Iraqi regime must reveal and destroy, under U.N. supervision, all existing weapons of mass destruction. To ensure that we learn the truth, the regime must allow witnesses to its illegal activities to be interviewed outside the country—and these witnesses must be free to bring their families with them so they [are] all beyond the reach of Saddam Hussein's terror and murder. And inspectors must have access to any site, at any time, without pre-clearance, without delay, without exceptions.

The time for denying, deceiving, and delaying has come to an end. Saddam Hussein must disarm himself—or, for the sake of peace, we will lead a coalition to disarm him.

Opposing Military Intervention

By Brent Scowcroft

As President Bush tried to build support for possible military action against Iraq in late 2002, many prominent people expressed opposition. One such opponent of Bush's policy was Brent Scowcroft, who had served as national security adviser to Bush's father, President George Herbert Walker Bush, during the Gulf War against Iraq in the early 1990s. Although Scowcroft vehemently condemned Saddam Hussein and expressed support for taking measures to try to remove him from power, he also feared that full-scale war would divert resources away from other national security priorities, such as the war on terrorism, and that it could prove to be more costly and consequential for the United States than the effort was worth. Scowcroft expressed these views in an editorial in the Wall Street Journal *during the summer of 2002, which is excerpted here.*

Our nation is presently engaged in a debate about whether to launch a war against Iraq. Leaks of various strategies for an attack on Iraq appear with regularity. The Bush administration vows regime change, but states that no decision has been made whether, much less when, to launch an invasion.

It is beyond dispute that Saddam Hussein is a menace. He terrorizes and brutalizes his own people. He has launched war on two of his neighbors. He devotes enormous effort to rebuilding his military forces and equipping them with weapons of mass destruction. We will all be better off when he is gone.

That said, we need to think through this issue very carefully. We need to analyze the relationship between Iraq and our other pressing priorities—notably the war on terrorism—as well as the best strategy and tactics available were we to move to change the regime in Baghdad.

Brent Scowcroft, "Don't Attack Saddam," *Wall Street Journal*, August 15, 2002. Copyright © 2002 by Dow Jones & Company, Inc. Reproduced with permission.

Assessing the Threat

Saddam's strategic objective appears to be to dominate the Persian Gulf, to control oil from the region, or both. That clearly poses a real threat to key U.S. interests. But there is scant evidence to tie Saddam to terrorist organizations, and even less to the Sept. 11 attacks. Indeed Saddam's goals have little in common with the terrorists who threaten us, and there is little incentive for him to make common cause with them.

He is unlikely to risk his investment in weapons of mass destruction, much less his country, by handing such weapons to terrorists who would use them for their own purposes and leave Baghdad as the return address. Threatening to use these weapons for blackmail—much less their actual use—would open him and his entire regime to a devastating response by the U.S. While Saddam is thoroughly evil, he is above all a power-hungry survivor.

Saddam is a familiar dictatorial aggressor, with traditional goals for his aggression. There is little evidence to indicate that the United States itself is an object of his aggression. Rather, Saddam's problem with the U.S. appears to be that we stand in the way of his ambitions. He seeks weapons of mass destruction not to arm terrorists, but to deter us from intervening to block his aggressive designs.

Given Saddam's aggressive regional ambitions, as well as his ruthlessness and unpredictability, it may at some point be wise to remove him from power. Whether and when that point should come ought to depend on overall U.S. national security priorities. Our pre-eminent security priority—underscored repeatedly by the president—is the war on terrorism. An attack on Iraq at this time would seriously jeopardize, if not destroy, the global counterterrorist campaign we have undertaken.

The United States could certainly defeat the Iraqi military and destroy Saddam's regime. But it would not be a cakewalk. On the contrary, it undoubtedly would be very expensive—with serious consequences for the U.S. and global economy—and could as well be bloody. In fact, Saddam would be likely to conclude he had nothing left to lose, leading him to unleash whatever weapons of mass destruction he possesses.

Israel would have to expect to be the first casualty, as in 1991 when Saddam sought to bring Israel into the Gulf conflict. This time, using weapons of mass destruction, he might succeed, provoking Israel to respond, perhaps with nuclear weapons, unleashing an Armageddon in the Middle East. Finally, if we are to achieve our strategic objectives in Iraq, a military campaign very likely would have to be followed by a large-scale, long-term military occupation.

War's Potential Consequences

But the central point is that any campaign against Iraq, whatever the strategy, cost and risks, is certain to divert us for some indefinite period from our war on terrorism. Worse, there is a virtual consensus in the world against an attack on Iraq at this time. So long as that sentiment persists, it would require the U.S. to pursue a virtual go-it-alone strategy against Iraq, making any military operations correspondingly more difficult and expensive. The most serious cost, however, would be to the war on terrorism. Ignoring that clear sentiment would result in a serious degradation in international cooperation with us against terrorism. And make no mistake, we simply cannot win that war without enthusiastic international cooperation, especially on intelligence.

Possibly the most dire consequences would be the effect in the region. The shared view in the region is that Iraq is principally an obsession of the U.S. The obsession of the region, however, is the Israeli-Palestinian conflict. If we were seen to be turning our backs on that bitter conflict—which the region, rightly or wrongly, perceives to be clearly within our power to resolve—in order to go after Iraq, there would be an explosion of outrage against us. We would be seen as ignoring a key interest of the Muslim world in order to satisfy what is seen to be a narrow American interest.

Even without Israeli involvement, the results could well destabilize Arab regimes in the region, ironically facilitating one of Saddam's strategic objectives. At a minimum, it would stifle any cooperation on terrorism, and could even swell the ranks of the terrorists. Conversely, the more progress we make in the war on terrorism, and the more we are seen to be committed to resolving the Israel-Palestinian issue, the greater will be the international support for going after Saddam.

Setting Priorities

If we are truly serious about the war on terrorism, it must remain our top priority. However, should Saddam Hussein be found to be clearly implicated in the events of Sept. 11, that could make him a key counterterrorist target, rather than a competing priority, and significantly shift world opinion toward support for regime change.

In any event, we should be pressing the United Nations Security Council to insist on an effective no-notice inspection regime for Iraq—any time, anywhere, no permission required. On this point, senior administration officials have opined that Saddam Hussein would never agree to such an inspection regime. But if he did, inspections would serve to keep him off balance and under close observation, even if all his weapons of mass destruction capabilities were not uncovered. And if he refused, his rejection could provide the persuasive casus belli which many claim we do not now have. Compelling evidence that Saddam had acquired nuclear-weapons capability could have a similar effect.

In sum, if we will act in full awareness of the intimate interrelationship of the key issues in the region, keeping counterterrorism as our foremost priority, there is much potential for success across the entire range of our security interests—including Iraq. If we reject a comprehensive perspective, however, we put at risk our campaign against terrorism as well as stability and security in a vital region of the world.

Iraq Stands Firm Against World Opinion

BY SADDAM HUSSEIN, INTERVIEWED BY TONY BENN

In 2003, the Iraqi leadership defended itself against charges that Iraq had behaved belligerently and denounced the threats of military actions against Iraq made by other nations, especially the United States. After not speaking with members of the Western press for many years, Iraqi leader Saddam Hussein gave an interview to Tony Benn, a former member of the British Parliament who had frequently opposed U.S. and British hard-line policies against Iraq. As the United States and other Western nations mounted campaigns to oust Hussein or force Iraq's total disarmament, Hussein denied that Iraq possessed weapons of mass destruction or had ties to terrorist networks. He also emphatically claimed that Iraq would stand up against aggression by the nations that were targeting it verbally and threatening military action against it. In March 2003, the United States and Britain led a military action to depose Hussein's regime. By mid-April, the nation's capital had fallen to U.S. troops. Hussein's whereabouts were unknown.

BENN: I come for one reason only—to see whether in a talk we can explore, or you can help me to see, what the paths to peace may be. My only reason, I remember the war because I lost a brother. I never want to see another war.

There are millions of people all over the world who don't want a war, and by agreeing to this interview, which is very historic for all of us, I hope you will be able to help me be able to say something to the world that is significant and positive.

SADDAM: Welcome to Baghdad. You are conscious of the role that Iraqis have set out for themselves, inspired by their own

Saddam Hussein, interviewed by Tony Benn, British Channel 4 News, February 5, 2003. Copyright © 2003 by The Press Association, Ltd. Reproduced by permission.

culture, their civilisation and their role in human history. This role requires peace in order to prosper and progress. Having said that, the Iraqis are committed to their rights as much as they are committed to the rights of others.

Without peace they will be faced with many obstacles that would stop them from fulfilling their human role.

BENN: Mr President, may I ask you some questions? The first is, does Iraq have any weapons of mass destruction?

SADDAM: Most Iraqi officials have been in power for over 34 years and have experience of dealing with the outside world. Every fair-minded person knows that when Iraqi officials say something, they are trustworthy.

A few minutes ago when you asked me if I wanted to look at the questions beforehand I told you I didn't feel the need so that we don't waste time, and I gave you the freedom to ask me any question directly so that my reply would be direct.

This is an opportunity to reach the British people and the forces of peace in the world. There is only one truth and therefore I tell you as I have said on many occasions before that Iraq has no weapons of mass destruction whatsoever. We challenge anyone who claims that we have to bring forward any evidence and present it to public opinion.

BENN: I have another which has been raised: do you have links with Al Qaida?

SADDAM: If we had a relationship with Al Qaida and we believed in that relationship we wouldn't be ashamed to admit it. Therefore I would like to tell you directly and also through you to anyone who is interested to know that we have no relationship with Al Qaida.

BENN: In relation to the [United Nations weapons] inspectors, there appears to be difficulties with inspectors, and I wonder whether there's anything you can tell me about these difficulties and whether you believe they will be cleared up before [inspectors] Mr Hans Blix and Mr El Baradei come back to Baghdad?

SADDAM: You are aware that every major event must encounter some difficulty. On the subject of the inspectors and the resolutions that deal with Iraq you must have been following it and you must have a view and a vision as to whether these resolutions [UN resolutions demanding Iraq comply with inspections] have any basis in international law.

Nevertheless the Security Council produced them. These resolutions—implemented or not—or the motivation behind these resolutions could lead the current situation to the path of peace or war. Therefore it's a critical situation. Let us also remember the unjust suffering of the Iraqi people.

For the last 13 years since the blockade was imposed, you must be aware of the amount of harm that it has caused the Iraqi people, particularly the children and the elderly, as a result of the shortage of food and medicine and other aspects of their life. Therefore we are facing a critical situation....

When Iraq objects to the conduct of those implementing the Security Council resolutions, that doesn't mean that Iraq wishes to push things to confrontation. Iraq has no interest in war. No Iraqi official or ordinary citizen has expressed a wish to go to war. The question should be directed at the other side. Are they looking for a pretext so they could justify war against Iraq? If the purpose was to make sure that Iraq is free of nuclear, chemical and biological weapons then they can do that. These weapons do not

HUSSEIN'S LONGTIME SPOKESMAN

Appearing on the ABC news program Nightline *in December 2002, Iraqi deputy prime minister Tariq Aziz claimed that the United States and its allies were being deceptive about their reasons for threatening to attack Iraq. He also accused the U.S. government of seeking to colonize and dominate the nation.*

TARIQ AZIZ: My conviction is that the war is not because of weapons of mass destruction, because the whole issue of weapons of mass destruction is a hoax. It has been used as a pretext in order to wage a war against Iraq. When they find that there are no weapons of mass destruction, they will use another pretext to attack. There is a plan to attack Iraq. There is a plan not to regime change in Iraq, there is a plan for region change, the whole region. To serve the imperialist purposes of the United States and to serve the purposes of Israel....

TED KOPPEL: As we sit here tonight, though, Dr. Aziz,

come in small pills that you can hide in your pocket. These are weapons of mass destruction and it is easy to work out if Iraq has them or not. We have said many times before and we say it again today that Iraq is free of such weapons.

So when Iraq objects to the conduct of the inspection teams or others, that doesn't mean that Iraq is interested in putting obstacles before them which could hinder the efforts to get to the truth. It is in our interest to facilitate their mission to find the truth. The question is does the other side want to get to the same conclusion or are they looking for a pretext for aggression? If those concerned prefer aggression then it's within their reach. The super powers can create a pretext any day to claim that Iraq is not implementing [United Nations] resolutions....

BENN: May I broaden the question out, Mr President, to the relations between Iraq and the UN, and the prospects for peace more broadly, and I wonder whether with all its weaknesses and all the difficulties, whether you see a way in which the UN can

---

is it your conviction, you've been in the diplomacy game a very long time, is it your conviction that Washington and London are determined to go to war against Iraq?

TARIQ AZIZ: I think Washington wants the war, you see. London, to a certain extent, yes. To a large extent it is with this plan. But Washington wants the war. It wants the war for its imperialist purposes. Allow me to use this word *imperialist* and *imperialism* because ...

TED KOPPEL: It's a very old word, it's out of fashion.

TARIQ AZIZ: It looks old, but now it's being renewed now. The American imperialism is at its peak. That's not only what Tariq Aziz is saying, many, many hundreds, thousands and millions of people in Europe, in Asia, in Africa, are saying that, you see. Especially this Administration. This [Bush] Administration is the peak of imperialism. So, they want to wage a war for imperialist purposes and they want to wage a war to serve the purposes of Israel in this region, they want to make Israel the empire in this region.

Tariq Aziz on *Nightline: In the Eye of the Storm*, December 4, 2002.

reach that objective for the benefit of humanity?

SADDAM: The point you raised can be found in the United Nations charter. As you know Iraq is one of the founders and first signatories of the charter.

If we look at the representatives of two super powers—America and Britain—and look at their conduct and their language, we would notice that they are more motivated by war than their responsibility for peace. And when they talk about peace all they do is accuse others they wish to destroy in the name of peace. They claim they are looking after the interests of their people. You know as well as I do that this is not the truth. Yes the world would respect this principle if it was genuinely applied. It's not about power but it is about right and wrong, about when we base our human relations on good, and respect this principle. So it becomes simple to adhere to this principle because anyone who violates it will be exposed to public opinion. . . .

BENN: There are tens of millions, maybe hundreds of millions of people in Britain and America, in Europe and worldwide, who want to see a peaceful outcome to this problem, and they are the real Americans in my opinion, the real British, the real French, the real Germans, because they think of the world in terms of their children. I have 10 grandchildren and in my family there is English, Scottish, American, French, Irish, Jewish and Indian blood, and for me politics is about their future, their survival. And I wonder whether you could say something yourself directly through this interview to the peace movement of the world that might help to advance the cause they have in mind?

SADDAM: First of all we admire the development of the peace movement around the world in the last few years. We pray to God to empower all those working against war and for the cause of peace and security based on just peace for all. And through you we say to the British people that Iraqis do not hate the British people. Before 1991 Iraq and Britain had a normal relationship as well as normal relations with America. At that time the British governments had no reason to criticise Iraq as we hear some voices doing these days. We hope the British people would tell those who hate the Iraqis and wish them harm that there is no reason to justify this war and please tell them that I say to you because the British people are brave—tell them that the Iraqis are brave too. Tell the British people if the Iraqis are subjected to aggression or humiliation they would fight bravely. Just as the

British people did in the Second World War and we will defend our country as they defended their country each in its own way. The Iraqis don't wish war but if war is imposed upon them—if they are attacked and insulted—they will defend themselves. They will defend their country, their sovereignty and their security. We will not disappoint those who believe in the principles of justice. And we will uphold the principles of justice and right that we strongly believe in.

Achieving Lasting Stability in Iraq

BY NIALL FERGUSON

After months of diplomatic stalemate and military posturing, an international coalition, led by the United States and consisting primarily of U.S and British forces, invaded Iraq in late March 2003. The coalition succeeded in deposing Hussein's Ba'ath regime within one month. However, the long-term outlook for better conditions in Iraq soon became doubtful. With no ruling authority, lawlessness prevailed with looters and violent gangs causing severe disruption. The religious and ethnic fragmentation of Iraq's populace, which had historically presented challenges to uniting the country under a single government, reemerged as a major obstacle. The occupying forces soon found themselves embroiled in ongoing skirmishes and ambushes, and a protracted guerrilla war seemed increasingly likely. These developments led some to question whether foreign forces should remain in Iraq.

In the following selection Niall Ferguson, an international historical author, argues that in order to ensure long-term stability in Iraq, the United States should mimic Britain's occupation of Egypt in the late 1800s and early 1900s. By offering nominal power to the Iraqis while retaining actual control of the political and economic systems, the United States can guarantee that Iraq will experience true autonomy in the future.

One month after the overthrow of Saddam Hussein, Iraq looks a lot closer to anarchy than to democracy. Looting is endemic because there are too few American troops to impose order. This week [June 2, 2003], 10,000 Shia took to the streets of Baghdad, exhorting the United States to quit the country altogether. And it is not only Iraqis who want the Yanks to go home. The other permanent members of the U.N. Security Council appear in no mood to give their blessing

Niall Ferguson, "Lessons from the British Empire: True Lies," *The New Republic*, June 2, 2003, pp. 16–19. Copyright © 2003 by The New Republic, Inc. Reproduced by permission.

to a protracted U.S. occupation of Iraq.

Somehow, then, the United States needs to impose order in Iraq while at the same time relinquishing power there. The good news is that there is a tried-and-tested way to accomplish this. The experience of the last anglophone empire in the Middle East offers a road map for the beleaguered American occupiers. But it is not Britain's occupation of Iraq that teaches valuable lessons; it is Britain's occupation of Egypt. Iraq was a relatively late addition to the British Empire, run only for a brief period during the 1920s as a League of Nations mandate. Egypt, acquired at the height of British power in the 1880s, was different. The resemblances between Britain's occupation of Egypt 121 years ago, touted at the time as the model of what a liberalizing imperial power could accomplish, and America's current occupation of Iraq are uncannily close, and Britain's Egyptian experience contains critical insights for the United States today. Most important, the Bush administration—and the American people—need to understand that successful imperialism (sorry, "nation-building") requires a kind of willful hypocrisy: The United States must stay in Iraq for a long time, but never stop promising to leave.

In 1882, A nationalist army officer named Said Ahmed Arabi seized power in Egypt, overthrowing the pro-British Khedive Tewfik. Arabi was no Saddam. And the pretext for foreign intervention was not the same as in Iraq today: violence against European residents in Alexandria as opposed to noncompliance with international calls for disarmament. However, the deeper causes for intervention are strikingly similar.

For a start, like George W. Bush on the 2000 campaign trail, the newly elected British government had pledged during the 1879 election campaign not to behave imperially. Liberal leader William Ewart Gladstone had condemned arch rival Benjamin Disraeli for meddling in Egypt and had made the avoidance of needless overseas entanglements a cornerstone of Liberal foreign policy. As late as January 1882, Gladstone was still advocating a policy of "Egypt for the Egyptians." But, like the United States in the Middle East today, Britain also had substantial economic interests in Egypt. More than 80 percent of the traffic going through the Suez Canal was British, and, in 1876, Britain had acquired a substantial shareholding in the Canal Company itself. What's more, a large chunk of Egypt's debt was owned by British bondholders—including the new prime minister himself.

A third factor reminiscent of America's Iraq war was Britain's initial expectation that any resolution of the Egypt crisis would need to involve the French, who also held Egyptian bonds and Canal shares. Since the Egyptian debt default of 1876, the country's finances had been under the control of a joint Anglo-French commission. Gladstone's immediate response to the Arabi crisis was to continue this cross-channel partnership. There was also a widespread belief that decisions governing what was then known as the Near East should be settled between all five great powers—Britain, France, Germany, Austria, and Russia, with Turkey (which still exercised formal suzerainty over Egypt) bullied as much as consulted. Great power conferences were the Victorian equivalent of the U.N. Security Council—and about as productive. Gladstone tried to secure international backing for military action against Egypt, just as President Bush sought backing from the United Nations. In both cases, the failure to achieve this backing, followed by the decision to act unilaterally, strained great-power relations.

Fourthly, as in Iraq today, there was no popular mandate in Egypt for a foreign occupation. As the future Conservative Prime Minister Lord Salisbury put it, "The Musselman [Muslim] feeling is still so strong that I believe we shall be safer and more powerful as wire-pullers than as ostensible rulers." Yet, once Gladstone had decided upon unilateral action, the British public was delighted by the swiftness of the military victory that ensued. The invading forces smashed Arabi's army in a matter of hours and with minimal British casualties. Even Gladstone was infected by the euphoric mood. "We and the whole country are in a state of rejoicing," he wrote shortly after Britain's victory. Indeed, commentators in London began to talk about imposing British rule not just on Egypt but also on neighboring Sudan, just as some hawks today propose that the United States now march into Syria.

Finally, there was the postwar reconstruction. After victory in battle, Britain quickly realized that Egypt's finances could be stabilized only through sweeping economic reforms and that these would require an ongoing British presence. Just as Americans today assume they know how to handle Iraq's reconstruction and democratization, the British were convinced they knew what would be good for Egypt. As Gladstone put it in his diary, the challenge was "how to plant solidly Western and beneficent [economic and political] institutions in the soil of a Mohamedan community." That, it swiftly became apparent, could not be done overnight.

Beneficial Deception

Immediately after conquering Egypt, Britain began vowing to leave. After occupying the country, Gladstone remarked, "Should the khedive desire it, a small British force may remain in Egypt." By August 1883, Gladstone had made no fewer than five public pledges to pull the British out of the country, an example followed by his successors. According to Gladstone's biographer, Colin Matthew, these were only the first of "what were to be at least sixty-six protestations of the temporary nature of the British presence in Egypt" between 1882 and 1922.

Yet, even as they made these promises, the British stayed in Egypt—and stayed and stayed and stayed. Britain maintained a fiction of Egyptian autonomy until World War I, when the "veiled protectorate" was converted into a real one. And, although in 1922 Egypt was formally declared independent, in reality the British continued to call the shots from behind the scenes. Indeed, they regarded the country as a de facto part of the Empire until the 1950s, when the Egyptian army overthrew the pro-British Egyptian monarchy. As late as October 1954, there were still 80,000 British troops in the Suez Canal Zone—a military base the size of Wales. Only that year did they finally go home, seven decades after the original invasion....

Steps Toward Stability

Promising to go while not actually doing so is of course a form of hypocrisy, and it is something all empires require. Indeed, only hypocrisy will solve America's current dilemma.

First, the United States must make it look like Iraqis are running the country. Indeed, [U.S. ambassador] L. Paul Bremer could learn from his Victorian predecessor Lord Cromer that it's quite all right to set up an interim ruling council of Iraqi notables and even to plan for a local national assembly in order to mollify local elites. But he has to ensure that ultimate control of military, fiscal, and monetary affairs remains firmly in American hands. This will not be easy. Repeatedly during their time in Egypt, the British had to resist the efforts of the country's nominal rulers to go it alone. In 1884, 1888, 1891, and 1919, the British were forced to sack recalcitrant Egyptian ministers. Anti-British forces sometimes fought back, and, in 1924, the British military commander in Egypt was assassinated. But the British remained in charge. In other words, it can be done.

Lesson number two from Britain's Egypt experience is economic. The United States must realize that Iraq's economic recovery requires not only troops but also an infusion of serious money into postwar reconstruction, just as the City of London helped stabilize Egyptian finances in the 1880s. Some American officials think that Iraq can finance its own recovery by boosting oil exports. But Iraq's oil fields are in dire need of repair and modernization. Given the country's current impoverishment, this simply will not happen without foreign investment. And investment in turn will not be forthcoming in the absence of an effective rule of law that secures private-property rights and a stable financial system that ensures a sustainable allocation of future oil revenue. Iraq, accordingly, needs something equivalent to the big loans floated by the Rothschild bank to stabilize Egyptian finances—which amounted to 50 million pounds between 1885 and 1893—in order to help resurrect its financial system. The trouble is that Iraq's existing foreign debts are daunting: more than $60 billion to foreign lenders plus another $200 billion in reparations claims dating back to the invasion of Kuwait. This is why the IMF—the modern equivalent of the Rothschilds—needs to help stabilize Iraq's finances and show foreign investors that they will not be throwing good money after bad if they lend to Iraq. In a briefing given in early May, Thomas Dawson, director of the IMF's External Relations Department, said the Fund was still collecting data and assessing a potential involvement in Iraq. That is not good enough. The Rothschilds moved faster in the age of steamships and telegraphs.

The third and final lesson is a diplomatic one. Like Gladstone, Bush is not so giddy with military, success as to disregard international opinion. Just as Gladstone sought to reach agreement with France about Egypt's finances after 1882, so too has Bush had to beat a path back to the United Nations to seek a lifting of sanctions on Iraq and to offer the U.N. a limited role in postwar reconstruction. Like Gladstone, Bush needs to give his foreign protectorate at least a semblance of international legitimacy. Gladstone did so because he needed France's agreement to reschedule Egypt's debts. Bush has an additional reason. Without international legitimacy, the United States can expect minimal help from Europe when it comes to policing Iraq. The humdrum work of peacekeeping is, after all, not what most American soldiers are trained for. As in Bosnia, the United States should hand over some of the dirty work of patrolling and manning checkpoints to European troops. But that will only be possible if the Europeans get what they want: the semblance of an imminent U.S. handover of power in Iraq.

Note the word semblance. As the British showed in Egypt, you can keep up this kind of hypocrisy for quite a long time before you actually have to restore self-government for real. Of course, hypocrisy is not terribly nice. It is, however, the only way the United States can reconcile its urgent need to remain in control of Iraq for the foreseeable future with the equally urgent need to appear on the point of departure.

Asked recently if he was worried about giving the impression that "the United States is becoming an imperial, colonial power," Defense Secretary Donald Rumsfeld retorted indignantly, "That's just not what the United States does. We never have, and we never will. That's not how democracies behave." Gladstone would have approved. Saying one thing and doing another is precisely how imperial democracies behave.

Chronology

ca. 6000 B.C.
The city-state of Sumer is settled.

ca. 5000 B.C.
Sumerian development of canals and irrigation systems leads to massive agricultural production and the emergence of modern civil society based on diverse economic activities.

ca. 2300 B.C.
The Akkadians conquer Sumer and the merging of the two cultures leads to the emergence of the city-state of Babylon.

1792–1750 B.C.
Hammurabi reigns over Babylon during the height of its power.

ca. 1300 B.C.
The Assyrians conquer Babylon.

612 B.C.
Babylonian revolts drive the Assyrians from power in Mesopotamia.

605–562 B.C.
Nebuchadnezzar reigns over another period of Babylonian supremacy and grandeur.

539 B.C.
Persian emperor Cyrus the Great conquers Babylon, ushering in a long era during which Mesopotamia is dominated by foreign powers.

331 B.C.
Alexander the Great conquers the territories of modern Iraq.

A.D. 227
After centuries of conflict between Romans and Persians for control of Iraq, the Persian Sassanids conquer the area and remain in power there for over four hundred years.

636
A Muslim Arab victory over the Sassanids at the Battle of Kadisiya paves the way for Muslim Arab domination in Iraq.

661
The Umayyad caliphate is established and based in Damascus, Syria, heightening tensions between Sunni Muslims and Shias, who are the majority in Iraq.

750
The Abbasids, based in what is now Iran, defeat the Umayyads and establish a new caliphate in the Muslim world.

762
The city of Baghdad is built as the center of the Abbasid caliphate.

786–833
Baghdad reaches its height of glory, becoming a center of high art, culture, science and intellect, and political power.

945
The Iranian clan the Buwayhids come to power in Iraq.

1055
The Seljuk Turks defeat the Buwayhids and take control of Baghdad.

1258
Hulagu Khan, descendant of Ghengis Khan, conquers Iraq and ends the rule of the Abbasid caliphate after more than five hundred years.

1401
Another Mongol descendant ruler, Tamerlane, wreaks yet more havoc and destruction upon Baghdad and commits massive massacres of its populace.

1534
The Turkish Ottomans defeat the Iranian Safavids to win control over Iraq.

1624–1638
The Safavids regain control of Iraq but are again driven out of the area by the Ottomans.

1869
After centuries of decline, a lack of centralized government authority, and regression to tribal primitivism, the Ottoman-appointed governor Midhat Pasha helps restore stability and promote renewed social progress in Iraq.

1908
Revolutionaries in Turkey known as the Young Turks overthrow the government, giving hope to a growing number of Arab-independence advocates in the Arab areas of the Ottoman Empire. However, the Young Turks seek to expand central Turkish control over the empire, galvanizing revolutionary sentiments among the Arabs against Turkey.

1914–1918
Iraq is a major theater of battle between Turkish and British forces in World War I.

1916
The Sykes-Picot Agreement between England and France secretly outlines postwar plans for the governing of Ottoman Arab territories.

1919
The League of Nations issues the British Mandate, giving control of much of the Ottoman Arab areas, including Iraq, to Britain.

1920
Iraqis revolt against the newly imposed British rule in a widespread uprising.

1921
The British create an Iraqi government with King Faisal, a descendant of the prophet Muhammad, as its leader.

1932
Iraq becomes a fully independent nation.

1936
Iraq experiences its first military coup, setting a precedent for instability in the central government that will last for many years.

1941–1945
British forces invade and reoccupy Iraq after Iraq shows signs of siding with the Axis powers in World War II.

1948
Another widespread uprising against British influence occurs among the Iraqi people as new agreements made after World War II again give significant power over Iraqi affairs to Britain.

1955
Iraq joins Britain, Turkey, Pakistan, and Iran in a mutual defense agreement known as the Baghdad Pact. This intensifies anti-British and independence sentiments among the Iraqi people.

1958
A group of military officers advocating Arab independence from foreign influence deposes the monarchy and announces the birth of the Republic of Iraq.

1959
The Ba'ath Socialist Party, a militant faction within Iraq, attempts to assassinate the military ruler Adbul Karim Qasim. Among those participating in the attempt is future Iraqi ruler Saddam Hussein.

1963
The Ba'ath Party, in cooperation with military officers opposed to the Qasim government, stages a successful coup, but the

Ba'ath factions are quickly purged from the new government.

1968
The Ba'ath Party stages another coup, this one led by Ahmad Hasan Bakr, a kinsman of Saddam Hussein. This time the Ba'ath purges members of the military who helped them stage the coup before they can be purged themselves.

1968–1979
Saddam Hussein rises to the level of second in command in the Iraqi government and plays a critical role in consolidating Ba'ath power and promoting nationalist unity in Iraq.

1979
When Bakr steps down from power for what he cites as health reasons, Saddam Hussein becomes supreme ruler of Iraq.

1980–1988
Iraq battles Iran in a war that is costly and destructive; however, it brings widespread international support to Iraq and enables the nation to emerge economically and militarily stronger than it has been in more than a thousand years.

1990
Iraq invades its southern neighbor Kuwait over territorial and financial disputes, causing fiercely negative reaction throughout the world.

1991
An international coalition led by the United States attacks Iraqi forces in both Kuwait and Iraq and drives them out of Kuwait.

1991–2001
International economic sanctions and occasional military strikes against Iraq, geared to prevent it from again becoming a military threat and to displace the Hussein regime, weaken Iraq both economically and militarily but have little adverse effect on Hussein's government.

2002

Claiming that Iraq has ties to international terrorists, U.S. president George W. Bush cites Iraq as one of three nations constituting an "Axis of Evil" and indicates a willingness to take military action against Iraq.

2003

Another U.S.-led coalition attacks and invades Iraq, topples the regime of Saddam Hussein, and occupies the country on an ongoing basis.

For Further Research

Books

Said K. Aburish, *Saddam Hussein: The Politics of Revenge*. London: Bloomsbury, 2001.

Stephen Bertman, *Handbook to Life in Ancient Mesopotamia*. New York: Facts On File, 2002.

Richard Butler, *The Greatest Threat: Iraq, Weapons of Mass Destruction, and the Growing Crisis of Global Security*. New York: Public Affairs, 2000.

Andrew Cockburn and Patrick Cockburn, *Out of the Ashes: The Resurrection of Saddam Hussein*. New York: HarperCollins, 1999.

Marion Farouk-Sluglett et al., *Iraq Since 1958: From Revolution to Dictatorship*. London: I.B. Tauris, 2001.

Andrew George, trans., *The Epic of Gilgamesh*. London: Penguin Books, 1999.

Cyril Glasse, *The New Encyclopedia of Islam*. Walnut Creek, CA: AltaMira Press, 2001.

Jason Goodwin, *Lords of the Horizons: A History of the Ottoman Empire*. New York: Henry Holt, 1999.

Dilip Hiro, *Iraq in the Eye of the Storm*. New York: Thunder's Mouth Press/Nation Books, 2002.

———, *The Longest War: The Iran-Iraq Military Conflict*. New York: Routledge, 1991.

Christopher Hitchens, *A Long Short War: The Postponed Liberation of Iraq*. New York: Plume, 2003.

Samuel Noah Kramer, *History Begins at Sumer: Thirty-Nine Firsts in Man's Recorded History*. Philadelphia: University of Pennsylvania Press, 1981.

Harold Lamb, *Cyrus the Great*. Garden City, NY: Doubleday, 1960.

Bernard Lewis, *The Arabs in History*. London: Hutchinson, 1966.

———, *The Middle East: A Brief History of the Last 2,000 Years*. New York: Scribner, 1995.

Helen Chapin Metz, ed., *Iraq: A Country Study*. Washington, DC: U.S. Government Printing Office, 1990.

Turi Munthe, ed., *The Saddam Hussein Reader*. New York: Thunder's Mouth Press, 2002.

Tim Niblock, ed., *Iraq, the Contemporary State*. New York: St. Martin's Press, 1982.

Kenneth M. Pollack, *The Threatening Storm: The Case for Invading Iraq*. New York: Random House, 2002.

Michael Prawdin, *The Mongol Empire: Its Rise and Legacy*. Trans. Eden and Cedar Paul. New York: Free Press, 1967.

Scott Ritter, *Endgame: Solving the Iraq Problem—Once and for All*. New York: Simon & Schuster, 1999.

Stanford J. Shaw and Ezel Kural Shaw, *History of the Ottoman Empire and Modern Turkey*. Vol. 2. Cambridge, England: Cambridge University Press, 1977.

Sumer: Cities of Eden. Alexandria, VA: Time-Life Books, 1993.

Clarice Swisher, ed., *The Spread of Islam*. San Diego, CA: Greenhaven Press, 1999.

Joseph Tragert and James S. Robbins, *The Complete Idiot's Guide to Understanding Iraq*. Indianapolis, IN: Alpha Books, 2002.

Tim Trevan, *Saddam's Secrets: The Hunt for Iraq's Hidden Weapons*. London: HarperCollins, 1999.

James Howard Wellard, *Babylon*. New York: Saturday Review Press, 1972.

Websites

Congressional Research Service: Iraq Research, www.iraqresearch.com. Produced by the public policy research office of the U.S. Congress, this site contains extensive background information on Iraq, as well as links to numerous reports on Iraq issued by the Congressional Research Service.

CountryReports.org, www.countryreports.org. This website contains information on all the nations of the world, including economic, political, geographic, demographic, and historical information on Iraq.

National Geographic Hot Spot: Iraq, www.nationalgeographic.com/iraq. The famous international magazine's website contains this page dedicated to news articles, pictures, maps, and lessons on Iraq and the Middle East.

Index

Abbas, Abu, 197
Abbasids, 21, 22, 24, 72, 78
  cities of, 73, 75
Abbas I (shah of Persia), 90
'Abd al-Hamid (Ottoman sultan), 102, 111
'Abd al-Rahman al-Kaylāni, 108
'Abdul-Ilah (prince regent of Iraq), 121, 138
Abdul-Kadir Gilani, 88
Abū-Bakr, 68, 69
Abu Hanifa, 88
Abu Nidal, 197
Aflaq, Michel, 127, 152
  on Saddam Hussein's promotion in Ba'ath Party, 150, 153
agriculture, 94, 124
  in city of Babylon, 44
  Sumerian developments in, 38–39
Ahali, 119, 120
al-Ahd, 103–104
A'ishah, 68, 70
Akkadians, 17, 40
Alexander the Great, 19, 40, 44, 63–65
Alexandria, 64, 69, 213
Algiers Agreement (1975), 167, 173
'Ali, 68, 70–71, 72, 96
'Ali Rida Pasha (governor of Aleppo), 98
Allen, Edmund, 112
Al'Ubaid, 48
al-Amiri, Hasan, 155
Antigonus, 65

Anu, 45
Arab Ba'ath Socialist Party (ABSP). See Ba'ath Party
Arabi, Said Ahmed, 213, 214
Arab League, 139, 178, 180
Arabs, 20–24
  as allies of British in WWI, 27
  conflict with Kurds and, 26, 29
  rivalry with Persians and, 23
  see also pan-Arabism
Arcacids, 66
Aref, Abd al-Rahman, 140, 141, 155–56
Aref, Abd al-Salam, 153–55
Ariaramnes, House of, 61
Armistice of Mudros, 105
army, 104, 119, 135, 144, 151
  involvement of, in politics, 120, 139, 141
  Khomeini's address to, 172
  monarchy not defended by, 133
  nationalism in, 144
art, 39, 44, 49
  Ishtar Gate decoration and, 56–58
  religious sculpture and, 45–48
  see also literature
Ashur, 43, 44
Ashurbanipal (Assyrian king), 43
Asia Minor, 62, 65, 74
  Tamerlane in, 88
al-Askari, Ja'far, 119
Assassins, 77, 80
Assyrian Empire, 18, 40, 43–44, 63–64

Astyages (Median leader), 61–62
Atomic Energy Commission (U.S.), 188
Axis powers, 29, 121, 122, 144
al-Ayyubi, Ali Jaudat, 118
Aziz, Tariq, 137, 208–209

Ba'ath Party, 127, 137, 140, 156
  education of youth and, 157–58
  influence on families through, 159
  militia of, 139
  violence of, 135, 136
  pan-Arabism of, 30, 140, 184
  power gained by, 141, 151
  reaction of, to fundamentalism, 169–71
  reduction of illiteracy rates by, 160–61
  rival factions in, 152
  Saddam Hussein's career in, 31, 148–49, 153–55
  standard of living improved by, 164
  status of women improved by, 162–63
  underground activity and, 150
Babylon, 15, 19, 63–64
  changes of power in, 65
  decline of, 44
  merging of two cultures in, 17
  as sacked by Hittites, 42–43
  two-thousand-year continuity of, 18, 40
  see also Ishtar Gate
Babylonia, 40–43, 63–64
  conquered by Parthians, 65–66
Baghdad, 15, 88, 124
  anti-British sentiment in, 107
  attack on Tariq Aziz in, 170
  British takeover of, 105
  as center for international trade, 73–74
  as center for pro-Axis activities, 144
  as center of Islamic/Arab civilization, 21–22
  decline of, 23–25, 76
  distinctive populations of, 95
  founding of, 72
  growth of political activity in, 101
  location of, between two rivers, 75
  mamluk rule in, 98
  Marco Polo's description of, 83–84
  members of al-Ahd in, 104
  Midhat Pasha as governor of, 26, 99
  military coups in, 119, 139, 151
  Mongol attack on, 24, 78–79, 80
  Ottoman power in, 89, 92, 100
  Persian takeover of, 90
  Saddam Hussein in, 146, 149, 154
Baghdad Pact (1955), 125, 126, 146, 147
Baghdad Radio, 133
Baker, James, 179
al-Bakr, Ahmad Hasan, 30, 137, 152–55, 169
  is relative of Saddam Hussein, 148, 151
  is replaced as leader by Saddam Hussein, 31
Basra, 25, 70, 90, 92, 174
  Arab establishment of, 69
  Bedouin control of, 89
  British occupation of, 105
  growth of political activity in, 101
  high commissioner Cox in, 108
  mamluk rule and, 97–98
  as port city, 75
  Safavid control of, 88

Index

Batatu, Hanna, 28
Bedouins, 69, 89
Begin, Menachem, 190–91
Bekr, Su Bashi, 90
Belshazzar, 62
Benn, Tony, 206
Bible, 40
  Daniel, 43, 60
bin Laden, Osama, 198
Bint al-Huda, Amina, 171
Borsippa, tower of, 54
Bremer, L. Paul, 215
Britain, 121, 166, 188, 210
  maintenance of sanctions against Iraq by, 33
  occupation of Egypt and, 213–17
  participation of, in attack on Iraq, 33–34
  presence of, in Iraq, 104–106
    anti-British sentiment and, 144
    Baghdad Pact and, 125
    following WWI, 27–28
    negotiations for independence and, 110, 113–15
    1920 revolt against, 107–108
    1958 closing of military bases and, 134, 215
    Portsmouth Treaty and, 123–24
    during WWII, 29, 122
  Suez crisis and, 147
British East India Company, 93, 97
Bureau of Special Investigation (Ba'ath enforcement office), 139
Bush, George H.W., 178, 202
Bush, George W., 34, 195, 202, 213, 216
Buwayhids, 23, 25
Byzantine Empire, 20, 87
  Muslim expansion into, 69

Cairo, 151

Conference of 1921 and, 108
calendar, 39, 65, 77
Cambyses I (Persian king), 61
Camel, Battle of the, 70
Canaanites, 40
Catal Huyuk, 38
Christians, 69, 78, 82, 83, 94
Churchill, Winston, 113
cities, 63, 75, 135
  Arabic, 69
  shift of rural dwellers to, 17
  Sumerian, 53
  see also Babylon; Baghdad; Basra; Mosul
civil liberties, curtailment of, 120, 137–39, 170
  for Communists, 123, 126
climate, 73
Cockburn, Andrew, 29, 31, 32, 33
Cockburn, Patrick, 29, 31, 32, 33
Committee of Union and Progress (CUP), 100
  centralizing policy of, 101
communism, 119, 126, 169–70
  supporters of, in violent militia, 136, 150
  suppression of, 123, 137, 151
Comprehensive National Campaign for Compulsory Eradication of Illiteracy, 160
Congress, U.S., 179, 196
Constantinople, 20, 87, 88, 112
Constitutional Union Party, 126
Cox, Sir Percy, 108
Croesus (king of Lydia), 62
Crusaders, 78, 80, 87, 143
cuneiform tablets, 16, 40, 47, 62
culture, 16, 74, 77, 93–94, 96
  effects of Islam on, 21–22
  merging of Akkadian and Sumerian, 17, 43
  in Mesopotamia, 18–19, 37
  see also art; religion; social

structure; writing
cylinder-seals, 48–49, 63
Cyrus I (Cyrus the Great) (king of Persia), 19, 44, 60–64
"Czech deal," 147

Damascus (Syria), 21, 69, 71, 151
   death of Yasin al-Hashimi in, 119
   King Faisal's capture of, 112
Da'ud Pasha (*mamluk* governor of Baghdad), 98
al-Dawah, 170, 171
Dawson, Thomas, 216
Diodorus, 44
Disraeli, Benjamin, 213
Dumuzi, 46

Early Dynastic period, 49
economy, 61, 77, 83, 105, 123
   decline of Mesopotamia and, 63–64
   effect of Iran-Iraq War on, 175–76
   need for foreign investment and, 216
   in postindependence Iraq, 119
   in postwar Iraq, 124–25
   see also trade
education, 83, 98, 136, 160–61
   in ninth century, 74, 77
   rise of nationalism and, 26
   of women, 162
Egypt, 19, 65, 80, 97, 126
   Britain's occupation of, 212–17
   effect of Six-Day War on, 140
   International Atomic Energy Agency and, 192–93
   Iraq's rival for Arab leadership and, 123, 146
   Saddam Hussein in, 30, 151
   spread of Islamic power and, 22, 69
   Suez crisis and, 147

E.hul.hul, 60, 62
En, 50–53
Enki of Eridu, 45
Enlil, 45
Euphrates River, 16, 40, 73–75, 88, 92
   Alexander the Great's plans for, 64

Faisal I (king of Iraq), 27, 29, 107, 108, 110
   as leader in Arab nationalism, 111–12
   moderate policy of, during process of British withdrawal, 113–14
   role of, in building Iraqi state, 115–17
   succeeded by son in 1933, 118
Faisal II (king of Iraq), 121, 124, 125, 138
   death of, 138
Faiziyeh Theological School, 167
Ferguson, Niall, 212
Ferneal, Robert A., 134
France, 110, 113, 168, 188
   Paris Peace Conference and, 112
Frazer, Sir James, 46

Gadd, Cyril John, 51
Gaugamela, Battle of, 64
General Federation for Iraqi Women, 163
George, Andrew, 50–51
Ghazi (king of Iraq), 118, 121
Genghis Khan, 80
Gibbon, Edward, 143
Gilgamesh (poem), 50–51
Gladstone, William Ewart, 213–17
Golden Bough, The (Frazer), 46
government of Iraq, 92–93
   British involvement in, 27–29, 104–106

revolt against, 107–108
end of monarchy and, 133–34, 138, 154
military authoritarianism in place of, 141
independence and, 15, 110
gradual process of acquiring, 113–17
instability in, 125–26, 144
European involvement and, 122
in postindependence period, 30, 118–21
in postrevolution period, 135–37, 139–40
in postwar period, 123–24
Ottoman rule and, 94–96, 98–101
weakened by tribal division, 97
Young Turks and, 102–103
see also Ba'ath Party
Great Iraqi Revolution, 28
Gulf War (1991), 195, 197, 203
objectives of, 179–82
prompted by Hussein's attack on Kuwait, 178

Habbaniya, 122
Hammurabi (king of Babylon), 17
Code of, 18, 41–42
Hamza, Khidhir, 183
Hart, Michael, 19
Hasan-i-Sabbah, 77
al-Hashimi, General Taha, 121
al-Hashimi, Yasin, 119
Herodotus, 64
Hiro, Dilip, 27–28
History of Iraq, A (Tripp), 92
History of the Ottoman Empire and Modern Turkey (Shaw and Shaw), 26
Hittin, battle of, 143
Hittites, 40, 42–43

Hulagu, 78–79, 80
Hurrians, 40, 43
Hussein, Saddam, 30, 141, 177, 202, 206
assassination attempt on Kassem and, 135, 150
attack on Kuwait and, 178–80
attack on Shi'ite political movement and, 170–71
childhood of, 144–45
on children's role in revolution, 158–60
education of, 146
in Egypt, 151
Iran-Iraq War and, 32, 172–77
overthrow of, 33–34, 212
in prison, 154–55
public relations campaign of, 174
quest of, for nuclear weapons, 183, 187–88
plan to infiltrate International Atomic Energy Agency and, 189–93
reaction of, to Ayatollah Khomeini's fundamentalism, 168, 169
regional interests of, 203–204
role of, in Ba'ath Party, 31, 139, 147–49, 153
threat posed to world by, 196–200, 202
need to disarm and, 201
need for evidence of, before U.S. attack on Iraq, 205
Hussein I (king of Jordan), 138

Ibrahim Pasha, 89
Imgur-Bel, 55
imperialism, 209
eradication of, the goal of revolution, 133, 134
Inanna, 46, 49
Independent Iraq: A Study of Iraqi

Politics from 1932 to 1958
(Khadduri), 110
India, 63–65, 73, 88, 97, 188
India Office Policy, 107, 108
International Atomic Energy
Agency (IAEA), 189–93, 199
Ionia, 62
Iran, 22, 62, 166
  defeat of, 176–77
  demands for reform in, 168
  Islamic revolution in, 31–32, 169
  nuclear power and, 190–91
  reason for war with Iraq and, 165
  Saddam Hussein's chemical
    attacks against, 197
  Saddam Hussein's perception of,
    172–73
  secularism vs. theocracy in, 167
  U.S. support for, 192
Iran-Iraq War, 31–33, 165, 174
  fundamentalist threat to Iraq
    and, 169–70
  Ba'ath regime's reaction to, 171
  Iraqi suffering and, 175
  nationalism of Iraqis encouraged
    by, 177
  role of Saddam Hussein in,
    172–73
  roots of, 166–68
  widening area of conflict and,
    176
Iraq, 15
  anarchy in, 212
  history of foreign involvement
    in, 16, 18, 23–25, 59, 76–81
    including British presence,
      27–29, 104–108, 110
    including *mamluk* pashas,
      93–97
    including Ottoman presence,
      87, 89–91, 98–100
  inhabitants of, described by
    Marco Polo, 82–85

  as member of regional defense
    organization, 146
  representation in International
    Atomic Energy Agency and,
    189–93
  sanctions against, 33
  self-defense in, intention of,
    210–11
  social regression in, 25
  status of, improved by war with
    Iran, 32
  Suez crisis and, 147
  threat posed by, 195–98
    need for new approach and,
      201
    nuclear weapons program and,
      199–200
    U.S. attack not justified by,
      203–204
  three provinces of, 25–26, 92
  2003 attack on, 33–34
  see also government of Iraq
Iraq: A Country Study (Metz), 18,
  20–23, 25–26, 28
Iraq: From Sumer to Saddam
  (Simons), 87
Iraqi Atomic Energy
  Commission, 183, 185, 186, 187
Iraqi Communist Party (ICP), 137
"Iraq: In One Swift Hour" (*Time*
  magazine), 138
Iraq in the Eye of the Storm (Hiro),
  27–28
Iraq Treaty of Alliance, 110,
  113–14
irrigation works, 16, 38–39, 119,
  120, 135
Isfahan, 176
Ishtar Gate, 54–56
Islam, 20, 71, 74, 77
  expansion of, 69
  social tensions caused by, 70
  influence of, on invaders, 81

Index

Ottoman adoption of, 87
regional variations in observance of, 94
strength of, 24
two main branches of, 23, 29, 71, 89, 97
  cooperation in anti-British movement and, 107
  in different areas of Iraq, 26
  see also Shi'ite Muslims; Sunni Muslims
Islam and the Arabs (Landau), 76
Islam: An Illustrated Historical Overview (Weiss), 68
Ismail I, 88
Israel, 123, 140, 188, 197
  Iraqi nuclear reactor raided by, 190–91
  is perceived as nuclear threat in Middle East, 185–86
  U.S. desire to promote, in Middle East, 209
  vulnerability of attack from Iraq on, 197, 203–204
Israeli Bomb, The (Jabir), 184–86
Istanbul, 90, 93, 98
  Iraqi delegates sent to, 103

Jabir, Fouad, 184–86
Jabr, Salih, 123, 126
Jacobsen, Thorkild, 51–52, 53
Jalili, 94, 95, 98
al-Jamali, Fadhil, 124, 125
Jerome, Saint, 44
Jerusalem, 18, 44, 140
  liberated from Christian rule, 143
  Muslim troops victorious in, 69
Jews, 95
Jordan, 140
al-Jumhuriyya (newspaper), 162

Kadisiya, Battle of , 20

al-Kailani, Rashid Ali, 118–19, 121–22, 144
Karbala, 96, 106, 107, 175
Karsh, Efraim, 143
Kassem, Abdul Karim, 30, 134, 138
  assassination attempt on, 135, 149, 154
  execution of, 136, 151
  responsibility of, for Mosul massacre, 150
Kassites, 43
al-Kazimiyya, 96
Kendall, J.P., 181
Kennedy, John F., 200
Khadduri, Majid, 110
al-Khalil, Samir, 157
Kharijites, 71
Khomeini, Ruhollah, 66, 167–69, 172, 176–77
Khurasanians, 72
kingship, 49–53
  see also monarchy
Kirkuk, 105, 107, 150
Koldewey, Robert, 54
Koppel, Ted, 208–209
Koran, 70, 74, 75
Kublai Khan, 82
Kufah, 69, 72
Kurdistan, 173
Kurds, 26, 83, 93–94, 167
  autonomy promised to, 134
  British-appointed government resisted by, 28
  lack of interest in Arab nationalism by, 107
Kuwait, 33, 175, 176
  war prompted by Hussein's attack and, 178–82

Landau, Rom, 76
Land Law (1858), 98, 99–100
land reform, 98–100, 134, 135

land tax, 124
language, 16, 40, 43, 85
  regional variations in, 93–94
  spread of Arabic and, 69
  of superpowers, 210
Lansing, Robert, 116
law, 83, 96, 103, 106, 126
  Babylonian, 43
  Code of Hammurabi and, 18, 41–42
  investment dependent on enforcement of, 216
  Islamic, 164
  origins of, 37
  see also land reform
Lawrence, T.E., 112
League of Nations, 27, 110, 147, 213
  Iraq admitted as member of, 114–15
Lewis, Bernard, 21, 22
literacy rates, 160–62
literature, 38, 50–51
Lloyd, Seton, 45
Longrigg, Stephen Hemsley, 118
Lydia, 62

Macedonia, 19
Mackey, Sandra, 133, 165
Madinat-al-Salam (City of Peace). *See* Baghdad
Mahmud II (Ottoman sultan), 97
al-Mallah, 183–87
Mamluks, 80, 87, 88
Manhattan Project reports, 188
al-Mansur, 21–22, 74, 75
Marduk, 43–45, 59, 60, 62–64
Marr, Phebe, 102
marriage, 42
Mas'udi, 75
Matthew, Colin, 215
Medes, 61, 62
Medina, 113

Mediterranean, 18
Mehmed II (Ottoman sultan), 87–88
Mesopotamia, 18, 19, 92, 93, 166
  as cradle of civilization, 15, 37
  decline of, 20, 63–64
  Mongol invasion of, 78
  various conquests of, 59–61, 64–66
  by Persians, 62–63
  see also Assyrian Empire; Babylonia; Sumer
Metz, Helen Chapin, 18, 20, 21–22
Middle East, 15, 32, 203–204, 209
  Iraq's strategic location in, 15
  Ottoman control of, 89
  territory of, divided by Western powers, 106, 147
Middle East, The (Lewis), 22
mid-Euphrates region, 96, 107
al-Midfa'i, Jamil, 118–22
Midhat Pasha, 26, 99
military coups, 119, 120, 121
  in 1958, 133, 138
  in 1963, 136, 139
  in 1968, 141
Modern History of Iraq, The (Marr), 102
Mohammad Reza Pahlavi (shah of Iran), 166–69, 192
monarchy, 104, 121, 141, 144
  end of, in Iraq, 133, 154
  bureaucracy of Iraq destroyed by, 135
  violent, 138, 149
  establishment of, in Iraq, 108
  replacement by Islamic government, in Iran, 31–32
  Saddam Hussein's hatred of, 145
  Sumerian concept of, 50–53
Mongol Empire: Its Rise and Legacy (Prawdin), 24, 78–79

Index

Mongols, 24
  Assassins defeated by, 80
  capture of Baghdad by, 78–79
  influence of Islamic religion and culture on, 81
Mosaic Code, 41
Mosul, 25, 90, 92, 105, 174
  conquered by Shah Ismail, 88
  growth of political activity in, 101
  massacre in, 150
  members of al-Ahd in, 104
  Muslims and Christians in, 82
  Ottoman authority and, 94, 98
  trade and, 83
Mu'awiyah, 70, 71
Muhammad 'Ali Pasha (provincial governor of Egypt), 97
Muhammad, Prophet, 23, 68
  descendants of, in Iraq, 94
Murad IV (Ottoman sultan), 90, 91
Mursilis I (king of Hittites), 43
al-Musta'sim, 22, 24, 78–79

Nabonidus (Babylonian king), 59, 60, 61, 62
Nabopolassar (Babylonian king), 43
Najaf (Shi'ite city), 96, 106, 107, 171
  Ayatollah Khomeini in, 168
  Ba'athist attempt to secularize, 170
al-Nasiriyyah, 106
Nasser, Gamal Abd al, 137, 146–47
  as president of UAR, 149
National Brotherhood, 118–19
National Council of the Revolutionary Command (NCRC), 137
National Guard (Ba'ath militia), 137, 139, 151, 152

nationalism
  Iraqi, 105, 107, 114–15, 126, 145
    Baghdad Pact and, 147
    demand for restoration of free political activity and, 123
    rebellion against British and, 27–28
    support for Kassem and, 135
  Persian revival of, 88
  support for, in army, 144
  Syrian, 112–13
  Western idea of, 111
  see also pan-Arabism
Nebuchadnezzar II (Babylonian king), 43–44, 56, 59, 60
New York Times (newspaper), 34
Nightline (ABC news program), 208–209
Nimitti-Bel, 54, 55
Nineveh, 43, 172
Nin-khursag, 46
Ninurta, 46
Nippur, 45, 63
Nizam-al-Mulk (Seljuk leader), 77

oil resources, 15, 105, 123, 176, 216
  effect of Iran-Iraq War on, 175
  exports of, 124–25
  Iran a threat to, 166–67
  used to pressure IAEA voters, 191–92
Omar Khayyám, 77
One Hundred: A Ranking of the Most Influential Persons in History (Hart), 19
Ottoman Empire, 25, 87, 92, 104, 106
  end of, 91, 147
  expansion of, 88
  into Iraq, 89–91
  influence of, in Iraqi cities, 94–95

Shi'ite resistance to, 96
military rulers of, 93
reassertion of power by, 97–100
Out of the Ashes: The Resurrection of Saddam Hussein (Cockburn and Cockburn), 29, 31, 32, 33

al-Pachachi, Hamdi, 122
al-Pachachi, Muzahim, 124
Paine, Thomas, 181
Pakistan, 125, 188
Palestine, 44, 69, 119
   capture of, by Sultan Selim I, 88
Palestine War, 124
pan-Arabism, 27, 29–30, 101, 103, 127
   Arif's support for, 139
   Ba'ath government support for, 140
   Baghdad Pact seen as betrayal of, 147
   Cairo, as center of, 151
   challenge of, to European imperialism, 110
   Hashimi government support for, 119
   King Faisal's leadership in, 111–13
   limit of, in prewar Iraq, 104
   Marxist ideology opposed to, 137
   meaning of, for individuals, 129
   struggle necessary for, 128
   unity the goal of, 123, 132
   view of past and, 130–31
Paris Peace Conference, 112
Parthians, 65–66
Partisans of Peace, 126
pashas, *mamluk*, 87, 93, 96–98
peacekeeping, 216–17
peace movement, 210
Persia, 19, 61, 80, 91, 96
   borders of, straddled by various tribal groups, 94
   national revival under Safavids in, 88
Persian Gulf, 166, 173, 175
   see also Gulf War (1991)
Persians, 23, 61, 64, 90
   Babylon and, 44, 62–63
Pioneers, 157
plough, 38
plutonium, 188
Political Report (ABSP), 160
Polo, Marco, 82, 85
Portsmouth Treaty, 123–24
Powell, Colin, 198
Prawdin, Michael, 24, 78–79
Press Law, 126
Protoliterate period, 45, 48, 49
Ptolemy, 65

Qadisiyyah, battle of, 69
al-Qaeda
   Saddam Hussein linked to, 198, 200
   con, 203, 207, 208
Qasim, Abd al-Karim. *See* Kassem, Abdul Karim
Qasr al-Nihayah, 139
Qom, 167, 168, 176

Rautsi, Inari, 143
Reckoning: Iraq and the Legacy of Saddam Hussein (Mackey), 133, 165
religion, 45–46, 49, 59–60, 70, 82
   see also Islam
Republic of Fear: The Inside Story of Saddam's Iraq (al-Khalil), 157
revolution, 127–28, 140, 160
   of 1958, 133–34, 138, 149
      pan-Arabic justification for, 129–32
   of Young Turks, 100, 104, 111
Revolutionary Command

Council, 160, 170
Roux, Georges, 45–46, 59
Rumsfeld, Donald, 217

Saddam Hussein: A Political Biography (Karsh and Rautsi), 143
Saddam's Bombmaker (Hamza), 183
al-Sadr, Muhammad Baqir, 124, 171
Safavids, 25, 92
 decline of, 89–90
 Persian national revival under, 88
Saffah, 72
Saggs, H.W.F., 51
al-Sa'id, Nuri (prime minister of Iraq), 29, 114–15, 119–25, 133, 146
Saladin (sultan of Egypt and Syria), 80, 143
Samarra, 74, 96
Samsu-iluna, 42
sanctions against Iraq, 33, 197
Sargon I (Akkadian king), 17
Sasanians, 19–20
Sassanids, 66, 69
Saudi Arabia, 122, 176, 191, 197
Sauvaget, Jean, 74
Schiffer, Shimon, 190–91
Scowcroft, Brent, 202
sculpture, 45–48
Seleucus, 65
Selim I (Ottoman sultan), 88
Seljuks, 23, 24, 76, 77
 decline of, 78–80
September 11 attacks, 33, 195, 197, 200, 203
Sharif, Husham, 183–87
Sharif Husayn of Hijaz, 111–12
Sharif Husayn of Mecca, 105
Shatt al-Arab, 120, 166, 173, 174, 176
Shaw, Ezel Kural, 26

Shaw, Stanford J., 26
al-Shawi, Husham, 190–92
al-Shaykhli, Abd al-Karim, 151, 155
Shi'ite Muslims, 28, 32, 71, 94, 137, 167
 appeal of Iranian Islamic rebellion for, 168–69
 Ba'ath repression of, 170–72
 in Basra, 97
 demonstrating against American occupation of Iraq, 212
 Iran-Iraq War and, 173, 175
 loyalty of, to Iraq, 177
 Persian roots of, 166
 resistance of, to British in Iraq, 107
 resistance of, to Ottoman influence, 96
 Safavids and, 88, 92
Sidqi, Bakr, 119–20
Siffin, Battle of, 70
Simon, Sir John, 115
Simons, Geoff, 37, 87
Sin, 46, 59, 60
 temple of, 61, 63
Six-Day War, 140
slaves, 39
social reform, 123, 125
 Ba'ath Party achievements and, 160–64
 following 1958 revolution, 134, 136
 see also revolution
social structure, 134, 135
 kingship and, 50–53
 rural, 94
 tribal differences and, 97, 100, 134
 army used to crush, 120
 King Faisal's ability to mediate, 116
 political use made of, 119

urban, 95–96
see also economy; social reform
Soviet Union, 125, 147, 191
Spain, 22
Stoakes, Frank, 118
Suez crisis, 140, 147, 213–14
Sufis, 94
Sulaiman, Hikmat, 119, 120, 121
Suleiman the Magnificent (Ottoman sultan), 88, 89, 90
Sumer, 16, 18, 38–40
  emergence of military warfare in, 17
  pantheon of, 45
  political structure of, 49–53
  sculpture of, 46–48
Sumer: Cities of Eden (Time-Life Books), 16–17, 47
Sunni Muslims, 28, 68, 71, 137, 174
  Basra elite and, 97
  in cooperation with Shi'ites, 107, 177
  Ottoman connections and, 90, 102, 166
  revolutionary government and, 135
  shrines of, desecrated, 88
  tension with Shi'ites and, 23, 29, 89, 92, 96
Supreme Council, 160, 161
al-Suwaidi, Taufiq, 123
Sykes-Picot Agreement (1916), 147
Syria, 21, 30, 44, 63, 154
  capture of, by Sultan Selim I, 88
  idea that U.S. should invade, 214
  Mongol invasion of, 78, 90
  Muslim troops in, 69
  nationalist propaganda from, 107, 112
  pan-Arabism of, 126, 149
  quest for independence in, 112–13

Saddam Hussein in, 150
Six-Day War and, 140
Tamerlane in, 88

Talfah, Khairallah, 144, 145–48
Tālib Pasha, 103
Tamerlane, 24–25, 88, 143
Tartars, 83–84, 143
Tauris, 84–85
taxes, 44, 64, 89, 93, 100
technology, 38–39
see also irrigation works
temples, 43, 44, 48, 60
  rebuilding of, 61–64
  Sumerian ziggurats and, 39
terrorism
  Iraqi links with, 195, 197, 198
  denied by Saddam Hussein, 207
  war on
    attack on Iraq consistent with, 199–201
    attack on Iraq may compromise, 202–205
  see also September 11 attacks
Tigris River, 16, 43, 73–75, 78, 92
  flooding of, 124
Tikrit, 143, 144, 146, 149
al-Tikriti, Hardan, 152
Time-Life Books, 16–17, 47
Time (magazine), 138
trade, 64, 73–74, 83–85, 94
  with India, 63, 97
  restoration of routes to Persian Gulf for, 91
  taxes levied on, 93
Transjordan, 69, 122
treaties
  of alliance with Saudi Arabia (1936), 120
  with Britain (1922), 113–14
  with Britain (1930), 123, 144, 146

with Persia (1937), 120
Tripp, Charles, 92
Troutbeck, John, 134
Tughril Beg (Seljuk leader), 76–77
Turco-Pakistani treaty (1954), 125
Turkey, 26, 105, 111, 125, 197
Turks, 23
  see also Ottoman Empire; Young Turks

Ubaidi, 94
'Umar, 68, 69, 70
al-Umari, Arshad, 123, 125
Umayyads, 21, 71, 112
UNESCO, 161
United Arab Republic (UAR), 149, 150
United Arab States, 149
United Nations (UN), 124, 178–80, 197, 209, 216
  Security Council, 201, 214
    Colin Powell's presentation to, 198
    Hussein seen as threat by, 196
    occupation of Iraq not approved by, 212
    resolution of, 177
    weapons inspection program of, 200–201, 205, 207
United Popular Front, 124
United States, 33, 147, 197
  attack on Iraq by, 34
    is counterproductive, 203
    is necessary, 200–201
  first atomic bomb produced by, 188
  hostility of Hussein toward, 196
  Iran backed by, 191, 192
  need for long-term stay in Iraq and, 212–17
  war on terror a priority of, 203–204
  war over Kuwait and, 178–82

Ur, 15, 42, 46, 60, 63
uranium, 188, 199, 200
Ur-Nammu, 42
Uruk, 45, 48, 63
Uta-napishti, 50
'Uthman, 68, 70
al-Uzri, Abdul-Karim, 124

Vanguards, 157, 158
Verse Account of Nabonidus, 59–60
Vienna, 189–93
Vilayet Law of 1864, 98, 99

Wall Street Journal (newspaper), 202
war, 76–81
  in ancient Mesopotamia, 17–21, 42–43, 61–66
  against Iraq (2003), 33–34
    case for, 195–201
    con, 202–205, 210
    imperialism the motive for, 208–209
    need for long-term U.S. involvement and, 212–17
  see also Gulf War (1991); Iran-Iraq War; terrorism, war on
Warka, 46, 48
Wars of Apostasy, 69
weapons of mass destruction, 207
  Iraq's efforts to develop, 183, 186–89, 195, 199, 202
    entry to the IAEA and, 190–93
    fear of Israel is motivation for, 184–85
    need for UN inspections and, 205
    Saddam Hussein's desire to terrorize world is motivation for, 196–98, 200–201
    Saddam Hussein's regional ambitions are motivation for, 203

used as pretext for U.S. attack, 208
Weiss, Walter M., 68
West Bank, 140
wheel, invention of, 39
Wiet, Gaston, 72
women, 162–64
  rights of, 42
Woolley, Sir Leonard, 60
World War I, 27, 91, 102, 105, 111
World War II, 29, 121, 122, 144
writing, 37, 39–40
  early historical texts and, 49–50, 53, 59–60, 63
  see also cuneiform tablets

Xerxes (king of Persia), 63, 64

Ya'qubi, 72–74
Yazidi, 94, 174
Yemen, 149
Young Turks, 26, 111
  authoritarian CUP government and, 101
  nationalism of, 103
  revolution of, 100, 104
  secular policies of, 102
Youth Organization, 157

ziggurats, 39